Canada and the Beijing Conference on Women

Canada and International Relations

Kim Richard Nossal, Brian L. Job, and Mark W. Zacher, General Editors

The Canada and International Relations series explores issues in contemporary world politics and international affairs. The volumes cover a wide range of topics on Canada's external relations, particularly international trade and foreign economic policy.

Elizabeth Riddell-Dixon

Canada and the Beijing Conference on Women: Governmental Politics and NGO Participation

UBC Press · Vancouver · Toronto

Printed in Canada on acid-free paper ∞

ISBN 0-7748-0842-X

National Library of Canada Cataloguing in Publication Data

Riddell-Dixon, Elizabeth, 1954-
Canada and the Beijing Conference on Women

(Canada and international relations, ISSN 0847-0510; 13)
Includes bibliographical references and index.
ISBN 0-7748-0842-X

1. World Conference on Women (4th: 1995: Beijing, China) 2. Canada –
Foreign relations – 1945- 3. Women – Social conditions – Congresses. I. Title.
HQ1106.R52 2001   305.42   C2001-910501-0

This book has been published with the help of a grant from the Humanities and Social Sciences Federation of Canada, using funds provided by the Social Sciences and Humanities Research Council of Canada.

The author gratefully acknowledges the assistance of the J.B. Smallman Publication Fund, Faculty of Social Science, The University of Western Ontario.

UBC Press acknowledges the financial support of the Government of Canada through the Book Publishing Industry Development Program (BPIDP) for our publishing activities.
Canadä

We also gratefully acknowledge the support of the Canada Council for the Arts for our publishing program, as well as the support of the British Columbia Arts Council.

Printed and bound in Canada by Friesens
Set in Stone by BN Typographics West
Copy editor: Judy Phillips
Proofreader: Leslie Timmins

UBC Press
The University of British Columbia
2029 West Mall, Vancouver, BC V6T 1Z2
(604) 822-5959
Fax: (604) 822-6083
E-mail: info@ubcpress.ca
www.ubcpress.ca

To Gretta Riddell-Dixon
Beloved mother, supportive friend, inspiring role model,
and life-long crusader for women's rights

Contents

Acronyms

CBFC	Canadian Beijing Facilitating Committee
CIDA	Canadian International Development Agency
CLC	Canadian Labour Congress
CPC	Canadian Preparatory Committee
CRIAW	Canadian Research Institute for the Advancement of Women
CSW	(UN) Commission on the Status of Women
DFAIT	Department of Foreign Affairs and International Trade
ECE	Economic Commission for Europe
FLS	*Forward-looking Strategies for the Advancement of Women to the Year 2000*
ICFTU	International Confederation of Free Trade Unions
ICPD	International Conference on Population and Development
IDC '95	Interdepartmental Committee on the Fourth World Conference on Women
ILO	International Labour Organization
JUSCANZ	An informal negotiating group of relatively likeminded states, including Japan, the United States, Canada, Australia, the Netherlands, Norway, and New Zealand
NAC	National Action Committee on the Status of Women
NGO	Nongovernmental organization
PFA	*Platform for Action*
SWC	Status of Women Canada
UN	United Nations
UNDP	United Nations Development Program
UNEP	United Nations Environment Program
UNFPA	United Nations Fund for Population Activities
UNICEF	United Nations International Children's Emergency Fund
UNIFEM	United Nations Development Fund for Women
VOW	(Canadian) Voice of Women for Peace
WHO	World Health Organization
WSSD	World Summit for Social Development

Preface

In late August 1995 I travelled to China to attend the Fourth World Conference on Women and the parallel NGO Forum on Women '95. Twenty-three hours after leaving home, I arrived at the Beijing International Airport to join the milling throngs waiting to clear customs. In spite of the hustle and bustle of large numbers of excited arrivals, we were processed relatively expeditiously and directed to buses bound either for Beijing – the site of the intergovernmental conference – or for Huairou – a resort town 42 kilometres north of Beijing where the NGO forum was being held.[1] I was spending my first four days at the NGO forum before moving to Beijing to attend the Fourth World Conference on Women.

Once in Huairou, we were directed into a two-storey reception centre. Getting my pass for the NGO forum was relatively straightforward, but sorting out my accommodations proved to be quite another matter. After much confusion and much jostling by the crowds, I arrived at the accommodations desk only to be told that my hotel had been changed and that they had no record whatsoever of my colleague from City University of New York, Charlotte Patton, with whom I had arranged to share a room. It was the merest coincidence that I did happen to bump into Charlotte six days later. She, too, had arrived to find her hotel reservation changed and no record of my registration.

After receiving my new reservation, I was directed outside to a shuttle bus, which left about half an hour later. Conversations in many languages could be heard on the bus as it toured around Huairou dropping off women at various hotels. Finally, the driver, his assistant, and I were the only ones left on the bus. They spoke no English or French. I spoke no Chinese. None of us had any idea where my hotel was. After an hour of driving around (and around) Huairou and of backing in and out of narrow alleys, my hotel was found. The next morning I saw that my hotel was only a ten-minute stroll from the registration centre.

What I refer to here as my hotel was in fact a brand new concrete apartment building which, I was later told, was quite luxurious by Chinese standards. After the conference, it became home to Chinese families. The building comprised five-storey blocks of apartments. Each block had a separate door to the outside and its own staircase. Each floor housed two apartments leading off the central staircase.

At the hotel, I was greeted by a group of friendly Chinese volunteers who led me to an office in which sat three officials. The first examined my hotel registration card, the second looked at my passport and NGO pass, and the third took the payment for my four days' accommodation in Huairou. After getting the receipt for the payment, I was directed back to the first person to get what I then thought was the key to my room but what turned out to be the key to the suite. Bedroom doors had no locks. Four volunteers led me outside and half way around the building to one of the many external doors. Here we entered and climbed five flights of concrete stairs to a locked suite. Inside was a stark common room off which were several closed doors. "Your room," announced a volunteer cheerfully as she swung open the door. Her expression changed suddenly to one of embarrassment and surprise as she saw that the bed was already occupied. "One minute please" – a phrase I was to hear many times over the next ten days – she added quickly. She scurried off to the office and the rest of us trundled down the five flights of stairs. Some time later she returned brandishing a key to a different suite and we climbed up another five flights of stairs. This time there was a vacant bedroom. It was some twelve feet long and the width of two single beds, allowing space for one bed and a narrow walkway. The room did open onto a small shared balcony with, what I saw the next morning, a lovely view of the town and the hills around Huairou. So I finally arrived after twenty-eight hours of travel.

Life seemed rather grim that first night. I was exhausted and feeling very alone. There were mosquitoes in the bathroom, and although UN officials and doctors in London had all insisted that one did not need to worry about malaria in either Beijing or Huairou, I could not help but wonder if they had really known for sure that these particular mosquitoes did not carry the virulent disease.

In spite of my exhaustion, the night was not restful. Three times – at spaced intervals – the bed board on which my grain-filled mattress rested collapsed onto the floor. It was too narrow to sit securely on the metal bed-frame and so slipped easily off, depositing me and my bedding uncere-moniously in a heap on the concrete floor. By the end of the night, I had become quite an expert at balancing bed boards – so much so that after that first night, I landed on the floor on only one other occasion during my remaining three nights in Huairou.

The next day dawned brightly and I met my suite-mates – Dr. Lily Tang, granddaughter of Dr. Sun Yat-Sen, and her son, Dr. Steven Tang, both of whom live in the United States. Having spent much of her youth in China,

Lily spoke the language fluently. Through their ongoing work with the Soong Ching Ling Foundation – a nonprofit NGO named after Lily's grandmother who had done much to promote the physical and mental health of women and children – Lily and her son knew the country well. They proved to be delightful and most interesting. We went to breakfast and dinner together each day during my stay in Huairou and it was, thanks no doubt to their excellent advice, that I never had any gastrointestinal problems. Their insights into China and its people were likewise very helpful and enriching.

It was quite a cultural shock to move from the rudimentary conditions in Huairou to the five-star Hotel Kempinski in Beijing – the hotel to which the Canadian delegation had been assigned. To facilitate research for this book, André Ouellet, Canada's minister of foreign affairs, had granted me unofficial academic observer status on the Canadian delegation. This meant that I paid my own way but that I was able to attend delegation meetings – a privilege for which I remain most grateful.

As the media proclaimed, there were organizational problems and, as Rhonda Ferderber, director of the External Relations and Communications Directorate at Status of Women Canada, says, "Mother Nature was not a feminist that year!" Nonetheless, the Fourth World Conference on Women and NGO forum were wonderful, enriching experiences. The conference documents, the *Beijing Declaration* and *Platform for Action,* represent new commitments on the part of the international community to achieve equality, development, and peace for all women throughout the world. Like their predecessors, they are not legally binding, but they are evidence of a growing international consensus on women's rights. As such, they establish standards by which we can measure the accomplishments of our government and of the 188 other states that participated at the Beijing conference. The existence of these standards does not guarantee compliance. Nonetheless, their existence heightens the cost of violations and increases the pressure for compliance. It is our responsibility as citizens to keep up the pressure to ensure that the Canadian government fulfils the commitments that its negotiators worked so hard to formulate.

To all who helped make the writing of this book possible, I would like to extend my heartfelt gratitude. It was a pleasure to work with the people at UBC Press. Special thanks are due to my Editor, Emily Andrew, whose excellent advice, support and admirable efficiency all facilitated the publication of this book. I am grateful to Holly Keller-Brohman, my Managing Editor, who oversaw and coordinated the production of the book. Her wide-ranging expertise and her sensitivity to an author's views made working with her a very pleasant and productive endeavour. I also wish to thank Judy Phillips for her thorough and thoughtful editing of the book and for her helpful comments. Her edited proofs were presented in the most user-friendly format that I have ever encountered. The book benefited from the comments of the anonymous reviewers, whose constructive suggestions helped to strengthen the final version.

Research for this book was made possible by a three-year grant from the Social Sciences and Humanities Research Council of Canada.

Much of the research for this project was drawn from personal interviews with federal and provincial public servants, UN officials, and representatives of NGOs. To all those who gave generously of their time and shared their insights with me, I thank you.

Three librarians were particularly helpful in locating UN and government documents and other useful reference information. Special thanks are due to Maureen Ryan at the D.B. Weldon Library at the University of Western Ontario, Céline Champagne at the library at Status of Women Canada, and Donna Burton at the Legislative Library of Ontario.

High praise goes to Carol Brookbanks, who persevered to decipher my illegible scrawl and to translate it into neat, legible print. In addition to her excellent keyboarding skills, Carol's kindness, encouragement, and good sense of humour were greatly appreciated.

Finally I owe a profound debt of gratitude to my friends and family, whose encouragement throughout this project has been invaluable. Pauline Bovey de Candolle warmly welcomed Thomas and I into her elegant home in Geneva, Switzerland, for four months in 1996, thereby providing an inspirational setting for the drafting of the initial chapters of the book. Frances Bauer generously made time on her summer vacation to read the entire manuscript. Her proofreading in both official languages was both insightful and meticulous. I am deeply grateful to Penny Brown, whose morale support and extensive assistance in many other walks of life greatly facilitated the completion of the project. Special thanks are due to my mother for her enthusiasm and encouragement and for the many times she babysat to facilitate my research and writing. Thomas, you patiently coped with my research trips and my preoccupations, while never letting me forget the importance of life outside academia. My mother pioneered women's rights, I have attempted to carry on the torch and Thomas is our hope for the future.

Canada and the Beijing Conference on Women

1
Introduction

On September 15, 1995, at the close of the Fourth UN Conference on Women – the largest UN conference ever convened – 189 countries unanimously adopted the *Beijing Declaration* and *Platform for Action*. The 361 paragraph *Platform for Action (PFA)* not only consolidated and reaffirmed gains for women realized at other recent world conferences, but it also made significant advances on diverse issues ranging from the reaffirmation that rape is a war crime, to the delineation of state responsibilities to eliminate violence against women, to the affirmation of sexual and reproductive rights for women.[1] The *PFA* is a major accomplishment that goes well beyond previous documents in prescribing norms to enhance the position of women worldwide.

Canada was an active player throughout the preparatory meetings leading up to Beijing and at the conference itself. Furthermore, the Canadian negotiators achieved some major successes both at the preparatory meetings and at the Fourth World Conference itself. At the 1995 New York Preparatory Meetings, for example, the Canadian delegation was instrumental in having the Health Section in the draft *PFA* expanded beyond a preoccupation with sexual and reproductive rights to include a more holistic approach that took account of the effects of poverty. Canada also played an important role in ensuring that a gender perspective was incorporated into the *PFA*. In Beijing, Canadian delegates chaired the majority of the working groups that were established to negotiate particularly contentious issues, such as parental rights, unpaid work, and sexual rights. Furthermore, several of the major precedent-setting advances in the *PFA* resulted from Canadian initiatives. They included the definition of rape as a war crime and crime against humanity, the requirement to develop international, gender-sensitive classifications for measuring unpaid work, and the stipulation that violence and gender-related persecution are grounds for claiming refugee status. Canadian NGOs, for their parts, played significant roles drafting composite texts for the international NGOs, chairing several international NGO caucuses, coordinating NGO activities for North America, and organizing and participating in workshops and panels at the NGO forum.

Canada uses a similar process when preparing for all UN conferences. There is always an interdepartmental committee as well as consultations with the provinces and NGO involvement. Nonetheless, the specifics vary and this book examines the process by which Canada's policies for the Beijing World Conference on Women were formulated – a process that involved federal government officials from some twenty departments, provincial representatives and NGOs from across Canada. The primary objectives of the study are to examine the decision-making process within the federal government and to analyze relations between the federal government officials and the NGO representatives, both within Canada and at the international negotiations. It concludes that the decision-making process within federal government circles was for the most part harmonious, in contrast to the tenets of the governmental politics approach that predict actors competing to determine outcome.[2] Three sets of factors account for this collegiality. First, and most importantly, the issues in the *PFA* all fell within existing government policies; hence, agreement had already been reached on the overall framework for establishing positions before preparations for Beijing began. Second, and closely related, there was a high degree of consensus on priorities and objectives. Third, the federal preparatory process began early and was well organized. Finally, all the key public servants had recognized expertise relevant to the negotiations on the *PFA,* and most were involved throughout the process; they understood the precedents that had already been set and the parameters within which they had to operate, both at home and at the international negotiations.

On the issue of government-NGO relations, the book examines federal government support of Canadian NGOs in the policy-making process, assesses the utility of the support in facilitating meaningful participation, and explores the extent to which NGOs were able to capitalize on the support given. The last decade has seen a large increase in the number of NGOs demanding input into the Canadian foreign policy-making process. Not only have Canadian NGOs increased in numbers but they have also gained considerable experience during this period and so are better able to voice their concerns. In 1993, the Chrétien government came to power with a promise to democratize the Canadian foreign policy-making process.[3] The promise reflected two widely held beliefs: that the Canadian foreign policy-making process was inherently undemocratic, and that this situation had to change. As Kim Nossal points out, a recurrent theme in the critical literature is that "foreign policy is undemocratic because it is elitist, made by a few in the interests of a few. In this view, the policy-making process is dominated by a minority of officials in the federal bureaucracy.

Decisions are made without public input or public consultation."[4] To operationalize its campaign promise, the Liberal government undertook a series of activities to increase public involvement in the foreign policy-making process. During its first year in office, it convened a two-day National Forum on Canada's International Relations, which drew over 100 experts from business, labour, NGOs, academia, and other members of the attentive public. It also established the Special Joint Committee Reviewing Canadian Foreign Policy (hereafter Special Joint Committee). The members of parliament and the senators on the Special Joint Committee "spent seven months considering 561 briefs, holding over 80 meetings in ten cities in Canada and three abroad, hearing from over 550 witnesses, and in the process generating over 10,000 pages in parliamentary testimony."[5] The national forums have since become an annual event convened by the Canadian Centre for Foreign Policy Development, which was created by the Chrétien government in 1995 in response to the recommendations of the Special Joint Committee. The government's commitments and subsequent efforts to consult widely on foreign policy issues sparked considerable debates among scholars of foreign policy.[6] Most of the discussion focuses on the work of the Special Joint Committee, though some authors consider the foreign policy-making process more broadly, while others focus on specific policy issues and areas.[7]

At the broadest level, the debate among Canadian scholars on this issue revolves around what constitutes democracy. Do higher levels of public involvement mean greater democratization? Kim Nossal describes the tendency to equate greater public participation with increased democratization of the policy-making process as "highly questionable" and asks, "What percentage of Canada's 27 million people need to be involved in the foreign policy-making process for that process to turn from being undemocratic to being democratic?"[8] This is a question to which neither Kim Nossal nor those he critiques for equating greater public participation with increased democratization of the policy-making process provide a direct answer. Nossal is, however, explicit in explaining why he finds the correlation between greater public involvement and increased democratization problematic. Those included in the consultations, he argues, are not the average man or woman on the street; instead, they constitute "Canada's conferencing classes" – representatives of business, labour, and NGOs as well as academics, all with expertise in the field of foreign policy, whose participation is actively sought by government officials.[9]

The question of what constitutes democracy can be raised at all levels of the Canadian political process. How democratic are Canadian elections? Of all the eligible voters in the 2000 federal election, only about 61 percent went to the polls to cast their ballots.[10] Does 61 percent constitute a sufficiently high voter turnout to warrant the designation of democratic election? Under Canada's single member plurality (or first-past-the post) electoral system, the candidate with the greatest number of votes in his or her constituency is elected. This candidate does not, however, need to have received an absolute majority of the votes cast. The system greatly benefits political parties whose support is geographically concentrated, such as the Bloc Québécois and the Reform Party, and it discriminates against parties that have a broad base of geographically dispersed support, such as the Progressive Conservative and New Democratic parties. In the 2000 election, the Progressive Conservative Party received 1 percent more of the popular vote than did the Bloc Québécois, yet the latter received over three times as many seats.[11] In the same election, the Progressive Conservative Party received almost half as much of the popular vote as did the Canadian Alliance, however, the latter received over five times as many seats.[12] In addition to discriminating against parties with geographically dispersed support, there are other ways in which the Canadian electoral system falls short of being fully democratic: women are grossly underrepresented in the House of Commons, few Aboriginals or visible minorities are elected, and the size of the populations being represented varies from riding to riding. Once in office, the ability of a member of parliament to respond to the demands of his or her constituents is severely curtailed by party discipline. In practice, all votes do not count equally in the Canadian electoral system.[13] Questions have also been raised as to how democratic it is to have a nonelected Senate.[14]

NGOs are clearly less representative of the Canadian electorate than are members of the House of Commons, even when the latter are elected by a far from complete electorate, from constituencies embracing significantly different numbers of voters and in a system that rewards the candidate in each riding who gets the most votes and ignores all other votes cast. It is, nonetheless, unfair to polarize members of parliament and NGO leaders at opposite ends of a continuum with the former labelled as democratic and the latter seen as unrepresentative. The system does not justify such stark juxtapositions. It is more realistic to see each group occupying space on a continuum, with the members of parliament closer to (but not at) the end representing complete democracy and the NGO leaders farther along the continuum towards (but still a considerable distance from) the end titled undemocratic. Debates over the ability of NGOs to contribute to democratization must be seen in the context of many concerns about the extent to which the Canadian political process is democratic.

Concerns have been raised in various quarters of the Canadian polity about the growing influence of NGOs in the policy-making process.[15] NGOs are frequently labelled as "special interests," which implies that they are pursuing their own selfish interests at the expense of the common good. Those raising such concerns rarely apply the same analysis to business leaders enjoying regular access to government officials. NGO leaders are not elected by universal suffrage, but they frequently seek to promote the well-being of a constituency broader than their own memberships. The Canadian Labour Congress, for instance, seeks to protect and promote the interests of all working people in Canada and not just those who belong to its member unions. Likewise, the National Action Committee on the Status of Women is concerned with the advancement of women in Canada, even though its membership is only a subset of the broader female population. Most importantly, NGOs play important roles in the Canadian democratic process.[16] They facilitate two-way communication between the government and their respective memberships. They provide an important mechanism by which people can articulate shared interests and positions to government. They also provide channels through which the government can convey information to the attentive public. NGOs monitor the government's development and implementation of policy, performing a watchdog function not only for their members but also for society more broadly. They can present new ways of conceptualizing problems, fresh perspectives, and creative solutions, thereby frequently providing a needed challenge to the status quo. Their unique expertise and experience can assist government officials in reaching more-informed decisions. In addition to their potential to make valuable contributions to policy making, they play important roles in program delivery. The Canadian government regularly channels significant amounts of international development assistance and humanitarian aid through NGOs, which are able to implement the programs abroad more efficiently and more economically than can the government. Thus, NGOs play important roles in the Canadian policy-making process that are useful not only to their members but also to the democratic process. Of course, not all NGOs perform all these functions all of the time, but, as a category of actors, they do make these contributions on an ongoing basis.

Clearly, government-sponsored consultations do not involve all Canadians. On the other hand, they do allow the voices of those whose concerns have been marginalized in the Canadian foreign policy-making process to be heard. Cranford Pratt used the term "counterconsensus" to describe the growing numbers of "internationally minded public interest groups which are in serious opposition to many components of the present consensus that underlies Canadian foreign policy."[17] The NGOs composing the counterconsensus include labour, development, human rights, peace, women's, indigenous, and environmental groups,[18] all of which were involved with the Beijing Conference on Women. In her study of the influence of women's groups which appeared before the Special Joint Committee, Sandra Whitworth points out that the process actually involved a key sector of society traditionally excluded from the foreign policy-making process: women in groups and as individuals.[19] The counterconsensus challenges dominant class assumptions. It offers valuable critiques of the direction and substance of public policies, and its participation in the policy-making process ensures that concerns frequently ignored in government circles are at least brought to the table for consideration. In providing venues through which the attentive public can express its concerns and opinions, consultations and other government-sponsored mechanisms to facilitate the participation of civil society in the foreign policy-making process contribute to greater – though by no means complete – democratization. Foreign policy issues rarely make election agendas; thus, it is even more important that members of civil society – or at least the attentive public – have ways of making their views known to those formulating policy and that these views receive serious consideration. In providing meaningful participation – participation that is taken seriously by government decision makers and offers real opportunities for influencing policy outcomes – for a broad range of NGOs, government-sponsored mechanisms can move the process farther along the continuum towards democratization.[20]

To determine if the government-sponsored mechanisms established in this case helped to democratize the policy-making process, it is important to consider several questions:

- Which NGOs participated in the government-sponsored mechanisms?
- Did the government-sponsored mechanisms facilitate meaningful participation?
- Whose interests were served by the government-sponsored mechanisms?

Each of these questions is addressed in Chapter 8. Overall, the book concludes that, in keeping with traditional wisdom on foreign policy making, government officials formulated Canada's positions with considerable autonomy from civil society. Although the motives they ascribed to government decision makers vary, most studies of Canadian foreign policy see government actors operating fairly autonomously from the direct influence of NGOs.[21] In this case, the trend was further encouraged by two factors, the most important of which was the prior existence of tension between the Canadian government and Canadian women's groups. In addition, there were problems with the timing and format of the NGO submissions to government.

Relations between feminist groups and the federal government had been deteriorating since the late 1980s, when the Conservative government had significantly cut funding for the Women's Program and withdrawn financial support for the Court Challenges Program, which had provided feminist groups with critical support in challenging Canadian laws that were deemed to discriminate against women.[22] At the same time, the Conservatives began funding the antifeminist group, REAL Women.[23]

From 1985 to 1988, the NAC and other members of the counterconsensus actively opposed a central priority of the Mulroney government: negotiating a free trade agreement with the United States. During this period, the NAC's strategy shifted from its earlier emphasis on maintaining cooperative relations with government officials to a much more confrontational approach.[24] Tensions continued to mount in the 1990s as the Conservatives persevered with policies inimical to women's needs, such as cutting social services, especially support for child care, pursuing a North American free trade agreement in spite of strong opposition from women's groups and other members of the counterconsensus, and promoting the Charlottetown Accord, whose provisions were seen as weakening sexual equality in Canada and further undermining social programs.[25] Feminist concerns faired no better after the Liberals came to power in 1993. Precious few references to women appeared in the government's 1995 policy document, *Canada and the World: Government Statement*.[26] In the very year of the Fourth World Conference on Women, the government's statement contains no substantial discussion whatsoever of women's rights or women's issues. Furthermore, the 1995 federal budget dramatically cut social programs of vital importance to women, slashed funding for women's groups, and disbanded the Canadian Advisory Council on the Status of Women. By the time preparations for the Beijing Conference on Women were underway, relations between the government and women's groups were already strained. Government policies since the late 1980s had been undermining the gains that feminist groups had previously worked so hard to achieve. The groups had responded with increased hostility and aggression, which in turn did little to endear them or their causes to government decision makers. These pre-existing tensions are critical to understanding the case study discussed in this book.

The timing and format of the NGO submissions to government also played roles in promoting state autonomy. NGO input arrived late in the process and was generally not presented in the most user-friendly format. The reasons for this were many. The UN process itself militated against early, systematic preparations. For example, the initial draft of the *PFA* was woefully inadequate and was sent back to the UN secretariat to be completely rewritten. The revised draft *PFA* was released in January 1995, just over one month before, what was then scheduled to be, the final preparatory negotiations. As a result, governments and NGOs had little time to prepare their responses.

Within Canada, the formal, government-sponsored mechanism to facilitate the participation of Canadian NGOs was established in April 1994 – less than a year and a half before the conference was convened. Furthermore, many of the key players in the Canadian Beijing Facilitating Committee had no previous experience preparing for a UN conference. As a result of these factors – the late release of the first substantive draft *PFA*, the tardy organization of a NGO facilitating committee, and the inexperience of some of its key members – the positions of the NGOs were presented relatively late in the process, and it was only in the summer of 1995 that they became more user-friendly.

The book provides a rich case study of women in the Canadian foreign policy-making process. Feminist theory raises important questions that need to be applied to all levels of policy making. How do the socially constructed roles ascribed to men and women affect their respective status in society? Where are the women and where are the men? Who does what work and why? Who makes which decisions and why? Who has access to resources and who controls resources? Whom is a policy or program targeted towards? Who will benefit? Who will lose? Who is consulted when solutions to a problem are being sought? Feminist scholars have demonstrated the invisibility of women in the foreign policy-making process. As Sandra Whitworth points out, "the study and practice of international relations in general, and foreign policy in particular, remain the most unrepresentative of women or of feminist analyses; resistance to any change in this respect is dependent upon the assumed, and regularly asserted, gender neutrality of these areas."[27] Assumptions of gender neutrality pervade analyses of Canadian foreign policy: "In foreign policy, current practices, which are primarily defined by men and within a masculine framework, provide the norm for explaining foreign policy. That which is feminine, and the areas where women predominate, is identified as outside the areas of "real" foreign policy and thus has little effect on the analysis or practice of foreign policy."[28] The book presents a detailed examination of a case that was rather unique: although the broader policy-making process remained male dominated, women were the key actors in the immediate decision-making process. As such, it provides important findings on which feminist scholars studying the gendered nature of Canadian foreign policy making and its implications may wish to draw. To understand this case, it is critical to recognize that there are tiers of power within government. At the macro-level, the Canadian government is male dominated. This is the level at which power resides and at which women's issues do not constitute a top priority. At the more micro-level, the public servants formulating positions on women's issues are generally women and most are personally, as well as professionally, committed to ensuring women's equality with men and to enhancing the well-being of women. Yet, they are relatively few in number and they tend to be relegated to positions within the overall structure that carry less weight than those occupied by others pressing for competing objectives. For example, the position of secretary of state for the status of women does not carry nearly the power, the authority, or the influence enjoyed by the minister of finance. Paul Martin, minister of finance, was able to implement his 1995 budget, many of whose provisions directly contradicted the positions that Canada was advocating vis-à-vis the *Beijing Declaration* and *Platform for Action*. When push came to shove, the views of the minister of finance prevailed over the concerns that the secretary of state for the status of women had for the advancement of women. The case supports the feminists' argument that the involvement of relatively small numbers of predominately elite women (i.e., white, well-educated women) has little effect on the overall structures of power.[29]

The findings of this study are related to two other broad concerns in the literature on Canadian foreign policy making. The first is the extent to which the external environment set the parameters for the direction and substance of Canada's positions on the *Beijing Declaration* and *Platform for Action*. To what extent did Canadian government officials and NGO representatives have to react to the actions of external actors and to developments at the UN negotiations? How much scope did they have to initiate and to exercise leadership? Why? The second inquiry relates the findings of the case to the ongoing debates about the impact and the effectiveness of government efforts to democratize Canadian foreign policy making that were introduced earlier. The book concludes by offering some points for NGOs to ponder when developing their lobbying strategies and some points for government officials to ponder when considering measures to facilitate NGO participation in the policy-making processes for future world conferences.

In making these recommendations, it is important to recognize four premises reflected in this work. First, NGOs have important roles to play in the policy-making process. The points for NGO representatives to ponder are, therefore, offered in the hope of assisting NGOs, generally, and women's groups, in particular, to lobby more effectively. The points for government officials to ponder are intended to encourage them to facilitate meaningful participation by a wide range of NGOs, especially those whose voices have frequently been marginalized.

The second caveat to the discussions of NGO roles and strategies to enhance their effectiveness is the recognition that structural barriers limit the potential for NGO efficiency. As discussed earlier, the government as a whole has not shown itself to be particularly receptive to the concerns of women's groups; it would be naïve and erroneous to assume that if only NGOs had lobbied more effectively, they would have exercised a major influence. On the other hand, just because there are limits to efficacy does not mean that women's NGOs could not lobby more effectively.[30]

Third, increased efficacy is important because improvements to the situation of women – even incremental changes – are nonetheless steps ahead. Each time norms and regulations are established to advance women, domestically or internationally, the pressure for conformity is heightened and the costs of violations are increased. This means that it is important to lobby effectively because even incremental change moves the agenda ahead.

Fourth, the government, for its part, needs to facilitate more meaningful participation for NGOs for both ethical and practical reasons. On ethical grounds, access to the policy-making process must be available to a broad range of NGOs and not just to those with the greatest resources. In practical terms, participants can provide valuable expertise and experience to assist government decision makers in making wise policies and in implementing them effectively. Furthermore, NGOs can serve as useful allies to government officials embroiled in intergovernmental competitions to affect policy outcomes. NGO support for a policy that directly affects its membership can serve to legitimize the policy. For example, the government's labour standards are likely to seem more credible to Canadians generally if they are strongly endorsed by the Canadian Labour Congress, which represents 2.3 million working Canadians.[31] Conversely, Greenpeace's vocal opposition to the seal hunt makes it more costly, in terms of the loss of prestige at home and abroad, for the government to pursue policies supportive of the hunt. In short, NGOs have important roles to play in the Canadian democratic process, and the participation of diverse groups needs to be facilitated.

Following this introduction, Chapter 2 examines developments that led to the convening of a Fourth World Conference on Women and that influenced the nature of its negotiations and the breadth and depth of its documents. It begins with brief overviews of the three previous UN conferences on women, as well as of the world conferences and summits convened by the UN in the 1990s, all of which influenced the tone and substance of the Beijing Conference. The remainder of the chapter focuses on preparations for the conference itself. This section presents the conference's mandate and then examines the process by which the *PFA* was drafted within the UN secretariat and negotiated in three key sets of preparatory meetings: the conferences convened in 1994 by each of the UN's five regional economic commissions; the 39th session of the UN Commission on the Status of Women (CSW), held in the spring of 1995, and the CSW Informal Consultations, convened in the summer of 1995.

Having established the broad framework within which Canadians had to operate, Chapter 3 examines the interaction among federal government actors in Ottawa in the formulation of Canada's policies for Beijing. It begins by identifying the key divisions/departments involved in the process and their interests and then examines the interdepartmental policy-making process and the work of the Interdepartmental Committee on the World Conference on Women.

Chapter 4 discusses the principal channels within Canada for facilitating NGO input into the Canadian foreign policy-making process: the Canadian

Beijing Facilitating Committee and the Canadian Preparatory Committee. These government-sponsored mechanisms are assessed in terms of their utility in facilitating meaningful NGO participation.

Having explored the policy-making process within Canada, in terms of governmental politics in Chapter 3 and NGO involvement in Chapter 4, the focus switches to the international arena in Chapter 5. Here the discussion begins by examining the work of the Canadian delegations at the three principal sets of preparatory negotiations in which they participated: the 1994 Vienna Regional Meetings for Europe and North America, the 1995 New York Preparatory Meetings, and the informal consultations that were convened by the CSW for five days in late July and early August 1995. The remainder of the chapter is devoted to the Canadian delegation at the Fourth World Conference on Women. Here the discussion is divided into two main sections: the controversies around the delegation's composition and the considerable achievements of the Canadian negotiators.

Chapter 6 explores the activities and contributions of Canadian NGOs at the international negotiations, commencing with the 1994 Vienna Regional Meetings and the 1995 New York Preparatory Meetings. The subsequent discussion of the Fourth World Conference on Women examines the key determinants of NGO access to the negotiations as well as their contributions. The chapter concludes with a brief discussion of the Canadian NGOs at the NGO forum, where networking was important, both in terms of orchestrating positions for the conference and, more especially, in terms of establishing linkages that will facilitate future cooperation between Canadian NGOs and those in other parts of the world.

Canada's chief reason for participating in the Beijing Conference on Women and the preceding preparatory negotiations was to influence the focus and the contents of the *Beijing Declaration* and *PFA*. Chapter 7 assesses the extent to which Canada was successful in achieving its objectives. The discussion begins with overviews of the two final conference documents. It then analyzes the extent to which Canada was able to realize each of its stated negotiating objectives. In the process of evaluating Canada's successes, a general assessment of the *PFA*'s effectiveness in advancing women is also provided.

The findings of this study are drawn together in Chapter 8. They are then related to the two broad concerns in the literature on Canadian foreign policy making that were discussed earlier: the parameters set by the external environment, and the democratization of the Canadian foreign policy-making process. The chapter concludes by offering some points that NGO leaders and government officials may wish to consider.

Research for the book was drawn from a variety of primary and secondary sources. The primary sources included government documents, UN documents, and NGO materials, as well as interviews with more than forty federal government officials, UN officials, and NGO representatives, both in Canada and at the 1995 New York Preparatory Meetings and the Fourth World Conference on Women. Most of those interviewed agreed to be cited, but some of the information provided by interviewees was given on the condition that it not be attributed to a particular individual. In order to use this information, while at the same time protecting the identity of the source, several footnotes are included that do not give the name or the precise title of the interviewee. Efforts have been made, however, to indicate the nature of the individual's involvement with the Beijing Conference on Women. A list of most of those interviewed appears at the end of the book. A few interviewees requested that their names not be included on the list, and their wishes have been respected.

2
The Road to Beijing

Several themes run through this book. Perhaps the most prominent is that the conference and Canada's preparations for it were part of a much larger process that had been under way since 1975. Although the UN Charter affirms the equal rights of men and women,[1] it took the organization thirty years to hold its first conference on women. This chapter provides an overview of developments leading up to the Fourth World Conference on Women: the three preceding UN conferences on women; the conferences and summits convened in the 1990s which addressed women's rights and which influenced the tone and the substance of the Beijing Conference and its preparatory meetings; and the process of preparing and negotiating the *PFA*, which was ultimately adopted in Beijing in September 1995. For Canada, the three most important sets of negotiations leading up to Beijing were the 1994 Vienna Regional Meeting, the 1995 New York Preparatory Meetings, and the CSW Informal Consultations convened in the summer of 1995. Canada's participation in each of these sets of negotiations is explored in greater depth in Chapter 5, where the role of the Canadian delegation is discussed.

Previous UN Conferences on Women
Between 1975 and 1985, the UN convened three sets of intergovernmental conferences on women and parallel NGO forums.[2] After years of urging by the UN Commission on the Status of Women (CSW),[3] the General Assembly finally agreed in 1972 to proclaim 1975 International Women's Year and to convene in 1975 an International Women's Year World Conference in Mexico City – the first global intergovernmental conference ever held on the status of women. Delegates to the Mexico conference recommended that the years 1976 to 1985 be declared a "Decade for Women" – a recommendation that was subsequently accepted by the General Assembly. The themes for the Mexico conference were "equality, development, and peace." The three themes continued to serve as the framework for the Decade as

well as for the subsequent three conferences on women. In Mexico, the international community adopted the *World Plan of Action for the Implementation of the Objectives of International Women's Year* (hereafter *Plan of Action*). Establishing guidelines and targets for enhancing the status of women over a ten-year period, the *Plan of Action* focused on "the more traditionally defined women's issues such as health, education, the family, political participation, and employment. Noticeably absent from the plan of action were any recommendations in the areas of the environment, women's inheritance rights, industry, science and technology, trade, transportation, violence against women, pornography, economic development policies and women, women's participation in the informal labour markets, and equal pay for work of equal value."[4]

The *Plan of Action* did, nonetheless, establish minimal targets in traditionally defined women's issues and prescribed actions to be taken at the national and international levels to ensure that substantial gains were realized by women in these areas. Its targets were concrete and specific for the first half of the Decade. In order to assess the progress made towards implementing its objectives, the *Plan of Action* recommended the convening of a Second World Conference on Women in 1980.

In 1980, mid-way through the Decade, the Second Conference on Women was convened in Copenhagen to assess progress made during the first five years of the Decade in implementing the standards and proposed actions outlined in the Mexico *Plan of Action*. The conference adopted a *Program of Action for the Second Half of the United Nations Decade for Women* (hereafter the *Program of Action*). Building on the Mexico *Plan of Action*, the *Program of Action* focused on three issue areas: health, employment, and education. It was more specific than its predecessor had been in identifying impediments to progress and in recognizing the need for practical solutions to overcome these barriers. The Copenhagen conference also witnessed the ceremonial signing of the *Convention on the Elimination of All Forms of Discrimination Against Women* by all the official delegations. The *Convention*, which had been adopted by the UN General Assembly in 1979, "laid out in detail the duties that states have to promote women's equality in all areas of life, from family to workplace to government."[5] Although the ceremonial signing was significant, the conference itself "failed to address the systematic barriers to women's participation in society and only included a footnote that said that defacto [sic] discrimination against women was called sexism in some countries."[6] North-South tensions were very much in evidence in Copenhagen where fierce debates were waged not only over the meaning of feminism but also over the merits of Zionism, apartheid, and the new international economic order.[7] In the end, it was geopolitical concerns that prevented the conference from achieving unanimous approval of the *Program of Action:* "the United States was left in the diplomatically awkward position of voting against a document it strongly supported because it would not accept language opposing Zionism, favouring the PLO, and blaming the West for Third World underdevelopment."[8] Canada, Australia, and Israel also voted against the *Program of Action* for similar reasons.

The Third World Conference on Women was convened in Nairobi in 1985 to assess progress made during the Decade, at national and international levels, towards realizing the goals of the Decade and to identify barriers to women's advancement. The conference adopted the Nairobi *Forward-looking Strategies for the Advancement of Women to the Year 2000 (FLS)*. Like the documents of the preceding women's conferences, the underlying themes in the *FLS* were equality, development, and peace. Nonetheless, the *FLS* were broader ranging in their coverage and more analytical than previous documents had been. In the political, economic, and social spheres, the document examined some of the obstacles to women's advancement and recommended strategies for overcoming these barriers: "The strategies provided a framework for action at the national, regional and international level to promote empowerment of women and their enjoyment of human rights."[9] Not only were governments and international organizations to advance women in the political, economic, and social spheres, but women were to be actively involved in the decision-making process. The *FLS* were described by former UN Secretary-General Boutros Boutros-Ghali as "a blueprint for women's future in all realms of life."[10] The *FLS* not only presented strategies for advancing women but also included some provisions for monitoring compliance. In particular, it called for a conference to be held ten years later to assess the progress made towards achieving the objectives laid down.

The lives of women around the world did not improve significantly as a result of the work undertaken during the UN Decade for Women. Nevertheless, the Decade was noteworthy on several scores. It saw the adoption of the *Convention on the Elimination of All Forms of Discrimination Against Women,* which has been described by former UN Secretary-General Boutros Boutros-Ghali as "a landmark treaty in the struggle for women's rights" and "an international bill of human rights for women."[11]

Although women's issues and programs never became central on the agenda at either the international or the national level, they were receiving greater attention and more resources by the end of the Decade than had been the case in 1975. Within the UN, several programs and bodies were established to support women, including the Development Fund for Women (UNIFEM) and the International Research and Training Institute for the Advancement of Women (INSTRAW). Yet in spite of these improvements, much remained to be done: "In all cases women's programmes and policies remain marginal in the system and rarely have the resources or authority to match the mandates given."[12]

Similar trends were evident at the national level. The Decade made it harder for state governments to continue to ignore women's issues: "The UN Decade for Women at the least forced governments to pay lip service to women's issues – and it sometimes encouraged them to do more. Ninety percent of the world's governments have created official bodies that are devoted to the advancement of women; half of these were created during the decade."[13] So while women's issues never became central on the political agenda, there was, during the course of the decade, a growing awareness of women's issues, reflected in the creation of programs and offices to facilitate the advancement of women.

The decade also saw major developments in the maturing of the women's movement on the international stage. In particular, the process became more democratic; valuable experience was gained both by states and by NGOs; the conference documents, themselves, came to cover increasingly broad ranges of issues and to deal more concretely with these issues; and the international networks mushroomed among women's groups worldwide.

The democratization of the process can be measured in terms of the quantity and the quality of the participation. In 1975, the First World Conference on Women was attended by 1,300 delegates from 133 countries and 113 NGOs, while 5,000 people from 82 countries participated at the parallel NGO Tribune.[14] Ten years later, 2,000 delegates from 157 states attended the Third World Conference on Women, in Nairobi, while 13,500 people from 150 countries participated at the NGO forum.[15]

The same period witnessed an increase in the number of female delegates and, more importantly, in the number of delegations headed by women. Of the official delegates to Mexico City, one third were men.[16] At Nairobi, over 80 percent of the delegates were women and some 85 percent of the delegations were led by women.[17] In Mexico City and Copenhagen, female delegates had yielded the microphones to male spokespersons from their respective countries when geopolitical issues were being discussed: "When the introductory and international sections were being discussed, male delegates representing the foreign ministries of various countries, began to move into the speakers' chairs, behind the microphone bearing the country's name. This was especially evident when troublesome international issues began to surface in the debate. There was often a flurry of activity as women delegates were moved aside and the men in virtually every delegation began to move into the chairs behind the microphones."[18] Such transfers of power were embarrassing and clearly incongruous with the objectives of the conference. This pattern of behaviour became less and less evident at subsequent conferences: "By the end of the Nairobi conference, in 1985, women delegates dominated the debate throughout the conference."[19] Thus, women were able to reclaim their voice – an indispensable prerequisite to the credibility of a conference devoted to the advancement of women.

A further demographic trend witnessed during the course of the decade was the considerable increase in the representation of women from the South: "The fact that African women had worked long and hard to have Nairobi as the site of the conference, and that Kenyan officials agreed to host the conference, demonstrated that the women's movement had become truly international. It could no longer be said that women's liberation or the demand for women's equality was a concern only of white, upper middle-class women in industrialized countries."[20] Southern countries accounted for 60 percent of the participants at the NGO forum in 1985.[21]

A great deal of learning took place during the Decade. The UN Commission on the Status of Women gained experience in running international conferences. State offices responsible for the women's issues learnt the intricacies of international conferences and how to develop effective negotiating strategies. The NGOs, for their parts, adopted increasingly productive tactics. Over time, they came to realize that it was critical to seek input early in the process when UN documents and state positions were being formulated. By the time an official conference was held, the scope and much of the specifics of the documents were already decided and state positions were already established.

In addition to gaining a deeper understanding of international negotiations and to developing more effective strategies, the participants learnt about each other. By 1985, participants at both the intergovernmental conference and the NGO forum had become more tolerant of diversity. In particular, women from the North and South sought increasingly to build on commonality in spite of recognized differences. By the end of the Decade, women had become increasingly determined not to let geopolitical issues derail progress on issues fundamental to the well-being of women.

The learning curve was not restricted to the conference participants alone. The work done during the Decade led to a growing awareness, at least in UN and governmental circles, of the interrelationship between women's well-being and the ability to make progress in other areas of concern, such as promoting economic development, addressing population concerns and preventing environmental degradation.

That the deepening understanding of women's issues and the growing awareness that the roles and status of women in societies has profound implications for all other areas of concern was reflected in significant improvements in the documents negotiated at each succeeding conference. The Mexico *Plan of Action* was described as a "shopping list of issues related to women."[22] The range of issues covered in the Nairobi *Forward-looking Strategies* was not only much broader but the issues were treated more concretely and with greater analysis. Furthermore, the *FLS* proposed measures for overcoming roadblocks to progress.

Finally the Decade saw enormous strides forward in the development of vast and expanding networks among women worldwide. The NGO forums provided venues for women from all over the world to come together to share their experiences, to discuss strategies for empowerment, and to develop relationships and networks to facilitate their ongoing work. The contacts forged at the intergovernmental conferences and parallel NGO forums were thereafter developed and expanded with the help of modern communications technology, such as computers and fax machines.

In many ways, the Beijing conference witnessed a continuation of the trends that had evolved over the Decade. The demographics for Beijing supported the trend towards greater participation. According to UN figures, the official Beijing conference and the accompanying NGO Forum on Women '95 in Huairou attracted nearly 50,000 people, of whom more than two thirds were women:[23] "The total number of people registered for the official UN Conference was 16,921, including 4,995 delegates, 4,035 NGO representatives and 3,250 media representatives."[24] The NGO forum, for its part, attracted 30,000 participants. Furthermore, 85 percent of the delegations to Beijing were headed by women.

The trend towards the inclusion of broader ranges of issues and the specific objectives and strategies was likewise seen in Beijing. At the Nairobi conference in 1985, governments were just beginning to recognize rape and domestic violence as social problems.[25] The Beijing *PFA* not only holds states responsible for protecting women from these and other forms of violence but it also prohibits "invoking any custom, tradition or religious considerations"[26] as excuses for neglecting this responsibility. For each of the twelve critical issues of concern, the *PFA* outlines specific objectives and provides detailed strategies for their attainment.

Not only were the range of issues broader and the treatment of issues more in-depth in the *PFA* but the whole conceptual framework had evolved since the early conferences on women.[27] In 1975, when the first World Conference on Women was convened, women's rights were seen as necessary to address other objectives, particularly economic development. Twenty years later, women's rights were seen as being intrinsically important; that is, important in their own right. Furthermore, the focus was shifting from women as a category of people to gender as a concept that examines the socially constructed roles of men and women. What has been constructed can also be deconstructed and reconstructed – a concept that threatens those committed to the status quo.

During the period between Nairobi and Beijing, the networks among international NGOs, generally, and women's groups, in particular, continued to expand, this time aided by the advances in information technologies. Electronic communication, particularly in the forms of websites and e-mail were used by UN bodies, governments, and NGOs to disseminate and redisseminate information pertaining to the conference. As a result,

NGOs were better informed and better able to coordinate their strategies. Furthermore, by the time the Beijing conference was convened, there existed some very experienced and sophisticated international NGOs dedicated to the advancement of women's rights in various domains with vast networks worldwide.[28] These networks were, for example, instrumental in organizing a worldwide campaign to have women's human rights included on the agenda for the 1993 Vienna Conference on Human Rights.[29] The strength of the women's global network was again in evidence when the Chinese government decided to move the NGO forum from Workers' Sports Service Centre in downtown Beijing to Huariou – a resort town 42 kilometres from the International Convention Centre, where the intergovernmental conference was being held: "UN Secretary-General Boutros Boutros-Ghali's office was flooded with calls, faxes, petitions, and letters from around the world. Women engaged in a global conversation about strategies to ensure an adequate site while simultaneously debating whether to boycott the Forum. The alacrity with which women responded to calls for action and the numbers who entered the debate reflected how seriously women took this event."[30] It also reflected the extent of the global NGO networks and their ability to orchestrate a massive campaign at short notice.

When the idea of holding a fourth world conference on women was being discussed in the UN in the early 1990s, the focus was on convening a conference to build on the work and achievements of the 1985 Nairobi conference on women.[31] Yet the progression from Nairobi to Beijing was less linear than had been the case between the previous three conferences. Several world conferences and summits were held in the 1990s that exerted major influences over the text of the *PFA* and, hence, over the agenda in Beijing.

Major UN Conferences and Summits in the 1990s
Each of the major world conferences and summits held in the 1990s addressed women's issues in their negotiations and in their final documents. The 1990 World Summit for Children established objectives for promoting the health, nutrition, and education of women and their children. The 1992 Rio de Janeiro Conference on the Environment and Development recognized the vital roles played by women in safeguarding the environment and in promoting sustainable development. It therefore pressed for their full participation in political and economic decision making. The 1993 Vienna Conference on Human Rights declared women's rights to be human rights and called for the mainstreaming of women's rights and gender concerns within the UN human rights system.[32] It stressed the importance of eliminating violence against women in both the private and public domains and called for the establishment of the new

position of special rapporteur on violence against women – a position created in March 1994. The same year, the Cairo Conference on Population and Development addressed issues of gender and recognized women's empowerment as being a prerequisite for health, population control, and economic development. The 1995 Copenhagen Summit for Social Development built on these achievements. Its *Declaration and Programme of Action* recognized that macro-economic policies have highly detrimental effects on women, that women have a crucial part to play in the eradication of poverty and in fostering social integration and that gender equality is an important component of sustainable development.

The documents emanating from these conferences were not legally binding. Nonetheless, their provisions relating to women's issues and women's rights were used as bases for moving ahead at subsequent conferences, particularly at the Fourth World Conference on Women, where a comprehensive program to enhance the social, economic, and political status of women and secure gender equality was adopted. As Secretary-General Boutros Boutros-Ghali said in his closing remarks to the Fourth World Conference on Women, "From each of these global conferences emerged a more powerful recognition of the crucial role of women in sustainable development and protecting the environment; of the human rights of women as an inalienable, integral and indivisible part of universal human rights; of violence against women as intolerable violation of these rights; of health, maternal care and family-planning facilities, and of access to education and information, as essential to the exercise by women of their fundamental rights."[33] The immediately preceding world conferences and summits all helped to set the stage for the Beijing conference. Yet of these conferences and summits, those whose language and approaches were most salient to the Beijing Conference on Women were the 1993 Vienna Conference on Human Rights, the 1994 Cairo Conference on Population and Development, and the 1995 Copenhagen Summit for Social Development.

The conferences and summits of the 1990s had additional spin-offs for the participants in the Beijing process. Through preparing for, and participating at, these conferences and summits, NGOs, in general, and women's groups, in particular, acquired greater expertise, expanded their networks and developed more effective strategies for coordinating their activities. On the other hand, the numerous meetings severely taxed NGO resources.

In spite of the progress made, it would be incorrect to see the twenty years leading up to the Beijing conference as a steady move towards enhancing the status of women in society. In both the economic and the political realms, the position of women actually got worse.[34] Furthermore, language adopted at one conference or summit was not always accepted automatically at subsequent sets of negotiations:

Although the term "gender" had been used in the Rio, Vienna, and Cairo documents, a group of Catholic, Islamic, and other countries insisted it be bracketed in the Beijing draft on the basis that its meaning was unclear and that it would be interpreted to endorse lesbianism and bestiality. The issue was resolved just prior to the Beijing conference by the formation of a special Gender Contact Group attended by sixty nations, chaired by Selma Ashipala of Namibia, which affirmed that "gender" was to be interpreted and understood as it is in ordinary, generally accepted usage![35]

At the start of the Beijing conference, brackets still remained around some of the provisions for sexual and reproductive rights that had previously been agreed to at the Cairo Conference on Population and Development.

The Beijing conference, like the three preceding conferences on women, was not without its polarizations, however, "as a 'post-Cold War' conference, the major divisions that had marked earlier women's Conferences, such as divisions between northern and southern women over what were women's issues or over Israel and Palestine, were replaced by political differences over issues like the global economy or the role of religion. And these debates crossed geographical and cultural boundaries."[36] The post-Cold War era, therefore, brought new constellations to the fore – new dichotomies that seriously challenged the prospects of success at the Beijing Conference on Women.

The twenty years preceding the Fourth World Conference on Women was not marked either by steady, large-scale improvements in the positions of women around the world or by the reconciliation of all polarizations. Nonetheless, the advances made profoundly affected the character and substance of the negotiations for the Fourth World Conference on Women. In particular, the Beijing conference reviewed and assessed the progress that had been made towards implementing the Nairobi *Forward-looking Strategies for the Advancement of Women to the Year 2000* and built on the provisions to advance women that had emanated from the series of conferences and summits held in the 1990s. Consequently, its mandate was expanded from that originally envisaged for the conference: to review the progress made on implementing the *FLS* and to accelerate the elimination of the major barriers preventing women from enjoying the full range of their human rights and from participating fully and equally in all spheres of life.

Preparations for the Fourth World Conference on Women

In 1990, the UN Commission on the Status of Women issued an evaluation of the progress that had been made towards implementing the *FLS*. The findings were mixed: "A greater proportion of women are literate, and more of them are visible at high political levels. At the same time, many women are poorer than ever before, and women's human rights are being violated on an unprecedented scale."[37] In other words, there had been progress in some areas, such as education and health, but overall the international community had not lived up to the commitments made in Nairobi. Vast numbers of women around the globe were no better off than they had been in 1985 and for many, the conditions under which they lived had actually deteriorated. In 1990, the Economic and Social Council recommended that the UN convene a Fourth World Conference on Women in 1995 and that the CSW serve as the preparatory body for the conference.[38] The recommendation was adopted by the UN General Assembly in December 1990.[39] In broad terms, the conference was to accelerate the implementation of the Nairobi *Forward-looking Strategies*; to examine the obstacles to achieving the objectives inherent in the themes equality, development, and peace; and to adopt strategies for overcoming the barriers by the year 2000. In more specific terms, the conference's mandate was to:[40]

1 review and assess the progress that had been made towards achieving the objectives spelled out in the *Forward-looking Strategies for the Advancement of Women in the Year 2000*
2 adopt a *PFA* that examined the major obstacles to the advancement of women in twelve interconnected critical areas of concern: poverty, decision making, education, human rights, health, media, violence, environment, armed conflict, girl child, economic equality, and national machinery for the advancement of women
3 specify in the *PFA* strategic objectives and actions to be taken by the international community, particularly by state governments but also by international organizations, the private sector, nongovernmental organizations, academic and research institutions, and the mass media, between 1996 and 2000, to remove the remaining barriers preventing women from enjoying the full range of their human rights and from participating fully and equally in all spheres of life
4 mobilize women and men at all levels of decision making to achieve the objectives outlined in the *PFA*.

Responsibility for drafting the *PFA* rested with the Secretariat of the Fourth World Conference on Women, part of the New York-based Division for the Advancement of Women. The secretariat was headed by Gertrude Mongella, the secretary-general of the Fourth World Conference on Women, who took office in December 1992. Mongella (United Republic of Tanzania) had previously served as a cabinet minister and as a diplomat who had led her country's delegation at the Nairobi Conference on Women. The draft texts were debated and revised by the UN Commission on the Status of Women (CSW), which served as the preparatory committee for the

Fourth World Conference on Women. Resolutions emanating from the CSW were forwarded to the UN Economic and Social Council for review. It, in turn, passed them on to the General Assembly for consideration, after which the draft texts were returned to the CSW for further elaboration and refinement.

The development of the draft *PFA* was a complicated and painstaking endeavour that spanned several years. During this period, the CSW convened three preparatory meetings that were held in conjunction with its annual sessions, in the springs of 1993, 1994, and 1995, an intersessional working group in January 1994 and five days of informal consultations in the summer of 1995. The earlier CSW negotiations focused on negotiations with China over the arrangements for the conference.[41] Not only was the discussion of the issues limited but it dealt only in generalities and not with the draft of the text that was to become the *PFA*.[42]

The first preparatory meeting was held January 1993. It was a "getting-to-know-you meeting. Many states sent delegates who knew little about women's issues. Some delivered set speeches focusing on geopolitical issues rather than on women's advancement. It was an unsettling experience for Gertrude Mongella."[43] In spite of these difficulties, the meeting produced a framework for the *PFA* that was adopted by the CSW at its 37th session in March 1993. Ten months later, the CSW convened an intersessional working group, from January 10 to 14, 1994, at which delegates from eighty-four countries struggled to transform the framework into a working paper for the Second Preparatory Meetings in March 1994. Madeleine Gilchrist, the only nongovernmental observer on the Canadian delegation, and in fact the only nongovernmental observer on any state delegation to the intersessional working group meetings, described the negotiations as a "growing pain process."[44] By this point in time, the draft *PFA* had identified eight areas of critical concern.

At the 38th session of the CSW in March 1994, a twenty-three-page version of the *PFA* was presented.[45] The draft was considered woefully inadequate by delegates to the meetings, who sent it back to the Secretariat of the Fourth World Conference on Women to be totally redrafted. Among other problems, its treatment of many issues was superficial, and it had failed to incorporate many of the advances that had been made at other recent conferences in the definition of women's rights. It was clear that the international community had moved far beyond the original concept of a more modest, short, succinct document outlining generally acceptable strategies for advancing women, such as literacy campaigns.[46]

The process of providing a more focused and in-depth coverage of the issues and of incorporating at least some of the advances in defining women's rights that had been made at other recent conferences took another ten months. In preparing the *PFA* that would be negotiated at the

Third Preparatory Meetings in March 1995, the secretariat drew on material from a wide variety of sources. As discussed earlier in this chapter, the three previous UN conferences on women as well as UN conferences in the 1990s exerted major influences on both the agenda in Beijing and on the substantive provisions in the *PFA*. But input into the *PFA* was not limited to these sources. As is evident in Figure 1, input came from a considerably wider range of sources.

As seen in Figure 1, these sources included meetings convened expressly to address issues in the *PFA*, national reports commissioned to serve as background for the meetings as well as for the conference itself and existing UN reports that addressed issues of initial concern to the work of the Beijing conference.

Between the Second and Third Preparatory Meetings, each of the UN's five regional economic commissions convened a conference to negotiate a regional Plan of Action. The five regional meetings were held as follows: the countries of Asia and the Pacific met in Jakarta, Indonesia, June 7 to 14, 1994; the Latin American and Caribbean states met in Mar del Plata, Argentina, September 20 to 25, 1994; the preparatory meeting for Europe and North America was held in Vienna, Austria, October 17 to 21, 1994; the states of western Asia met in Amman, Jordan, November 6 to 10, 1994 and the African states met in Dakar, Senegal, November 16 to 23, 1994. In each case, a parallel preparatory meeting was held for NGOs from the region. The regional meetings were important on several scores. They constituted the first substantial multilateral negotiations on the issues in preparation for the Beijing Conference on Women. They produced regional plans of action that were used as a basis for totally redrafting the *PFA* that was subsequently negotiated at the March 1995 New York Preparatory Meetings. They also were an important phase in the evolution of state policies.

Each regional intergovernmental meeting produced a *Plan of Action* that identified the key issues for women in its respective region, assessed the main barriers to their advancement, specified the region's needs and priorities and recommended actions to advance women in their regions. The regional meetings expanded the original agenda of the *PFA*. For instance, the African states, with the support of UNICEF, recommended that the girl child be added to the existing eleven areas of critical concern. This recommendation was accepted at the Third Preparatory Meetings in March 1995 – a move that actually reversed a previous decision that the Beijing conference would deal with women throughout their life cycle and that it would not focus on separate age groups. Following the regional meetings, the conference secretariat had to distil the five regional texts into one coherent document and to place their various findings into a global context.[47]

Figure 1

Sources of input into the PFA

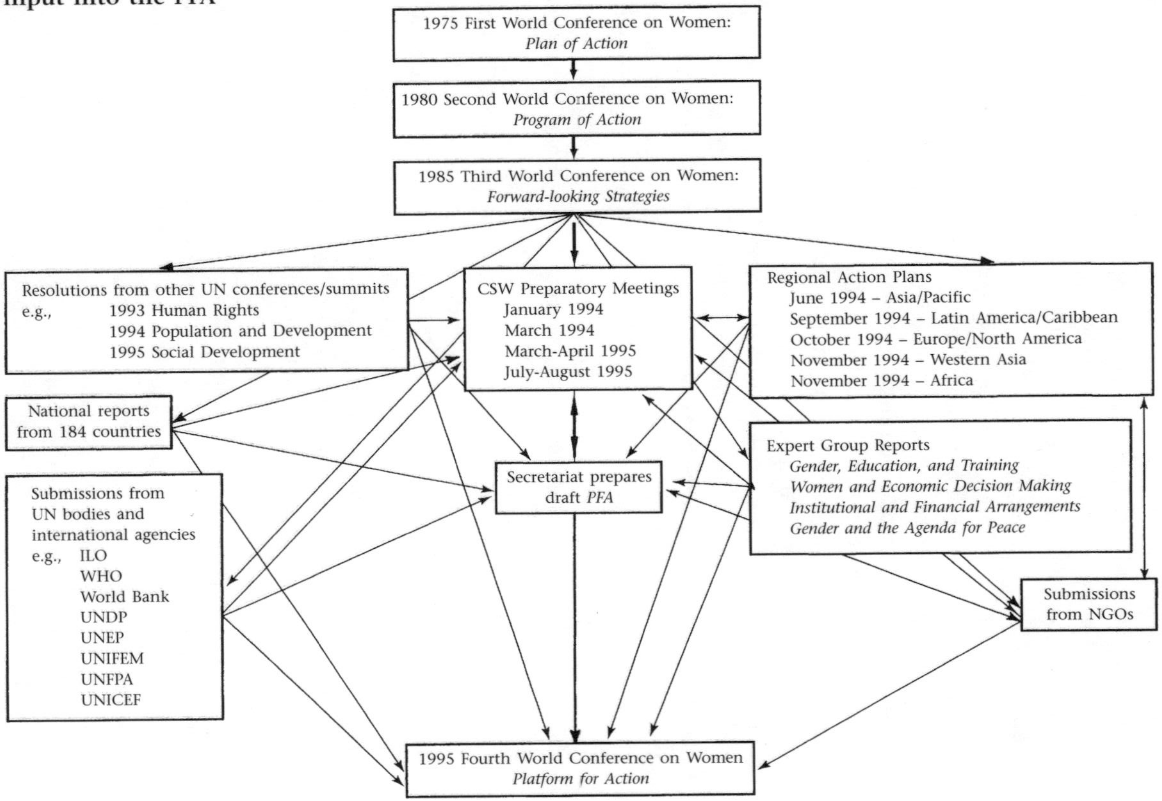

1975 First World Conference on Women: *Plan of Action*

1980 Second World Conference on Women: *Program of Action*

1985 Third World Conference on Women: *Forward-looking Strategies*

Regional Action Plans
June 1994 – Asia/Pacific
September 1994 – Latin America/Caribbean
October 1994 – Europe/North America
November 1994 – Western Asia
November 1994 – Africa

Expert Group Reports
Gender, Education, and Training
Women and Economic Decision Making
Institutional and Financial Arrangements
Gender and the Agenda for Peace

Submissions from NGOs

CSW Preparatory Meetings
January 1994
March 1994
March-April 1995
July-August 1995

Secretariat prepares draft PFA

1995 Fourth World Conference on Women
Platform for Action

Resolutions from other UN conferences/summits
e.g., 1993 Human Rights
1994 Population and Development
1995 Social Development

National reports from 184 countries

Submissions from UN bodies and international agencies
e.g., ILO
WHO
World Bank
UNDP
UNEP
UNIFEM
UNFPA
UNICEF

One of the key sources of data and analysis for the regional meetings, as well as for the CSW's preparatory negotiations, was the national reports that each of the UN's 185 member states was asked to submit. In its national report, each government was to assess the status of women in its country as it had evolved since the early 1980s in terms of specific quantitative and qualitative indicators such as participation in decision making, poverty, violence, and access to health, employment, and education. The report was to review and appraise the effectiveness of programs to advance women that had been implemented both by government and nongovernmental organizations and to define future goals for each of the indicators, and the strategies and financial arrangements to secure their attainment. Collectively, the national reports were designed to provide information on the status of women worldwide and a registry of pilot projects and programs designed to advance the status of women. Of course, each government wanted to put its best foot forward and so the accuracy and comprehensiveness of the reports varied from country to country.

In addition to the regional preparatory conferences, four meetings of experts were convened in the autumn of 1994 to examine specific areas in *PFA*. The issue areas examined were gender, education, and training; women and economic decision making; institutional and financial arrangements; and gender and the *Agenda for Peace*. The reports emanating from these meetings of experts provided specific analyses of the problems in their respective issue areas and recommendations for overcoming barriers to progress.

In drafting the *PFA*, the secretariat also drew on a series of UN reports. They included the 1990 evaluation by the UN Commission on the Status of Women of progress made towards the implementation of the Nairobi *Forward-looking Strategies;*[48] the 1994 *Update of the World Survey on the Role of Women in Development;*[49] an updated review of progress made towards the implementation of the *Convention on the Elimination of All Forms of Discrimination Against Women*[50] and *The World's Women: Trends and Statistics.*[51]

These documents, as well as the national reports and the reports of the regional meetings and experts groups, were used by the Secretariat of the Fourth World Conference on Women in drafting the *PFA* presented to the CSW meetings in New York in March-April 1995. The redrafting process was complicated by the vast amounts of material that had to be carefully considered and by severe time constraints. The last of the regional meetings ended in late November and the fourth expert group did not complete its meeting until December 9, 1994 – only three months before the Third Preparatory Meetings. States, for their part, expected to receive the document well in advance of the negotiations so as to have time to analyze the new provisions and to prepare their positions.

The Herculean task of redrafting the *PFA* to incorporate the advances made at other recent UN conferences and summits, the work of the regional conferences and the expert groups, the national reports and the UN documents discussed above had to be completed under tight time constraints. There were, moreover, organizational complications with which to contend. In October 1994, the Division for the Advancement of Women moved back to New York after being based in Vienna for ten years: "When the division moved back to New York, it took time to install telephones and to acquire computers. Some staff decided not to move and had to be replaced. Documents and resource materials, which had been shipped from Vienna, came late and were hard to find amid all the packing boxes."[52] Thus, the division underwent a major relocation just at the point when it was designated the conference secretariat responsible for drafting the *PFA*.

On February 27, 1995, less than a month before the Third Preparatory Meetings, a new and almost totally rewritten draft *PFA* was officially released.[53] The Division for the Advancement of Women was required to get the document to the editors four to six weeks before its publication so as to allow time for translation into the official UN languages. As a result, only the unedited English version was available to state governments by mid-January 1995. Just as the secretariat had operated under a tight time frame to complete the document, states and NGOs were left scrambling to analyze the virtually new document and to prepare their positions.

The Third Preparatory Meetings made up a large portion of the agenda of the CSW's 39th session, held March 15 to April 7, 1995. It was at these meetings that the first substantial international negotiations took place on the document that ultimately became the Beijing *PFA*.[54] By the 1995 preparatory meetings, the number of critical areas addressed in the draft *PFA* had risen to eleven, and, during the 39th session, the number was increased to twelve with the addition of the girl child.

Although substantial progress was made, the 1995 New York Preparatory Meetings faced several obstacles. First, the late release of the draft *PFA* had afforded participants little time to prepare their responses. Second, the preparatory meetings were convened immediately after the Copenhagen Summit for Social Development. As a result, there was no time to incorporate text agreed to in Copenhagen into the *PFA*. Furthermore, many of the delegates came straight from the summit to attend the preparatory meetings. The Group of Seventy-Seven, in particular, had not had time to prepare its joint positions on the *PFA*. Third, religious and conservative forces, which opposed much of the direction and substance of the *PFA*, were strong and vocal in their criticisms in New York. At the state level, they consisted of the Holy See[55] and its allies (most notably Guatemala, Ecuador, Honduras, Argentina, and Malta), as well as fundamentalist[56] Islamic states (in particular, Iran, Sudan, Algeria, and the Gulf states). Their antifeminist stances were supported by conservative NGOs, such as

Catholic Campaign for America, Focus on the Family, and Canada's REAL Women. On the other side, taking profeminist positions, were the European Union, Canada, Australia, and the Caribbean countries. The NAC, along with the vast majority of Canadian NGOs involved in the Beijing process, were profeminist in their orientations. Needless to say, this polarization rendered the process of reaching consensus on the *PFA* much more arduous.

In light of the number of delegations, the diversity of their views, and the broad range of issues under negotiation, it was not surprising that numerous amendments were proposed to the text during the first week of the meetings. To address this huge negotiating agenda, the 39th session of the CSW was extended by three days. Considerable progress was made during the three week period, and on April 7, the final day of the session, the CSW adopted the *Draft PFA*,[57] from which 65 percent of the previously existing brackets had been removed.[58] This was no small achievement in light of the facts that the delegates had little time to prepare their positions (given the late arrival of the document from the UN), they were dealing with a virtually new document and a great many of the issues were highly controversial. Nonetheless, 35 percent remained in brackets and so still had to be agreed upon. Some of the brackets were considered "soft," which meant that they were placed around text that was not negotiated because of time constraints (e.g., the delegates did not have time to consult with home governments and therefore could not negotiate) but on which there are probably not fundamental differences. In essence, the main reason the brackets remained was that time ran out in the negotiations. "Hard" brackets refer to brackets around text where ideological or substantial differences are involved – issues difficult to resolve. Most of the remaining 35 percent constituted "hard" brackets. The bracketed text included references to the universality of human rights, to sexual orientation, to cultural and ethical values, and to philosophical convictions. Also in dispute was language pertaining to sexual and reproductive rights that had previously been adopted at the 1994 Conference on Population and Development.

In light of the number of items remaining to be negotiated in the draft *PFA,* the CSW decided to hold an additional intergovernmental meeting July 31 to August 4, 1995, in New York to try to remove as many of the brackets as possible. As a cost-cutting measure, these informal consultations were to be conducted in New York by delegates posted to their countries' missions to the UN. It was understood that those sections requiring experts from the home countries who were not based in New York would be left to be negotiated in Beijing. The informal consultations focused on human rights, constitutional arrangements, resources, and macro-economics. These issues were divided between two working groups. Working Group One dealt with macro-economic concerns (e.g., structural adjustment programs, debt, sustainable development, and the respective roles of international financial institutions and transnational corporations), institutional arrangements, and additional commitments of resources. Working Group Two examined the human rights provisions pertaining to armed conflict, the girl child, and diversity.

To expedite the negotiations, Patricia Licuanan (Philippines), chair of the Commission on the Status of Women and chair of Working Group One, proposed ground rules that were adopted at the start of the informal consultations. The ground rules were as follows:

- Delegates should avoid making statements of position and should instead concentrate on resolving differences.
- Once agreement is reached on a particular text, delegates should not try to reopen the discussion.
- The only document under discussion is *A/CONF.177/L.1* [i.e., the *Beijing Declaration* and *Platform for Action*].
- Agreed language from other UN conferences should not remain bracketed.
- No new proposals should be entertained.
- The consensus reached this week should be confirmed by the Main Committee of the Fourth World Conference for [sic] Women.[59]

Participants at the informal consultations were assisted by three reference documents that the Secretariat of the Fourth World Conference on Women had prepared in advance. These three informal notes were as follows:

- Informal note 1 – Clustering of Bracketed Elements in the *Platform for Action*. This note arranges the bracketed paragraphs into twelve issue-related clusters to help the delegates focus their discussions on similar issue areas.
- Informal note 2 – Possible Arrangements of Titles in the *Platform for Action*. This note examines the consistency of titles and makes suggestions for a possible restructuring and harmonization of titles in the document.
- Informal note 3 – Relationship of Bracketed Text in the *Platform for Action* with Agreed Text from Recent United Nations Conferences. This note cross-references text from the Beijing document to passages from the Vienna *Programme of Action and Declaration*, the *ICPD Programme of Action and Declaration*, the *WSSD Declaration and Programme of Action*, and the *Convention on the Elimination of All Forms of Discrimination Against Women*.[60]

These ground rules helped focus and expedite the negotiations, but the fact remained that some issues were much more difficult to resolve than were others: "Progress was made in removing brackets from references to a number of economic and human rights issues, including structural adjustment programmes, sustainable development, international human rights instruments and economic rights. Other issues, such as references to the concepts of equity/equality, proved more difficult and remained bracketed. All issues related to health were held over for discussion in Beijing."[61] Notwithstanding the controversial nature of many of the issues under negotiation, significant progress was made at the informal consultations. A further 10 percent of the brackets were removed from the text. The report of these consultations was transmitted to the Fourth World Conference on Women.[62]

When delegates arrived in Beijing to attend the largest conference ever convened by the UN, 468 brackets[63] remained in the text. These brackets indicated words, phrases, and paragraphs on which agreement had yet to be reached. About 25 percent of the text remained to be negotiated.[64] Although some brackets remained because time had run out in the preparatory negotiations, most reflected the highly controversial nature of the issues themselves. This is part of what makes formal UN conferences so demanding: the issues left to negotiate are usually the most contentious.

This chapter has provided an overview of developments and preparations leading up to the Beijing Conference on Women. The remainder of the book focuses on Canada's positions and contributions and on the participation of Canadian government officials, nongovernmental representatives, and individuals in the policy-making process at home and at the international negotiations. The focus on Canada begins in Chapter 3 with an examination of the process by which government officials in Ottawa developed Canada's positions relating to the *PFA*.

3
Governmental Politics

Some may be tempted to dismiss the interactions discussed in this chapter as rather dull since there were no major fights among government officials and no graphic examples of crisis management. Instead, relations among government officials were relatively harmonious and the preparations for the Beijing process went smoothly. Broad objectives were established early and subsequent decisions were made in accordance with those objectives. As such, the process was logical with little of the "pulling and hauling" generally associated with governmental politics.[1] While crisis management may be considered more glamourous, it is every bit as important to understand cases in which the participants succeed in avoiding crises and in ensuring that the process functions smoothly.

Developing positions on the *PFA* was a complicated task for several reasons. The *PFA* dealt with twelve interrelated issue areas: poverty, decision making, education, human rights, health, media, violence, environment, armed conflict, girl child, economics, and mechanisms for the advancement of women. The number of interrelated issues was in itself a determinant of complexity. It also resulted in some twenty federal departments participating at various points in the policy-making process.[2] Preparations for the Beijing conference involved an even larger number of government departments and agencies and divisions within departments than do preparations for the Group of Seven summits.[3] Then there was the problem discussed in Chapter 2: governments (and NGOs, for that matter) had to respond on an ongoing basis not only to an evolving text but also to one that was radically transformed at least once in the process. The revised document for the 1995 New York Preparatory Meetings was so fundamentally changed from the previous version that it was virtually a new document. Furthermore, the draft was issued just one month before the session, leaving government policy makers only a few weeks to formulate their response. Thus, the number of issue areas under negotiation, their interrelatedness, the number of federal government departments participating in the policy-making process, and the late arrival of a significantly expanded and altered draft *PFA* just weeks before what was then slated to be the final negotiating session before Beijing all made the development of Canada's policies a complex process.

On the other hand, the issues under negotiation in Beijing were not new to Canadian government officials. In fact, all the recommended priorities and objectives for the Beijing conference were in accordance with existing policies that had received ministerial approval prior to previous conferences such as the 1993 Vienna Conference on Human Rights, the 1994 Cairo Conference on Population and Development, and the 1995 Copenhagen Summit for Social Development. Therefore, most of the interdepartmental conflicts that these issues might have triggered had already been resolved in interdepartmental negotiations for previously held UN conferences. Canada's policies and priorities for the Beijing Conference on Women were being formulated within existing guidelines: "In essence the proposals for Beijing sought to further strengthen the language pertaining to women's rights that had been negotiated at previous conferences and to build on their achievements."[4] The fact that positions had already been established on most of the issues under negotiation reduced the likelihood of conflict occurring at either the ministerial or the bureaucratic level.

The fact that the Beijing conference came at the end of a long string of conferences also had a down side. As Rhonda Ferderber, who initiated the government preparations for the Beijing conference, commented, "We were all suffering from conference fatigue. It was hard to get people enthused about the prospect of preparing for yet another conference."[5] Nonetheless, they rose to the occasion, and the time and energy they devoted to the process as well as their commitments to moving the agenda ahead are commendable.

This chapter begins by identifying the key departments, their main interests pertaining to the Beijing conference, and the ways in which each sought to develop its policy positions in response to the *PFA*. The respective roles of cabinet ministers and public servants are included in the discussion. After discussing the key departments individually, the interaction among departments and the work of the Interdepartmental Committee on the World Conference on Women is examined. Before drawing its conclusions, the chapter considers, albeit briefly, the interaction between federal officials and representatives of provincial and territorial governments. The provinces and territories have been included in this chapter for several reasons. They are clearly governmental, as opposed to nongovernmental, actors. Furthermore, their status in the Canadian foreign policy-making process is quite different to that of nongovernmental actors. Unlike the constitutions of most other federated countries, which give the federal government exclusive authority to conduct foreign policy, Canada's

Constitution Act neither assigns nor denies the provinces competency in foreign affairs.[6] What the Constitution Act does do is give the provinces jurisdiction over a wide range of issues that are often subjects of international negotiations. For instance, many of the issues in the *PFA*, such as education, health, and some of the economic provisions, involve provincial or territorial jurisdiction. The federal government was well aware of the practical imperatives of getting provincial or territorial support before committing itself on these issues. Such approval had, however, been secured before the Beijing process even began. As mentioned earlier, Canada's positions regarding the *Beijing Declaration* and *PFA* fell within existing government policies, and provincial or territorial approval had been sought before these original guidelines had received federal cabinet approval. Because the involvement of the provinces and territories in the policy-making process in this case was, for the most part, minimal, it does not warrant a separate chapter. Their involvement consisted mostly of being briefed several times a year at meetings convened by federal officials.

The chapter concludes with an assessment of the policy-making process within the federal government. It seeks to explain both policy outcomes and the relatively harmonious nature of the process.

Key Departments
Although some twenty government departments and agencies were involved at one time or other in the formulation of Canada's polices for the UN World Conference on Women, three were pivotal throughout the process: Status of Women Canada (SWC), Department of Foreign Affairs and International Trade (DFAIT), and Canadian International Development Agency (CIDA). In addition, the Women's Program, which was first part of the Department of Secretary of State, then part of Human Resources Development, and subsequently moved to Status of Women Canada on April 1, 1995, was intimately involved throughout the process. Thus, when the Women's Program was still part of Secretary of State, there were four pivotal departments: Status of Women Canada, Department of Foreign Affairs and International Trade, Canadian International Development Agency, and Secretary of State. Other departments played active roles as issues directly related to their mandates were featured on the agenda. For example, the health provisions were particularly weak in the first (February 1995) substantive version of the *PFA*, which prompted the executive director of the Women's Health Bureau (Health Canada) to become active in advocating stronger language both in interdepartmental consultations and at the New York Preparatory Meetings in March 1995. The Department of Justice was active in reviewing the language in the *PFA* to ensure that it both reflected Canada's interests and was consistent with UN language.

The full cabinet never became involved with Canada's policies for the

Beijing Conference on Women. Cabinet approval is required when a change in government policy is proposed or when there is a proposal for a new government policy. Such was not the case here, since the positions developed within the Canadian public service were compatible with existing government policies. Public servants from each of the departments and agencies that participated in the work of the interdepartmental committee were responsible for keeping their respective ministers apprised of their work.

There was some ongoing friction between the minister of foreign affairs and the secretary of state for the status of women, largely over questions of jurisdiction, but that was at times exacerbated by personality clashes. The DFAIT is responsible for international affairs, and the minister of foreign affairs was ultimately responsible for the Canadian delegation to Beijing. SWC was responsible for the coordination and development of policies for the Beijing conference and the conference was more important to its secretary of state than it was to the minister of foreign affairs. The time that the minister of foreign affairs was willing and able to devote to the Beijing conference was minimal. The demands on a minister of foreign affairs today are daunting: in addition to being responsible for the large departments (DFAIT and CIDA), the minister is expected to represent Canada abroad in numerous bilateral and multilateral meetings. André Ouellet lacked experience in foreign policy and was appointed minister of foreign affairs in 1993 by newly elected Prime Minister Jean Chrétien as a political move to place a senior francophone from Quebec in a major portfolio.[7] While the minister of foreign affairs was officially responsible for two of the three key departments involved in this case, his personal involvement was very minor.[8]

In the end, the instructions to the Canadian delegation were approved by André Ouellet, minister of foreign affairs, and Sheila Finestone, secretary of state for the status of women.[9] Since the instructions reflected existing Canadian policies that had been agreed to interdepartmentally, there was no need to seek full cabinet approval.[10]

Overall, those interviewed from the lead departments as well as from Health Canada described their respective ministers as supportive of women's issues, in general, and of their work for the Beijing conference, in particular. In most cases, positions and briefs were sent to the ministers on a "for your information" basis. None of the ministers was directly involved in the formulation of policies and position.

Status of Women Canada

Throughout the process, Status of Women Canada (SWC) was the lead department and served as the secretariat of the interdepartmental policy-making process. As the federal agency devoted to advancing women's equality, it was "responsible for policy co-ordination, research, funding and technical assistance, and communications activities related to the promotion of women's equality in all spheres of Canadian life."[11] It played a central role "advising the federal government on the potential impact of all proposed policies and programs, and in promoting measures to improve the economic, social and legal conditions of women in Canada."[12] SWC was also active in Canada's efforts at the international level to promote the full participation of women in society worldwide and to promote their advancement.

Preparations for the Beijing conference were in full swing when the Women's Program was being integrated into SWC. The Women's Program had been established in 1973 in response to the 1970 Report of the Royal Commission on the Status of Women, which recognized explicitly the pivotal role of voluntary women's groups in the struggle to combat wide-ranging discrimination against women and recommended that government funds be provided to facilitate their work for equal rights.[13] As noted above, the Women's Program was first part of the Department of Secretary of State and then part of Human Resources Development, before moving to Status of Women Canada in January 1995. Incorporating this important unit into SWC, while in the middle of preparing for a major world conference, was a tall order. Nonetheless, working relations within SWC were good.

The coordinator of SWC, Louise Bergeron-de Villiers, oversaw the process and acted as a liaison between the secretary of state for SWC and the public servants in her department, briefing the minister on an ongoing basis on the preparations for Beijing and keeping others aware of the minister's views and interests. She also ensured that adequate resources were allocated to the preparatory process.

The initial preparations for the conference were handled by Rhonda Ferderber, then director of Inter-Governmental and Non-Governmental Relations. Ferderber, who had been an active member of SWC since 1988, was well organized and is to be commended for beginning the preparations early (discussed later in this chapter). By the summer of 1994, she was not only responsible for her department's external communications and its relations with the provinces, NGOs, and the UN, but she was also coordinating preparations for the Beijing conference. Clearly, the workload was too heavy for one person. The inevitability of this development had been foreseen; in fact, the need to create a position dedicated to coordinating preparations for the conference had been recognized when the Beijing process first began.[14]

In August 1994, with the Vienna Regional Meetings only two months away, Valerie Raymond was seconded to SWC from the DFAIT to handle the overall coordination of Canada's policies for the conference. Raymond brought extensive experience, both in international negotiations and women's issues, to the newly created position of executive director of the

UN World Conference on Women Secretariat at SWC. She had served on the Canadian delegation to the 1985 Nairobi Conference on Women and as the women's rights advisor on the Canadian delegation to the 1993 Vienna Conference on Human Rights. Before being seconded to SWC, she had been director of the Human Rights, Women's Equality and Social Affairs Division (DFAIT). This meant that Raymond had already been working closely with Ferderber on the preparations for the Beijing conference. Once Raymond arrived, Ferderber, who had by then become director of the External Relations and Communications Directorate, focused on the external communications for the conference (e.g., public and media relations), as well as on her regular SWC work.

Government policy cannot be formulated effectively without good interdepartmental communications. The task of facilitating such communications rested with Janet Burn, chief of Communications Services. As part of her earlier responsibilities at SWC, Burn had actively participated in the 1991 establishment of the Canadian Panel on Violence Against Women, which was the first comprehensive study on violence against women conducted anywhere in the world. Burn chaired the interdepartmental subcommittee that was established to handle communications relating to the Beijing conference. She also worked with UNESCO to organize the 1995 International Symposium on Women and the Media, held in Toronto. At this symposium, which is discussed later in the chapter, agreement was reached on some of the most contentious media issues in the *PFA*.

Sheila Regehr did not join the Beijing secretariat until "the day after the briefing notes for Copenhagen were completed" (late February 1995).[15] The 1995 New York Preparatory Meetings were, therefore, the first UN meetings pertaining to the Beijing conference that she attended, though she had experience with other international negotiations, including the Copenhagen Summit for Social Development. She had worked on women's issues for the federal government since 1983, primarily in SWC but also for a period in the Women's Bureau, Human Resources Development Canada (HRDC). During this time, her responsibilities had included coordinating for the 1985 Nairobi conference and developing Canada's policies for the OECD and the Commonwealth Ministers' Meetings (especially their 1990 meeting in Ottawa, where the Commonwealth heads of government adopted the *Ottawa Declaration on Women and Structural Adjustment*). Regehr was seconded from SWC to the Women's Bureau to assist with domestic policy development in the newly created HRDC and also became Canada's negotiator on employment for the Copenhagen Summit for Social Development, before returning to SWC to work on the Beijing Conference on Women.

Primary responsibility for facilitating the participation of NGOs in the Canadian policy-making process rested with the Women's Program, "the primary government source of financial and advisory assistance to women's groups and other voluntary organizations working to improve the status of women."[16] Women's groups were funded to enable them to perform a watchdog function, to facilitate networking among themselves, and to assist them in participating more fully in the political process.[17] Financial and technical support to assist Canadian NGOs in preparing for and attending the UN negotiations on women was channelled though the Women's Program. The director, Jackie Claxton, had good coordinating skills and had established long-standing working relationships with women's groups across the country. In addition, she had attended the 1985 Nairobi Conference on Women and so had experience with the dynamics of an international women's conference and its accompanying NGO forum.

Louise Bergeron-de Villiers, Valerie Raymond, Rhonda Ferderber, Sheila Regehr, Jackie Claxton, and Janet Burn had worked together in other capacities, which facilitated working together in preparation for the Beijing conference. Although formal meetings were held, much of their work was conducted informally.

Department of Foreign Affairs and International Trade

Responsibility to "conduct and manage international negotiations as they relate to Canada" is a key component of the department's mandate.[18] It was, therefore, to be expected that the department legally and operationally responsible for conducting Canada's foreign policy, negotiating international agreements, and representing Canada at international conferences would play a major role in the Beijing process.

The priority for DFAIT, like that for the government of Canada, was to advance women's equality issues globally.[19] Of the twelve issue areas in the *PFA*, those of highest priority for the DFAIT were human rights, violence, armed conflict, reproductive rights, economic equality, and the girl child. On matters regarding international human rights, and peace and security, the DFAIT assumed the lead, as these were areas in which it had established expertise and they involved international treaties and covenants.

Within DFAIT, the key division was Human Rights, Women's Equality and Social Affairs. Adèle Dion, the departmental coordinator for International Women's Equality, was the principal voice of DFAIT and was considered "very good" by her colleagues.[20] She attended the Vienna Regional Meetings as well as the New York Preparatory Meetings for Beijing that were convened by the UN Commission on the Status of Women. In addition, she had been actively involved with the World Conference on Human Rights in Vienna.

Ruth Archibald, director of the Refugee, Population and Migration Division, became actively involved after the New York Preparatory Meetings when the issues relating to reproductive rights were more clearly defined and had assumed higher priority. Archibald had been consulted on issues of migration, refugee rights, and reproductive health when these issues were being discussed in Ottawa, but she had not attended the CSW preparatory meetings for Beijing.[21] Archibald had been Canada's principal negotiator at the Cairo Conference on Population and Development and head of the Canadian delegation to its preparatory meetings. She was, moreover, Canada's expert in international negotiations on reproductive rights.[22] In addition, she had a long-standing involvement with women's issues and had served as chief of staff for Barbara McDougall from 1988 to 1991, when the latter was Minister Responsible for the Status of Women.

Although there was some consulting with the Legal Operations Division, there was overall less than there had been for other recent conferences. This was because Kerry Buck, who had worked on human rights in the Legal Operations Divisions before being posted to New York in 1994, continued to be actively involved in the Beijing process. Buck had worked on the 1993 *Declaration on the Elimination of Violence Against Women* and had attended the Vienna Conference on Human Rights. In New York, she continued to work on human rights and women.

No formal mechanisms for consultations were established within DFAIT. Instead, the people involved consulted informally as the need arose. For example, Dion and Archibald consulted each other two to three times a week.[23] Within DFAIT, Dion also consulted regularly with her director, Ross Hynes, as well as with Gilbert Laurin of the Legal Operations Division, in the development of departmental positions. Outside the department, Dion conferred regularly with SWC colleagues. She consulted officials in the Department of National Defence on issues pertaining to peace and security, in the Department of Citizenship and Immigration on provisions for refugees, and in the Department of Justice on matters involving international treaties and covenants.[24]

Raymond was the key point of contact outside the department for all DFAIT officials involved in the interdepartmental decision-making process for the Beijing Conference on Women. This was logical in light of her position as the executive director of the UN World Conference on Women Secretariat. In addition, Raymond continued to be viewed as part of the DFAIT by her colleagues in that department even after her secondment to SWC.[25]

Based on her consultations inside and outside DFAIT, Dion drafted her priorities relating to the *PFA*. These priorities were discussed with the other DFAIT players, particularly Archibald and Laurin, as well as with Diana Rivington (CIDA), before she sent them to her assistant deputy minister for approval.

Canadian International Development Agency

The Fourth World Conference on Women was important to the Canadian International Development Agency (CIDA) on several scores. The conference's three themes (equality, development, and peace) coincided with CIDA's mandate, which is "to support sustainable development in developing countries, in order to reduce poverty and to contribute to a more secure, equitable and prosperous world."[26] Furthermore, advancing the well-being of women in development encompassed one of CIDA's key priorities. In particular, CIDA had a commitment:

- To increase women's participation as decision makers in the economic, political, social and environmental spheres;
- To improve women's economic conditions, basic health, education and human rights;
- To promote activities aimed at eliminating discrimination against women;
- To support developing country partners in voicing their concerns on gender issues in development.[27]

CIDA's mandate focused on working with Southern countries, which accounted for the majority of participants in the UN negotiations leading up to Beijing and at the conference itself. Yet in addition to its focus on integrating women into the development process within the South, CIDA was committed to enhancing "the understanding of gender and development issues among all Canadians."[28]

Of major concern to CIDA was the need to combat poverty, in general, and the ongoing feminization of poverty, in particular. Therefore, it gave highest priority to ensuring that the *PFA* addressed adequately the following objectives:

- to respect, nurture, and educate the girl child
- to recognize the economic contributions of women, since so much of women's work as wives, mothers, and caregivers goes unnoticed and unrewarded
- to combat AIDS, a disease that is spreading most rapidly among women
- to promote human rights and preserve the Vienna language
- to establish institutional arrangements to ensure that governments carry out the provisions to advance women to which they have agreed.[29]

Within CIDA, the process of preparing for the Beijing Conference on Women went smoothly, thanks to seven factors. First, Marnie Girvan, director of the Women in Development and Gender Equity Division was, like Rhonda Ferderber (SWC), a good planner and so the preparations within CIDA began early. Second, CIDA already had established policies on Women in Development, on poverty reduction, and on the environment, all of which served as guidelines for developing positions on the *PFA*. Third, CIDA officials developed their objectives pertaining to the *PFA* early and so had easy reference points for making subsequent decisions. That is, everybody knew the parameters within which decisions were to be made. Fourth, there was consistency in personnel; most of those within CIDA who participated were involved for the duration and there was relatively little turnover. Fifth, communications between those involved was good. Sixth, CIDA personnel had experience in the international arena – that was, after all, CIDA's primary area of operations – and CIDA's emphasis on Women in Development meant that those involved with the Beijing process already had considerable expertise on women's issues. In short, they had expertise at the international level and with women's issues. Finally, when the workload became too heavy for the existing staff to handle in addition to their regular duties, permission was granted to hire a coordinator.

The meeting convened by Rhonda Ferderber in August 1992 to begin the process of interdepartmental consultations for the Beijing conference prompted Girvan to establish what became CIDA's "1995 Network," which drew its membership from every branch of CIDA. The network first met on September 15, 1992. Thereafter it met as need arose, initially every six weeks. Closer to the conference, meetings became more frequent and were held every couple of weeks.[30] About fifteen people attended the network meetings on a regular basis.[31] The objective of the network was to facilitate the sharing within CIDA of information pertaining to the conference. In between meetings, there was constant consultation among members of the group.[32]

At the same time as the network was being established, telexes were sent to CIDA's posts and missions abroad informing them of the upcoming conference. It was expected that Southern groups would begin requesting CIDA funding for Beijing-related activities within their communities and for their representatives to attend the regional meetings and the preparatory meetings, as well as the Beijing conference. To facilitate communications both within CIDA and with the posts abroad, the *Beijing Bulletin* was produced. The *Bulletin* outlined what CIDA was doing in preparation for Beijing. The publications put out by the International Women's Tribune Centre in New York were also circulated.[33]

Two years before the conference, the 1995 Network held an all-day planning session which produced a mission statement and a detailed list of goals and objectives. By this point, the work had mushroomed to the extent that Marnie Girvan could no longer handle all the coordination process in addition to her regular responsibilities.[34] Permission was obtained to hire a Beijing conference coordinator, who would report to Girvan. Nicole Vaillancourt was appointed to the newly created position. Although one coordinator was significantly less than the three additional staff members originally requested, it was considered significant to get any increase in personnel in a time of fiscal restraint.[35]

The core members of CIDA's team responsible for preparing for the Beijing conference also included two other officers in the Women in Development and Gender Equity Division: Diana Rivington and Rajani Alexander. Both women had worked extensively on international development and on women's issues. Rivington, a senior policy advisor, had managed CIDA's aid programs in Latin America. Her involvement with women's issues dates back to 1984, when she had participated in the development of CIDA's Women in Development Action Plan. She had attended the 1994 Cairo Conference on Population and Development, which served as valuable background for negotiating the *PFA*. Alexander, a policy analyst, had experience working in both Canada and India to promote international development with particular concern for the status of women. She had been actively involved in the 1995 Copenhagen Summit for Social Development, which had tackled some of the key issues that were also on the agenda in Beijing. In broad terms, Marnie Girvan handled issues relating to education, human rights, AIDS, and violence against women, while Rajani Alexander concentrated on economic issues and poverty reduction, and Diana Rivington focused on health, population, and the girl child.[36]

In keeping with its mandate, CIDA facilitated the participation of Southern NGOs in the Beijing process and provided valuable expertise to the Canadian policy-making process. At first glance, these functions may appear unrelated but in fact they were complementary. Through its close working relations with Southern countries and Southern NGOs, CIDA officials gained a wealth of information that was highly valuable in the formulation of Canada's positions and strategies during the Beijing process.

Facilitating the participation of Southern NGOs took two forms: providing funds to attend the preparatory negotiations and the Beijing conference, and furnishing money for projects in Southern countries that related to the Beijing conference. As expected, requests from Southern groups seeking funding for projects began to arrive early in the process. The 1995 Network established a program committee and set out a list of criteria by which the committee was to judge the submissions. The criteria were designed to ensure that diverse activities related to the twelve critical areas of concern in the *PFA* were supported and that funding went to a wide range of NGOs, so as to reflect regional and ethnic diversity and to include grassroots groups as well as those more structured.[37] According to Girvan, the procedures proved effective and the allocation of funds went "smoothly."[38]

When it came to funding women to attend the actual negotiations, the 1995 Network gave priority to the regional meetings, though some more-limited funds were provided to assist Southern women to attend the New York Preparatory Meetings and the Beijing conference. This allocation of priority was based on several considerations. First, it is much easier to get input earlier in a process rather than later when positions are set. Second, the Southern NGOs with which CIDA worked would benefit most by meeting with NGOs dealing with similar concerns and problems. Violence against women was, for example, a major concern of women's groups in Latin America, Asia, and Africa.[39] Third, there were regional concerns that warranted attention. Each region was different; it was, therefore, important for women to hear from, and to interact with, women from their own region. Tackling these concerns was considered to have major impact on the programs of Southern NGOs and, hence, on CIDA's programs.

Southern NGOs were nominated by branches within CIDA, as well as by its posts abroad, to receive funding to attend the international negotiations. These nominations, like the applications for project funding, were reviewed in light of detailed, established criteria by the program committee that decided who received funding.[40]

In supporting Southern NGOs with their projects and in facilitating their representation at the international negotiations, CIDA assisted groups with which it had established working relationships. The Beijing conference was seen as part of a process rather than as an isolated event: facilitating the participation of Southern NGOs was considered a building block in ongoing relationships.[41] These relationships also had direct and immediate benefits for the process of formulating Canada's priorities on the *PFA*. CIDA sent observers – regional specialists – to each of the regional meetings. For example, Diana Rivington attended the Regional Meeting for Latin America and the Caribbean, while Rajani Alexander went to the Asian meetings, and Marnie Girvan went to the Vienna Regional Meetings. Through attending these regional meetings, CIDA officials gained valuable insights into how the UN preparations were proceeding and what positions were being taken by whom. The latter provided useful intelligence on where the Canadian delegation could expect to find support and where it was likely to encounter opposition in the upcoming negotiations. All this information, as well as that gained from CIDA's ongoing relationships with government officials and NGOs in the South, was fed into the policy-making process in Ottawa and provided valuable insights into the context within which Canadian negotiators would have to operate.[42]

Health Canada
Health Canada became involved rather late in the Beijing process, and its interests were far more narrowly focused than were those of the three lead departments. While the latter's concerns spanned most of the twelve critical areas in the *PFA*, Health Canada focused predominately on the health sections. As such, it sought to broaden their focus from a preoccupation with sexual and reproductive rights to include socioeconomic factors, such as the effects of poverty.

The Women's Health Bureau in Health Canada was part of the Interdepartmental Committee on Status of Women Mechanisms and, as such, had been consulted in the preparations of Canada's national reports to the UN Committee on the Elimination of Discrimination Against Women as well as in the drafting of the *Fact Sheets*, both of which are discussed later in this chapter. As a member of the Interdepartmental Committee on Status of Women Mechanisms, it regularly received information on activities of relevance to its work that were taking place domestically and internationally.[43] Nonetheless, the Women's Health Bureau became involved in the process of preparing for the Beijing conference considerably later than did the three key departments. Several reasons explain this late involvement. First, the conference was not a high priority for the department as a whole.[44] Second, the issues of health and the family did not become major issues on the international agenda before the 1995 New York Preparatory Meetings; therefore, the involvement of Health Canada was less important earlier in the process. Third, Abby Hoffman took over as executive director of the Women's Health Bureau just before the September 1994 Cairo Conference on Population and Development – after the preparations for Beijing had begun. The first request for her substantive input pertaining to the *PFA* came just ten days before the start of the Vienna Regional Meetings.[45] SWC itself had received the documentation for these meetings only shortly in advance; it could not have circulated the material any sooner.[46] Nonetheless, Hoffman was faced with the daunting task of having to respond to the *PFA*, while "getting up to speed" on the complex issues in her new portfolio.[47]

In light of limited resources, the decision of whether or not to participate in a process that was undoubtedly going to be very time-consuming was not taken lightly. Hoffman hired a recent law school graduate to research and write a report assessing the potential benefits of the conference. The report concluded that the *PFA* would be useful, especially to the women's movement, and Hoffman decided to invest scarce resources in the process. Her decision was accepted in the department but without enthusiasm.[48]

In June 1994, a Beijing advisory group was established within Health Canada. Its nine members met almost weekly to analyze proposals and develop departmental positions that formed the basis for the Health proposals. The researcher continued on a part-time basis to provide secretariat functions within the department, distributing documents to members of the advisory group, conducting research, reviewing the documents – those emanating from both the UN and from other departments within the Canadian government – and verifying that Health's proposals were indeed being incorporated into the Canadian position papers.

The Interdepartmental Committee

The policy-making process for any conference is not an isolated event but, rather, part of an ongoing process. Canada's experience at the three previous UN Conferences on Women and at the 1993 Conference on Human Rights, 1994 Conference on Population and Development, and 1995 Summit for Social Development all affected the positions it assumed in Beijing. Long before the Beijing conference was called, there existed established patterns of cooperation among SWC, DFAIT, CIDA, and the Women's Program. One of the ways in which this cooperation was manifest was in the production of two sets of publications: the *Fact Sheets* and Canada's reports to the UN Committee on the Elimination of Discrimination Against Women.

The development of the *Fact Sheets* began the process of interdepartmental coordination that evolved into the preparatory process for Beijing.[49] The *Fact Sheets*, which have been produced every two to three years since 1985, evaluated Canada's actions in terms of the recommendations in the Nairobi *Forward-looking Strategies*. They are, in a sense, the government's report card assessing its own progress towards implementing the *Forward-looking Strategies*.[50] Its facts, figures, and information about Canada's programs were useful resources for the Canadian delegations to the preparatory meetings as well as to the Beijing conference.[51]

SWC, DFAIT, CIDA, and the Women's Program also cooperated and collaborated in the production of Canada's reports to the UN Committee on the Elimination of Discrimination Against Women. These reports discussed Canada's compliance with the *Convention on the Elimination of All Forms of Discrimination Against Women*. In the process of drafting these documents, ideas were developed and clarified. In addition, the process involved consultations with the NGOs, and the provinces and territories, which resulted in ongoing exchanges of views. Thus, the preparation of the *Fact Sheets* and the national reports served as useful preparations for the Beijing conference. These documents also facilitated the dissemination of information about the conference and Canada's policies.[52]

In August 1992, once it was clear that the Fourth World Conference on Women was to be held, Rhonda Ferderber (SWC) called a meeting of Valerie Raymond (DFAIT), Jackie Claxton (Women's Program, secretary of state), and Marnie Girvan (CIDA) to discuss preparations for the conference and participation in the preparatory process.[53] From this meeting was born the Interdepartmental Committee on the World Conference on Women (IDC '95, as it was commonly called), which convened its first meeting in August 1992. It was chaired by SWC and included representatives from DFAIT, CIDA, Human Resources Development, Health, Agriculture, Justice, Citizenship and Immigration, Indian Affairs and Northern Development, and the Privy Council Office. Its mandate was to oversee the government's preparations for the conference, to coordinate the government's positions pertaining to the conference documents, and to develop strategies for the international negotiations.

SWC called the meetings, solicited agenda items from the committee members, established the agendas, and circulated documents and materials to all members of IDC '95 for comment. Positions were developed collaboratively. The SWC would compile the document outlining Canada's positions, circulate it to IDC '95 members for comment, and produce a final version to reflect these comments.[54] The IDC '95 recommendations were then given to Sheila Finestone, secretary of state for the status of women, by Valerie Raymond, and to André Ouellet, minister of foreign affairs, by Adèle Dion.[55] Since all the recommendations were in keeping with existing policy guidelines already approved by cabinet for previous conferences, further cabinet approval was not required.

In the course of preparing for the Copenhagen Summit for Social Development, the issue of financial resources had been broadly debated and the three key ministers, André Ouellet (DFAIT), Paul Martin (Finance), and Sheila Finestone (SWC), had agreed that no additional funds would be committed.[56] The ministers subsequently decided that the same principle would apply for Beijing: the conference would involve political commitments but no additional financial contributions.[57] This decision paralleled one taken at the international level: the UN had specified that the Beijing conference was to involve political commitments but that it was not to be a pledging conference. Canada supported the UN directive, since its official position specified that the UN budget was to have zero real growth.[58] Consequently, early on in the process, it was clear to the public servants preparing for the Beijing conference that no additional resources would be forthcoming; they had to be creative in spreading the program dollars out. This creativity included incorporating Beijing activities into programs and events that drew on existing resources. For example, funds were already allocated in the budget of SWC to support International Women's Day celebrations. Such events provided forums for informing participants of the World Conference on Women. They also drew media attention, which helped to disseminate the message to larger audiences.

In February 1993, Rhonda Ferderber (SWC) organized a two-day strategic planning session to establish broad objectives for Beijing. The session was attended by public servants from SWC, CIDA, DFAIT, and the Women's Program. The participation of Louise Bergeron-de Villiers reflected the importance accorded to the session by the senior administration in SWC. An external coordinator was brought in to facilitate the process, thereby ensuring that all the public servants could participate fully without having to divide their attention between the discussion of the issues and their administrative responsibilities. The meeting exemplified good planning in advance. At the time it was convened, the participants were still in the process of planning how to get the *Declaration on the Elimination of Violence Against Women* through the UN General Assembly, and they had only a vague idea of what the issues in the *PFA* would be. Nonetheless, many of their 1993 goals were achieved, at least to a significant extent, in Beijing.[59] The objectives agreed to at the February 1993 meeting remained the guiding principles, not only for preparing Canada's policies for the Beijing Conference on Women but also for addressing women's issues in other international negotiations, including the Vienna Conference on Human Rights (June 1993) and the Copenhagen Summit for Social Development (March 1995).

Given the large range of issues covered in the *PFA*, it is not surprising that many departments participated in the IDC '95 at some point – if not continuously – during the preparatory process. Most issues were broadly within the mandates of the key department. Officers from SWC, DFAIT, and CIDA were each handling several chapters, while those from other departments, such as Health, focused on the particular chapter relevant to their respective mandates. A subcommittee on communications was established to develop and implement strategies and plans for producing and disseminating information relating to the UN negotiations and Canada's positions at them. In addition, the IDC '95 established six working groups to deal with specific issue areas, such as health, human rights, and the economy and poverty.[60]

It was recognized that each division, bureau, or department had its own areas of expertise and that each would and should give priority to the issues most relevant to its mandate. But there was also a recognition that not only were the issues interrelated but that a symbiotic relationship existed between the domestic and the international levels – what one IDC '95 member described as "a yin-yang kind of effect."[61] Domestic decisions impinge on foreign policy options just as the external environment establishes parameters within which foreign policy makers operate. For instance, Canada's policies for the Beijing conference fell within existing policy guidelines, but the conference also served as leverage for developing policies and actions within Canada. During the process of preparing for the Beijing Conference on Women, cabinet approval was sought, and received, for a formal mandate to promote the equality of women and men and to ensure that gender-based analysis was used in the development of all future Canadian policies.[62] This initiative was not sought solely for the Beijing conference; instead, it was designed to apply to a broad range of Canada's domestic and international policies that addressed such issues as women's economic autonomy, their employment, their health, their participation in decision making, and the elimination of violence against women. Although the application of the policy extended well beyond

Canada's response to the *PFA*, preparations for the Conference on Women nonetheless provided the impetus and the justification for seeking cabinet approval at that particular time.

When the substantially revised *PFA* finally arrived a month before the 1995 New York Preparatory Meetings, SWC allocated each section to the members of the relevant working group. SWC set the stage by outlining the focus for each group and posing the central questions each group was to consider:

1 Which provisions in the *PFA* must be protected?
2 What is unacceptable and thus needs to be deleted or amended?
3 What priorities are omitted from the documents that need to be included?
4 Which areas in the document reflect acceptable ideas but need to have the wording redrafted (alternative wording proposed)?
5 What changes, if any, are required to the process or to the organization of the document?[63]

Naturally, all positions had to be consistent with Canadian legislation. The time frame in which to examine the actual provisions in the *PFA* was short, but because the working groups had already developed broad responses to the five questions outlined above before the text arrived, each had a frame of reference to assist with its textual analysis.[64] In addition to formulating positions, the working groups, in particular, and the IDC '95, in general, devoted considerable time to developing strategies for the upcoming negotiations.[65] Which states were likely to be allies? How could alliances be built to ensure that the provisions considered necessary were indeed included in the text?

The working groups submitted their reports to Valerie Raymond and her colleagues in SWC, who "lived in the office for four weeks" to produce a coordinated and consolidated document,[66] which was subsequently approved by the two key ministers. In spite of time constraints, Canada's positions were clearly defined before the 1995 New York Preparatory Meetings.

During the period when the members of IDC '95 were busy reviewing the new draft *PFA* and developing Canada's positions for the upcoming New York Preparatory Meetings, Canada hosted an "International Symposium on Women and the Media: Access to Expression and Decision-Making" from February 28 to March 3 in Toronto. The symposium was organized jointly by UNESCO and the Canadian Commission for UNESCO, in consultation with Janet Burn (SWC). It was the culmination of seven regional preparatory workshops that had been held between August and October, 1994, and had drawn participants from seventy countries. The participants at the Toronto Symposium included some 200 journalists, media experts, and researchers, as well as representatives of intergovernmental organizations and NGOs.[67] Together they discussed "ways to foster a more accurate and equitable portrayal of women in all forms of media, and strategized on how to increase women's participation at all levels of traditional, alternative and modern media industries."[68]

Strategies for achieving these objectives were outlined for governments, international organizations, media enterprises, NGOs, and professional associations in the *Toronto Platform for Action* that was adopted by the symposium participants. In addition, they critiqued the section in the *PFA* relating to the media and achieved some major breakthroughs in the resolution of several contentious issues. They were, for example, able to reach agreement on the need to ensure that the media presented the positive contributions women made to society. These agreements were subsequently incorporated into the *PFA* with the approval of the delegates to the preparatory meetings. In proposing solutions to several issues of contention in the media sections of the *PFA,* the symposium played a vital role in laying the groundwork for the resolution of these issues and, therefore, they did not need to be negotiated in Beijing.

It was not necessary to revert to the use of working groups after the New York Preparatory Meetings because IDC '95 was beyond the stage of developing its basic positions. IDC '95 did, however, hold a debriefing session after the New York Preparatory Meetings. At this point, the focus was on removing the remaining brackets in the *PFA.* The revised version of the *PFA* that appeared in May 1995[69] reflected the progress made at the New York Preparatory Meetings. Still 35 percent of the text remained in brackets, indicating passages on which agreement had yet to be reached.[70] Clearly, 35 percent did not bode well for the prospects of success in Beijing. The CSW decided to convene an additional set of negotiations from July 31 to August 4, 1995, in New York. These negotiations were designed to be carried out primarily by those already posted to the member countries' missions to the UN in New York; only issues within their competencies were to be addressed.

The preparations for these negotiations followed the same basic procedures as had been developed for previous negotiations. Departments were asked to review the sections of the May document most relevant to their mandates and to identify those provisions needing protection, those needing revising, and those that should be deleted; in other words, to answer the questions addressed to the working groups earlier in the process. Positions were worked out in close collaboration with Kerry Buck, who was posted to New York and who played a pivotal role in the ad hoc negotiations.

Assessing the Interdepartmental Process
The range of differences among members of the IDC '95 was relatively small and members of the committee even disagreed on the extent to

which differences of opinion existed at all. Finances did not cause interdepartmental wrangling in this case, since the ministers had agreed in
advance that no additional funds would be allocated. As a result, there was
no controversy between the Department of Finance and the lead departments over how much new commitments would cost. While such differences were normal in the interdepartmental bargaining surrounding
the allocation of regular departmental budgets, they were not part of the
Beijing process, per se.

There was, however, some disagreement over the priority accorded to the
health issues. According to Adèle Dion, the lead departments had sought
the participation of Health Canada for both IDC '95 and the Canadian delegation to the 1995 preparatory meetings precisely because priority was
given to health issues.[71] Abby Hoffman maintains that she had difficulty
getting the others to take the health provisions seriously.[72] The document
that emanated from the Vienna Regional Meetings took a narrow perspective: health and social services were lumped together, and the focus was on
medical intervention. Furthermore, the health section and the international
negotiations were preoccupied with sexual and reproductive rights. Hoffman
wanted the Canadian government to give high priority to broadening the
focus and to promoting a more holistic approach to health.[73] IDC '95 members from other departments tended to agree, for the most part, that health
issues had received inadequate attention in previous negotiations, but they
were nonetheless unwilling to accord the highest priority to these issues.[74]

Following the 1995 New York Preparatory Meetings, where the conservative and religious forces (in particular, the Vatican; the strongly Roman
Catholic, largely Latin American, countries; and the fundamentalist Islamic
states) had been especially active, there were some philosophical differences in approaches, again between Health, on one hand, and SWC and
DFAIT, on the other. Here, the main issue was the extent to which new
issues and approaches should be introduced into the text. Health sought
to move beyond previous accomplishments "to broaden the agenda and to
move the bar up higher."[75] The SWC and DFAIT were concerned with consolidating the positive language that had been adopted at previous conferences, and they sought to build on this foundation. In the health section,
this meant consolidating the gains made on sexual and reproductive rights
in Cairo. According to Valerie Raymond, "the introduction of broad new
language and new initiatives at this late stage in the negotiations would
have been unlikely to find support among the other government delegations. Furthermore, it would have reduced Canada's credibility and the
resources that it had available to negotiate the hard issues which the IDC
'95 had identified as key Canadian priorities."[76] Within SWC and DFAIT
there was concern that to push too hard would trigger a conservative backlash aimed at rolling back the progress already achieved.[77]

There was a sense, at least among some of the members of the IDC '95, that policies were being determined by an "inner circle" rather than being developed collaboratively. On the other hand, Raymond confided that the process of "trying to get everyone on board" (i.e., of trying to develop consensus) was at times challenging.[78] Nonetheless, these differences in priorities and in the degree to which progress was feasible should not be exaggerated. All members of the IDC '95 sought to build on past accomplishments and to move the agenda ahead. In the grand scheme of bureaucratic infighting, the differences among members of the IDC '95 were minor.

Consultations with the Provinces and Territories

Canada's federal system demands that federal government officials consult the provincial and territorial governments when developing foreign policies that affect areas under provincial jurisdiction.[79] Within SWC there have long existed mechanisms for consultations with the provinces at both the political and bureaucratic levels. The 1985 Task Force on Program Review commended SWC for its success in bringing "the provinces together for national awareness of issues relating to women and for consensus building."[80] Federal ministers responsible for the status of women and their provincial and territorial counterparts have been meeting annually for more than twenty years. At the bureaucratic level, senior officials in SWC have been meeting with their provincial and territorial counterparts throughout the same period, at least three times a year.[81] The agenda for the meetings is mutually agreed to in advance by the provincial and federal officials. The meetings are held in SWC headquarters and chaired by its officials. Thus, the process of consultations between federal officials and their provincial and territorial counterparts was well established long before the Beijing conference was called. The provinces and territories had, for example, been asked for their input in the preparation of Canada's national reports to the UN Committee on the Elimination of Discrimination Against Women and the *Fact Sheets*. The Beijing conference was first placed on the agenda of these meetings in 1992.[82]

Generally, international matters pertaining to women receive little attention from the provincial and territorial governments. In this case, most of the provinces and territories did respond to SWC's requests for input, and they kept SWC informed of their concerns and of their activities related to the Beijing conference. SWC officials, for their part, shared information and documents pertaining to the conference with their provincial and territorial counterparts. The latter's involvement in the Beijing process varied from province/territory to province/territory, but overall it was relatively minor. This level of involvement did not reflect a lack of interest either in the conference or in the issues on its agenda on the part of the status of women bureaus in the various provinces and territories; instead, the key determinant of the extent to which provincial and territorial status of women officials were able to participate was their respective budget.[83] They just did not have the financial resources or the personnel to devote greater resources to this particular area of foreign policy making.

On January 25, 1995, a joint meeting of the Canadian Preparatory Committee and the senior status of women officials from the provinces and territories was held, at which the reports from the regional meetings were presented and preparations for the 1995 New York Preparatory Meetings were discussed. Likewise, after the Beijing conference, a major debriefing meeting was held with the provincial and territorial officials to examine Canada's plans for implementing the *PFA* and to consider the provincial and territorial interests pertaining to these plans.

In the spring of 1995, every province and territory was invited by SWC to nominate representatives to the Canadian delegation. The decision of whether to send representatives rested with the provinces and territories and once they submitted their nominations, these representatives became members of the delegation. Of Canada's ten provinces and two territories, only Manitoba, Quebec, and the Northwest Territories sent representatives on the official delegation. Since the provinces and territories were responsible for the travel expenses of their delegates, cost appears to have been the major factor inhibiting greater representation.[84]

Relations between the federal officials and their provincial/territorial counterparts were cordial and fit within a pre-existing framework of regular consultations. Throughout the Beijing process, federal officials kept their provincial counterparts apprised of developments and solicited the latter's response. The provincial and territorial officials were relatively minor players for three reasons: their resources were minimal, which precluded a major involvement; their priorities focused on domestic rather than international matters and they were in general agreement with the direction and substance of federal policies. Nonetheless, the relationship between the federal and provincial and territorial governments was symbiotic. The former considered the latter to be informed and necessary players in the work to advance the status of women, while the gains made by the Canadian negotiators in Beijing could be cited by the provincial and territorial officials in their efforts to improve the position of women within their jurisdictions.

Conclusion

The chapter has considered three categories of actors: federal cabinet ministers, federal public servants, and provincial and territorial officials responsible for the status of women within their respective jurisdictions. As discussed, the provincial and territorial officials responsible for the status of women consulted regularly with federal officials and were kept apprised of developments pertaining to the Beijing conference. They did not, however, exert any major influence over the substance or the direction of Canada's policies.

Canada's policies for the Fourth World Conference on Women were developed through interdepartmental negotiations at the bureaucratic level. Full cabinet approval of these positions was not sought or needed, as they fell within existing policy guidelines. Public servants kept their respective ministers apprised of relevant developments and of the positions they were taking. Canada's formal positions were approved by the minister of foreign affairs and secretary of state for the status of women.

At the bureaucratic level, where Canada's negotiating positions were formulated before being forwarded to the ministers for final approval, the policy-making process went smoothly and was relatively harmonious. Four factors account for this. First, and most importantly, the policies being formulated fell within existing policy guidelines. Canada had a long history of involvement with most of the issues in the *PFA* and had already developed clear policies in these areas. For example, there already existed a clear policy framework in the area of violence that could easily be translated into positions for the Beijing conference.[85] Thus, most – if not all – of the significant interdepartmental differences on these issues had been resolved prior to the Beijing process, when the policy frameworks themselves were being negotiated.

Second, and closely related to the first factor, there was a high degree of consensus within government on what the priorities and objectives should be.[86] All the key participants shared the macro-level objective: to build on language to advance women that had been agreed to at previous UN conferences. There was consensus that all of the twelve critical areas of concern within the *PFA* were important, though departmental affiliation was the key determinant of the priority and focus that each participant was willing to accord to a given issue. For example, in the area of violence, the primary concerns for SWC were its ramifications for the well-being of women within Canada, whereas CIDA was concerned with violence against women in the Southern countries. Priorities differed but broad goals, such as eliminating violence against women, were shared.

Third, the planning process began early. Rhonda Ferderber convened the first meeting three years in advance of the conference, an interdepartmental committee began functioning shortly thereafter, and this pattern of careful, advanced preparation was replicated in all the key departments. Clear objectives were established early, and these objectives were used as guidelines for subsequent decisions. The result was a smooth and relatively harmonious policy-making process.

Finally, the consistency, the experience, and the perspectives of the key participants facilitated the process. Most of the key participants from

SWC, DFAIT, CIDA, and the Women's Program were involved throughout the policy-making process. They had, moreover, experience predating the Beijing process, not only with the issues but also in working together on these very issues. As Archibald (DFAIT) comments, "We had fought the good fight together through the development of domestic policies."[87] Furthermore, most also had experience with international negotiations. The public servants in the Women's Program and the three lead departments, in particular, had "long standing collaborative relations working together in the context of other international negotiations affecting women's rights. It was an effective partnership: we relied on each other for specific policy language in our respective areas of expertise."[88]

All the key participants were personally committed to the issues – though their commitments to, and notions of, feminism varied considerably. Several remarked that the process had worked particularly well because most of the participants were women, which resulted in more cooperative, collaborative teamwork than they had experienced in male-dominated decision making.[89]

While there were some differences over priorities and tactics, one did not see the kind of interdepartmental wrangling that has occurred in some other cases, including the formulation of policies for the UN Third Conference on the Law of the Sea.[90] Overall, the policy-making process within the federal government was marked by careful planning and cooperation. So often there is a tendency to focus on crises and to give credit only to those who overcome crises. There is also a need to give credit for smooth, ongoing work.

4
Nongovernmental Organizations within Canada

Canadian nongovernmental organizations used three major strategies to exert influence in the Canadian policy-making process for Beijing: utilizing government-sponsored mechanisms to facilitate their participation, lobbying individually, and working through transnational NGO networks both prior to and at the UN negotiations. Of course, the extent to which a group employed a particular strategy depended on a variety of factors: its resources, its priorities, its perception of the receptivity of government, and the extent to which its objectives coincide with those of other groups within Canada and abroad. This chapter examines the principal channels for facilitating NGO input into the Canadian foreign policy-making process for the Beijing Conference on Women: the Canadian Beijing Facilitating Committee and the Canadian Preparatory Committee. The decision to focus on these government-sponsored mechanisms was made for several reasons. Most importantly, the majority of the government officials interviewed say that direct lobbying efforts by individual groups resulted in very little influence on Canada's positions.[1] Then there are the pragmatic considerations: so many individual groups approached the various government departments during the Beijing process that it would be hard to know where to draw the line.[2] Finally, the focus is justified because the government-sponsored mechanism involved a broad spectrum of groups. Transnational networking among NGOs is discussed in Chapter 6.

Demographics
The participation of nongovernmental actors in the Beijing process was greater than it had been for other recent UN conferences, in terms of numbers and the length and intensity of their involvement. Three reasons account for the higher level of participation. First, women's groups had a history of involvement dating back to the First World Conference on Women in 1975 and their participation had gathered momentum both in terms of quality and quantity over the ensuing twenty years. Second, the

Beijing process began early, allowing time for interest to mount. Third, the *PFA* addressed twelve interconnected issue areas: poverty, decision making, education, human rights, health, media, violence, environment, armed conflict, girl child, economics, and mechanisms for advancement of women. As a result, the process attracted input from national women's groups with broad mandates, such as the National Action Committee on the Status of Women (NAC), as well as from local organizations, such as shelters for battered women. Labour, peace groups, human rights organizations, and environmental groups also sought input.

It should be noted that the Canadian Labour Congress (CLC) considers itself as having a different status from NGOs in terms of entitlements.[3] Nevertheless, it is included in this chapter, as well as in the discussion in Chapter 6 of Canadian NGOs at the UN negotiations, since it is clearly a nongovernmental, as opposed to a governmental, organization. The CLC participated in the government-sponsored Canadian Preparatory Committee as a nongovernmental actor. Representatives of the CLC attended the UN negotiations leading up to Beijing and the conference itself.

The nongovernmental actors were extremely diverse in terms of the specific issues on which they focused, the range of their interests, their geographic bases, their lobbying tactics, the intensity of their lobbying efforts, their knowledge of the Canadian foreign policy-making process, and their experience with UN negotiations. All the issues in the *PFA* were relevant to the NAC; hence, it had designated representatives to deal with poverty, health, violence, economic equality, financial arrangements, national machinery, human rights, the environment, and the girl child.[4] In areas where it did not have its own experts, it worked closely with other women's groups, such as Canadian Voice of Women for Peace (VOW) in the area of armed conflict and the Canadian Congress for Learning Opportunities for Women in the area of education and training. In contrast, small, locally based groups focused on particular issues, such as violence or health, and their involvement in the process were generally minimal.

Just as there were differences among NGOs in terms of the range of the interests they were pursuing and in the degree to which they participated in the process, there were also major differences in their levels of experience. The CLC has a particularly long history of involvement with international negotiations. In addition to its long-standing participation in the work of the International Labour Organization, it had sent an observer on the Canadian delegation to the Third World Conference on Women in Nairobi, its president had addressed the plenary at the Vienna Conference on Human Rights, and its vice-president was on the Canadian delegation to the Copenhagen Summit for Social Development as well as on the Canadian delegation to the Beijing Conference on Women. The NAC and VOW also had considerable experience attending UN negotiations.[5] Other groups, including the Canadian Research Institute for the Advancement of Women, which volunteered to administer the government-sponsored Canadian Beijing Facilitating Committee, had no prior experience with UN negotiations.

Ideologically, the NGOs ranged from groups with strong feminist orientations, such as NAC, to conservative groups, such as REAL (Realistic, Equal, Active for Life) Women, which opposed the feminist agenda, in general, and the provisions for sexual, reproductive, and lesbian rights, in particular. Nonetheless, the vast majority of the NGOs that sought input into Canada's policies for the Beijing Conference on Women espoused a feminist approach to advancing the status of women and pushed the government to go further in promoting a feminist agenda.

Government Support for NGOs

Government support for NGOs within Canada took four forms:

1 creating and funding the Canadian Beijing Facilitating Committee (CBFC) to facilitate and coordinate the participation of NGOs
2 providing funds, channelled through the CBFC, to assist NGOs in preparing their positions prior to the Vienna Regional Meetings (October 17 to 21, 1994), the New York Preparatory Meetings (March 15 to April 4, 1995), and the Beijing conference (September 4 to 15, 1995)
3 establishing the Canadian Preparatory Committee (CPC) to facilitate consultations between members of the federal interdepartmental committee (IDC '95) and NGOs in the preparations of Canada's positions
4 disseminating information pertaining to the 1995 World Conference on Women.

The discussion begins with a brief look at the fourth category of support: government efforts to inform Canadians about the 1995 Women's Conference. Thereafter, it moves on to assess the work of the CBFC and CPC, which together form the focus of this chapter.

Dissemination of Information

Since the Canadian government had decided not to allocate additional funds for the Beijing conference, SWC officials had to use ingenuity to get the message out. This was evident in their use of pre-existing venues to publicize the conference. SWC included information on the Beijing conference in publications that it was already producing and distributing, including the *Fact Sheets* and its national reports to the Committee on the Elimination of Discrimination Against Women, which were discussed in Chapter 3. SWC also capitalized on events, such as International Women's

Day celebrations across the country, to disseminate information about the Beijing Conference on Women.

In addition to tapping into existing venues, SWC officials undertook some modest, new initiatives. In 1994, the Communications Subcommittee of the Interdepartmental Committee '95 commissioned a public opinion poll in Montreal and Toronto to see what type of communications they would find most useful. Based on the result of the poll, *Beijing Update* was first published by SWC in the autumn of 1994. Although less detailed than the *Fact Sheets,* it was, nonetheless, a useful source of information on the Fourth UN Conference on Women and on activities and developments pertaining to it. *Beijing Update* was sent out to all those who had expressed, to SWC and other government departments, an interest in the conference. SWC also used existing publications, such as its quarterly, *Perspectives,* to disseminate information about the conference. CIDA published the *Beijing Bulletin,* which outlined its preparations for the Beijing Conference on Women. Thus, through the creation of new publications, as well as through the use of existing reports and periodicals, government officials kept the attentive public apprised of relevant developments, and it provided helpful advice for those planning to attend the preparatory meetings and World Conference. As is discussed in Chapter 6, both SWC and Health sent out comprehensive briefing packages before the Beijing conference, outlining Canada's positions for the negotiations.

SWC also funded special activities relating to the Beijing agenda. For example, funds were provided to produce a video on violence against women and to publish a special volume of *Canadian Woman Studies* entitled *Women's Rights Are Human Rights.*[6] In partnership with *Homemaker Magazine,* SWC ran a writing challenge to select two youth delegates for the Canadian delegation to Beijing. The contest generated a lot of media coverage.[7] In several instances, SWC cosponsored public meetings to inform those interested about the conference. For example, on November 22, 1993, SWC, the International Development Research Centre, and the North-South Institute together hosted a public forum on the Fourth World Conference on Women, at which Gertrude Mongella, the secretary-general of the conference, was the guest speaker.

Government officials used a variety of avenues to make Canadians, generally, and women's groups, in particular, aware of the Beijing process. They deserve commendation for doing much with relatively little to make Canadians aware of the conference. Their efforts were, however, not aimed at providing detailed explanations of Canada's policies and priorities or in-depth analysis of the issues. Instead, they provided general overviews of the conference, its issues, and developments relevant to it, as well as tips for those hoping to attend the negotiations.

These efforts to disseminate information about the Beijing conference were aimed at reaching as broad an audience as possible. For groups wishing to conduct in-depth analysis of the *PFA*, to develop the priorities in response to its provisions, and to participate in the policy-making process, the principal channels for securing the text and for gaining access to key government decision makers were the government-sponsored mechanisms.

Government-Sponsored Mechanisms to Facilitate NGO Participation in the Canadian Policy-Making Process

Government preparations for the 1995 conference began early, and meetings were held with NGOs a full three years in advance to inform them about the conference. As the government did not provide travel funds, most of the groups represented at the meetings were Ottawa-based, though a few came from Montreal. Yet in spite of these early consultations, the formal mechanisms for facilitating NGO participation were not set in place until April 1994 – one-and-a-half years before the conference – when a Canadian Beijing Facilitating Committee was established.

Early on in the Beijing process, SWC initiated a meeting of government officials who had been involved at Nairobi to consider the questions: What had gone well? What had not worked? What could have been done better?[8] It was decided that the major weakness in the preparatory process for Nairobi had been that NGOs had enjoyed few opportunities to prepare positions and to coordinate strategies prior to the conference. It was recognized that the women's movement had grown in strength in the ensuing decade and that women's groups in the 1990s had more expertise and experience to offer and were demanding greater participation than had been the case for the Nairobi conference.[9] There was a need to make the process more democratic.

On June 4, 1992, SWC convened a national consultation for Canadian women's groups to inform them about the upcoming conference and to encourage them to start preparing for it. The meetings were convened at SWC headquarters in Ottawa and were attended by Mary Collins, secretary of state for the status of women, who provided an overview of international developments pertaining to the Beijing conference. During the one-day session, the NGO representatives brainstormed in working groups on their priorities and on ways of organizing themselves.

Yet in spite of holding this initial meeting more than three years in advance of the 1995 conference, NGO involvement in the policy-making process was slow in coming. Several of those who became key members of the CBFC saw the government's preoccupation with the 1993 federal election as a major factor delaying preparations for Beijing.[10] "Because of the election we could not get SWC and the bureaucrats to move on anything,"[11] says Pat Beck, of the National Council of Women. Government officials saw things quite differently: "The election gave us a reprieve from some of our other policy work to focus on preparations for Beijing while the minister was otherwise pre-occupied."[12] In retrospect, these differing perspectives over the impact of the election were indicative of a key characteristic of relations between NGO representatives and government officials. As is quite common in such relationships, the NGO representatives expected government officials to devote more time and energy to ensuring the meaningful participation of the former than government officials were willing to allocate.

In any case, before government officials had decided on a mechanism for involving NGOs, events overtook them. The Manitoba UN End of Decade Committee was the only group in Canada that had, every year since the Nairobi conference, held a conference to assess what progress was being made in Canada towards the implementation of the *Forward-looking Strategies*. In March 1993, it added an extra day to its annual conference, to which federal government officials were invited. The objective of the meeting was to discuss preparations for the Beijing conference. The federal government not only sent Jackie Claxton to the meeting but also provided funding to allow some of the major national women's groups, which were not members of the Manitoba UN End of Decade Committee, to send representatives.[13]

The meeting was attended by some forty people.[14] They represented national women's groups[15] and local women's groups, as well as several national organizations concerned with international development, poverty, and human rights, such as the North-South Institute, MATCH International, and the National Anti-Poverty Organization. Although some of these groups, such as Zonta and the YWCA, had consultative status with the UN Economic and Social Council, very few of the women present had ever had any direct experience with the UN.[16] Representatives from organizations not considered "women's" groups, such as the North-South Institute, were invited to participate in the discussions but only women's groups were allowed to vote.

Much of the substantive focus for the meeting came from a survey that Deborah Stienstra and Barbara Roberts had just completed for the Canadian Advisory Council on the Status of Women.[17] The study described the terms of the *Convention for the Elimination of All Forms of Discrimination Against Women* and the Nairobi *Forward-looking Strategies for the Advancement of Women by the Year 2000* and assessed the progress made by provincial, territorial, and federal governments in the implementation of their obligations arising from these two documents. The study was particularly timely since the Beijing conference was to build on the *Forward-looking Strategies,* especially since it was to move the agenda ahead in areas where progress had been weakest. The idea of establishing a Beijing Coordinating

Committee to encourage and assist NGOs to participate fully in the Beijing process was proposed and accepted.

Volunteers were then sought to sit on a steering committee. The process was informal: the thirteen women who raised their hands in response to the call for volunteers were said to compose the committee.[18] In this way, an ad hoc steering committee emerged from this meeting. There were also several offers to carry out specific preparatory work before the first meeting of the ad hoc steering committee. Joanna Kerr (North-South Institute) volunteered to write a proposal that could be presented to the next meeting of the steering committee, outlining strategies for NGOs seeking input into the Beijing process and the objectives, principles, and operating procedures for a CBFC.

Madeleine Gilchrist, one of the very few participants with UN experience, explained that four days later she would be representing VOW and its international affiliate, Women for Mutual Security, at the UN Commission on the Status of Women meeting in Vienna.[19] She offered to send information to those interested in the Vienna meetings once she returned to Canada, and several women asked to be kept informed.[20] Once in Vienna, Gilchrist met for over an hour with Rhonda Ferderber (SWC), during which time Gilchrist presented Ferderber with a list of the women who had participated in the Winnipeg meeting, their groups, their groups' affiliations (if any) with international groups, and the topics of particular concern to each group. The issue of primary concern to most in Winnipeg was violence, although health issues, the media, and economic issues were listed by a few as major concerns. This illustrates that, beginning early in the process, there was a two-way flow of information between the federal government and the women's groups.

On May 27, 1993, SWC held a consultation to which it invited the steering committee and the Group of Twenty-Three, an existing coalition of national women's groups. The objective of the meeting was to develop mechanisms for facilitating and coordinating the participation of Canadian women's groups. The NGOs decided to meet one day before the consultation to organize their positions. At the NGO meeting, there was some jockeying for control of the process, though views vary as to who the main contenders were. Members of the Manitoba UN End of Decade Committee had for years been the only ones working on a follow-up to Nairobi, and they had begun the preparatory work for Beijing; they did not want to be squeezed out after getting the process moving. The NAC, the largest women's umbrella group in Canada, with its well-established history of being the leading voice of women to government, expected to play a large – if not the pivotal – role in the preparations for Beijing.[21] Some saw the North-South Institute as a third contender for the lead role, since Joanna Kerr was drafting the first proposal for a formal facilitating committee and her director, Maureen O'Neil, had headed the Canadian delegation to the

Third Conference on Women in Nairobi.[22] In the course of the NGO meetings on May 26, Stella LeJohn, chair of the steering committee and a North-South Institute board member, suggested that the North-South Institute had offered to consider housing the secretariat of a NGO facilitating committee.[23] Joanna Kerr denied that such an offer had been made. Her version of events was supported by Jackie Claxton, who had pointed out that it would be preferable for the secretariat to be housed within a women's group.[24] Yet, in the end, neither the Manitoba UN End of Decade Committee nor the NAC nor the North-South Institute assumed leadership of the CBFC, as is discussed later in the chapter. The issue of leadership, however, continued to be a sore point for the NAC as well as for groups at the opposite end of the ideological spectrum, such as REAL Women.

One day after holding their own consultations, the NGO representatives met with government officials. In the course of this meeting, the groundwork was laid for creating a Canadian Beijing Facilitating Committee to act as a liaison between the government and NGOs and to facilitate the latter's participation in the Beijing process. But working out the actual details of a proposal was left to the Canadian Beijing steering committee.

The Canadian Beijing steering committee held its first meeting in July 1993. NGO attendance at this weekend meeting was facilitated by funds received from the federal Women's Program.[25] On the Friday evening, Joanna Kerr presented a proposal for Canadian women's groups and NGOs to prepare for Beijing.[26] The proposal outlined a range of research, communication, and lobbying activities, including preparing issue-specific positions and lobby tools; developing strategies to facilitate communications and outreach with Canadian women and to form linkages with women's groups internationally; establishing a fund for small strategic activities by Canadian women; and facilitating the participation of women at the international preparatory meetings. These activities were to be managed by a small secretariat. In preparing the proposal, Kerr had examined the extensive existing literature on NGO participation vis-à-vis both the UN Conference on the Environment and Development and the UN Conference on Human Rights and had talked to government and NGO representatives who had organized Canadian participation in previous UN conferences.[27] The proposal came with a verbal offer from the International Development Research Centre of free office space and one half-time staff member for three years – a contribution in kind worth approximately $250,000.[28] The overall budget was approximately $1 million.[29] The proposal stressed that Beijing was a watershed in an ongoing process to further feminist activities across the country and that it provided a strategic opportunity to seek additional money to advance women's equality.

The proposal was not greeted with widespread approbation at the steering committee meeting. Quite to the contrary, it immediately came under fire from all sides.[30] The focus of the criticism was not the overall strategy outlined in the proposal but, rather, the structural and financial details.[31] There were widespread concerns that the size of the budget would cut into core funding for women's groups. A lot of time was spent criticizing the secretariat's budget because, for example, it did not include money to translate written texts into Braille, to provide telephone access for the hearing impaired, or to ensure adequate salaries and benefits for staff. A deep-seated distrust of the federal government was evident.[32] The offer from the International Development Research Centre of staff and office space was seen by some as an effort by government to co-opt NGOs and so was rejected.[33] Furthermore, the representative of the Women's Program was asked to leave the room on the ground that NGOs alone were to be party to the discussions. Although most of the discussion focused on criticizing the details of Kerr's proposal and debating whether the groups assembled were sufficiently representative to be able to make decisions for all Canadian women, there was general agreement that a CBFC had to be established, that nominations for the committee had to be sought from women's groups across the country and that a secretariat had to be established.[34] There was considerable support among members of the steering committee for locating the secretariat in Winnipeg, since it was the Manitoba UN End of Decade Committee that had to this point played the key role in systematically getting Canadian women's groups to think about the follow-up to Nairobi and the preparations for Beijing. On one hand, it seemed only fair to let this group continue to take the lead. On the other hand, there were distinct advantages to locating in Ottawa, close to government, both for reasons of convenience and of finance.

Through a series of consultations organized both by government officials and, most especially, by NGOs themselves, the concept of a CBFC and the procedures for its establishment were developed. Among the NGO representatives and government officials there was agreement that a CBFC was needed, that it had to be run by women's groups for women's groups and that the process of selecting members for its board had to be democratic.

The Canadian Beijing Facilitating Committee

The model for NGO participation developed for the Beijing conference differed from those used for previous UN conferences on women.[35] For the Nairobi conference, for instance, women's groups had been invited to submit applications for funding. Government officials had then reviewed these applications and decided which groups would receive funding. The Beijing process departed from the more traditional pattern of groups approaching government on an ad hoc basis; instead, a structure was set in place to assist NGOs to develop their input into the policy-making processes both within Canada and at the UN negotiations. According to interviewees, Canada was the only country known to provide funds to assist groups in preparing composite NGO position papers prior to the preparatory meetings and the Beijing conference.[36] The specific mandate of the CBFC was as follows:

> The role of the Canadian Beijing Facilitating Committee (CBFC) is to facilitate Canadian Women's NGOs participation in the Beijing process.
>
> The CBFC will work through its seats on the Canadian Preparatory Committee (CPC) to lobby on behalf of women's groups in terms of process, access, and representation. In this capacity, it will bring Canadian women's voices to the CPC and will strive to influence the government's preparations.
>
> Through the Secretariat in Ottawa, the CBFC will serve as a clearinghouse for information in preparation for Beijing. The CBFC newsletter will play a crucial role in this networking. As well, the CBFC will be compiling a list of Canadians who will be going to New York and Beijing.[37]

The CBFC was not only to distribute information relating to the Beijing conference and to facilitate the participation of Canadian NGOs but it was also to lobby on their behalf.

Efforts were made to make the process of selecting members for the new committee democratic. The interim CBFC sent letters to 2,000 women's groups across the country requesting nominations in three broad categories: national women's groups, provincial/regional groups, and women's groups representing specific constituencies (e.g., indigenous, visible minorities, lesbian, immigrant, and disabled).[38] Each group was allowed to nominate a single candidate.[39] Some groups chose their candidate democratically. For example, the board of VOW solicited names of potential candidates from its members. From this list, board members elected Madeleine Gilchrist. Other groups simply nominated their presidents. From all the nominations, the groups then elected six representatives from national women's groups, six representatives from provincial/regional groups, and eight representatives from the specific constituencies.[40] Membership in the CBFC encompassed some twenty organizational representatives (see Appendix 1). The CBFC attracted the participation of federal and regional groups. Local grassroots organizations did get involved, but their activities were designed to raise consciousness about the upcoming UN Conference on Women rather than to affect policies.[41]

The name of the new committee became the Canadian Beijing Facilitating Committee. Two co-chairs were elected: an anglophone, Chandra Budhu of the YWCA of Canada, and a francophone, Charlotte Thibault of L'Association des collaboratrices et partenaires en affaires.

Then there was the question of where the new committee was to have its headquarters. The CBFC had to be run by and for women; it could not be an adjunct to government.[42] Among Canadian women's groups there was a strong preference for housing the committee within the women's movement rather than in the NGO community more broadly.[43] Ottawa was the logical location for the headquarters both for reasons of convenience – it facilitated contact between the CBFC staff and government officials – and of budgetary constraints, since there was little money for travel or long-distance telephone calls.

The Canadian Research Institute for the Advancement of Women (CRIAW) was the only group to volunteer space and staff time. CRIAW is a national organization that encourages and promotes research conducted by and for women that addresses all aspects of women's experiences within Canada. As such, it had established links with Canadian women's groups. What it lacked was UN experience. CRIAW donated a day of staff time a week to the CBFC, the time of its financial officer to do the paperwork for both the administrative budget and the travel funds for those sponsored to attend the UN negotiations, and the time of the desktop publisher's secretary to format the CBFC newsletter. These were significant contributions for a small organization with a staff of four people.[44] Furthermore, Linda Clippingdale, director of the CRIAW, and her staff were dedicated and frequently devoted additional time to the work of the CBFC beyond what they were contracted to provide.[45] Thus, the CBFC was administered out of the CRIAW national office in Ottawa by CRIAW staff. CRIAW staff who worked for the CBFC saw their role as facilitating the participation of Canadian NGOs in the policy-making process and not as providing expertise on the twelve issue areas.[46] Lise Martin (CRIAW), the coordinator for the CBFC, maintained regular contact with Duy Ai Kien and Jackie Claxton in the Women's Program, largely regarding budgetary matters.[47] Claxton and Kien attended portions of most CBCF board meetings.[48] The federal Women's Bureau paid for one-and-a-half days per week of a staff member's time and provided a small administrative budget to facilitate liaison work with Canadian women's groups. Interest in the Beijing conference was considerable, and the CBFC's one telephone line rang constantly.[49]

Limited resources posed serious challenges to an organization designed to coordinate NGO positions and their input into the policy-making process. In the year and a half leading up to the Beijing conference, the CBFC members met only three times.[50] The rest of the time they had to rely on a few conference calls, e-mail, and faxed messages to keep in touch. The modest budget limited the opportunities for communications both among members and with Canadian groups more broadly. These were significant limitations, made all the more serious by three facts. First, the CBFC, as a new organization, had to start from scratch to work out ways of facilitating NGO participation and, later, of coordinating and articulating NGO policy positions to government. Second, it was facilitating input from diverse groups responding to twelve separate yet interconnected issue areas. Third, it had only a year and a half to do all these tasks.

There was some friction during the early stages over the issue of whether Quebec groups should receive separate funding to conduct their own preparations. Although the CBFC remained the key NGO facilitating body, twenty-three Quebec women's groups did form a Quebec Preparatory Committee for Beijing in the autumn of 1994. Some Quebec groups participated in the CBFC, but the government also provided funds directly to the Quebec Preparatory Committee for Beijing, just as it funded activities in several other provinces, including Nova Scotia and Manitoba. The Quebec Preparatory Committee was well organized, and it continued to function after the Beijing conference. Most of the government funding, however, was channelled through the CBFC, which, in keeping with its mandate, worked to assist Canadian NGOs in preparing for the Beijing conference and in participating in the policy-making process. It did not work with groups outside the country.[51]

In May 1994, within one month of its inception, the CBFC began producing an informative newsletter, *Onward to Beijing*. The newsletter provided information on what was happening within the UN vis-à-vis the conference. It described the key issues and presented lists of contacts in the various issue areas and advice to those attending UN negotiations. In short, *Onward to Beijing* provided up-to-date, useful information that facilitated the participation of NGOs. In addition to producing its own newsletter, the CBFC circulated relevant government publications and other pertinent information about the conference.

When it came to coordinating the development of policy positions, the achievements were more modest. The CBFC held its first conference in August 1994 in order to prepare for the Vienna Regional Meetings. Government officials and many NGO representatives in attendance describe the meeting as a disaster: "ill-planned," "a bitch session," and "the worst organized meeting I went to in my entire life."[52] The major problems were inadequate prior planning and insufficient forethought in the selection of participants. The meeting was unfocused. People were asked at the last minute to act as workshop facilitators without being given a clear sense of what the discussions were to accomplish.[53] Translators were hired, but the equipment needed for simultaneous translation was not procured. The choice of participants was likewise problematic. Some of the nearly 200 participants were representatives of the major women's groups from across the country, while others were individuals working to advance women within their local communities. The latter category lacked the background and expertise to prepare a policy document in response to the *Draft Platform for Action*. Not only did most lack the expertise to do the analysis, but "few women at the meeting had even seen the March [1994] UN draft *PFA* before arriving in Winnipeg."[54]

Two days of workshops produced sixty pages of statements, most of which bore little relation to the *PFA* or the Beijing agenda.[55] For example, "a paper produced in a workshop titled 'Developing Mechanisms for Women's Advancement' focused exclusively on Canadian problems with no mention of the UN while others made only passing reference to the *Platform for Action.*"[56] Although "there was some meat among the higgledy-piggledy compilation that emerged from the conference, it was not in any shape to present to government."[57]

These problems meant that the Winnipeg meeting achieved little. Furthermore, the credibility of the CBFC was weakened in the eyes of some of the major women's organizations, which bluntly told the fledgling organization that it was not the voice of the Canadian women's movement.[58] To be fair, the period between the creation of the CBFC and the deadline for preparing for the regional meetings was short. It would have posed a challenge for the most experienced, and it was insurmountable for those without extensive experience preparing for international negotiations.

Clearly the CBFC had its growing pains. As one CBFC member explains,

> the CBFC hadn't been together long enough to even get to know each other, let alone to put together a working group to organize a national conference. And the staff member we hired did not do her work.
>
> The conference took a toll on the CBFC members. We met for one full day following the Winnipeg conference. It was a very difficult meeting. The secretariat staff member who had been responsible for organizing the conference was fired. Chandra Budhu, whose excellent negotiating skills had managed to inject some order into the conference, announced that she was resigning to take on the New York-based position of plenary program coordinator of the NGO forum, so we were left without her experience and leadership.[59]

In response to the vacancy created by Chandra Budhu's resignation, the CBFC elected a new co-chair: Marge Friedel of the National Métis Women of Canada, who had participated in the process from the beginning.

The Manitoba conference was, nevertheless, a learning experience that galvanized the CBFC members to work to avoid similar problems at subsequent sessions. The Winnipeg discussion groups began the process of identifying women's needs in particular issue areas. Furthermore, several of the more experienced members pulled together a document that was much more substantial than the discussion at the meeting had been.[60] The recommendations were, nonetheless, compiled at short notice and were without priorities or clear focus.

The Vienna Regional Meetings marked a watershed in the preparatory process. The NGO representatives who attended the meetings saw – many for the first time – how the process worked; they had thereafter a much better idea of what it was they were preparing for, and the need to develop more effective strategies for seeking influence was apparent. On the final day of the Vienna meetings, Canadian NGOs got together to discuss new approaches to their preparatory work. While some remained focused on complaining about the lack of government support, others recognized the need to move on and to produce some useful analysis and recommendations.[61]

Following the Vienna Preparatory Meetings, Irene Santiago, executive director of the NGO Forum on Women '95, decided to appoint regional focal points. The position of regional focal point for North America was delegated to Stella LeJohn, chair of the Manitoba UN End of Decade Committee and member of the CBFC, who became the key contact for North American NGOs.

The experience gained from the Vienna Regional Meetings prompted the CBFC to adopt a more effective strategy in developing its response to the *Draft Platform for Action* prior to the New York Preparatory Meetings in March 1995. In the December 1994 edition of *Onward to Beijing*, groups were asked to volunteer to take the lead in coordinating the NGO response to specific sections of the *Draft Platform for Action* that corresponded with their respective areas of expertise (e.g., human rights, health, armed conflict, poverty).[62] Each lead group was to identify five priorities within its issue area and to develop strategies and recommendations for their implementation. The objective of the exercise was to produce line-by-line analysis to assist Canadian NGOs in lobbying SWC. Such analysis involves providing precise wording inserted in bold type into the document to replace or augment existing text.

Seven of the ten groups that volunteered to assume this responsibility were organizations based in Toronto, which caused some rumblings about geographic concentration.[63] Each lead group received $5,000, paid in instalments, to prepare textual analysis prior to both the New York Preparatory Meetings and the Beijing conference, and, following the conference, to provide an assessment of progress achieved in Beijing.[64]

Before the individual "lead" groups began their tasks, the CBFC invited their representatives to a meeting chaired by Madeleine Gilchrist (VOW). At this meeting Shelagh Day, a long-time advocate of human rights with considerable UN experience, explained the purpose of UN documents, outlined approaches to analyzing their contents, and described methods for channelling input into the policy-making process. The composite text produced by the international NGOs in Vienna was given as an example of line-by-line analysis.[65]

Time was tight. The lead groups had only four weeks to produce their analyses and to present their visions for Beijing.[66] Furthermore, the *Draft Platform for Action* was available only in English, which disadvantaged francophone groups. The nature of the exercise required groups to respond to the agenda and the parameters set forth in the *Draft Platform for Action:* to be reactive rather than proactive vis-à-vis the agenda and its substance.

The lead groups faxed out the relevant sections of the *Draft Platform for Action* to their members and to other groups involved in the same issue area and compiled analyses for their respective sections. In two weeks, over 2,400 women were contacted by e-mail and fax for their input.[67] Each lead group submitted its text, some of which contained several versions of the same section of text. Madeleine Gilchrist, Bruna Nota, and Monique Lavoie (all members of VOW) undertook the task of compiling a single document out of the submissions. Since the objective of the exercise was to produce a line-by-line analysis, they had to choose language which they thought reflected the majority view in cases where lead groups had submitted multiple versions of the same text.[68] It was in many respects a thankless job: "We knew we were likely to be crucified for our choices and we did receive criticism from several whose language was not included in the final version."[69] The line-by-line analysis for each of the twelve issue areas was then stapled into a 126-page document. Within one month of receiving the *Draft Platform for Action*, the CBFC had produced a "Coordinated Response."[70] It was the first composite line-by-line analysis produced by Canadian women's groups in response to an international document.[71]

It is to the credit of the CBFC that it was able to produce a coordinated line-by-line analysis at such short notice. However, the document was somewhat unwieldy since the proposed changes were numerous and, for the most part, extensive, and they were generally listed in the numerical order in which they appeared in each lead group's report rather than in the numeric order of the paragraphs as they appeared in the *Draft Platform for Action*. For instance, the NGO document begins with paragraph 28a in the section on Education prepared by the Canadian Congress for Learning Opportunities for Women and Réseau national d'action éducation femmes. A third of the way into the document are the NAC's proposed changes to the section on the Globalization of the Economy, which begins with paragraph 1 of the Mission Statement in the draft *PFA*. Two-thirds of the way through the document is the section on Peace that was prepared by VOW, which begins with paragraph 62 of the *Draft Platform for Action* and then addresses the Mission Statement.

Government officials received the document only one day before their March 9, 1995, meeting with the ten lead groups.[72] This meeting, in turn, was held just before the Canadian delegation left for New York. So while the CBFC had done well to canvass so many groups and to pull together a response in a short period, it nonetheless arrived after the Canadian government's positions had been established. Furthermore, to read a 126-page document and to compare its proposed changes to the wording in the *Draft Platform for Action* was a time-consuming endeavour.

On the morning of March 9, the lead NGOs met in Ottawa to discuss their strategies for their meeting with government officials later that day. The government representatives at the afternoon meeting included Louise Bergeron-de Villiers, Valerie Raymond, Rhonda Ferderber, Sheila Regehr, and Jackie Claxton. Each lead group presented its own issue. When the NGOs asked for the government position, they were told that the government officials first needed time to review the NGOs' line-by-line analysis.[73] They never did receive the official government position.[74]

The idea of using lead groups was continued in final preparations for Beijing, and again a composite document was submitted to government and circulated among the NGO community. The format for this coordinated document differed from its predecessor in several respects. It was not a line-by-line analysis; instead, the lead group in each issue area provided a preamble explaining the importance of the issue and the need for change. They then proposed between four to six priorities, with five priorities being identified in most issue areas. Under each priority, strategies for its attainment were outlined. While not providing specific wording for the Canadian delegation, it clearly identified the principal concerns in each issue area, specified priorities rather than trying to fix everything in the *PFA* and provided succinct strategies for their attainments. This final document was 53 pages long rather than the daunting 126 pages of its predecessor. The final product fell short of the ideal: a composite text providing line-by-line analysis for identified priorities. Nonetheless, a dramatic learning curve was evident: as time went on, the NGO documents became more focused and more "user-friendly." The key forum for discussing these NGO position papers with government officials was the Canadian Preparatory Committee.

Canadian Preparatory Committee
The Canadian Preparatory Committee (CPC) was established to facilitate consultations between members of the federal Interdepartmental Committee on the World Conference on Women (IDC '95) and NGOs in the preparations of Canada's positions pertaining to the UN Conference on Women.[75] In a sense, it integrated two parallel processes: the intergovernmental preparations for the Beijing conference and the NGO preparations that were being coordinated through the CBFC. The CPC meetings were chaired by the coordinator of SWC, Louise Bergeron-de Villiers, reflecting the importance accorded to them. On the government side, its members were drawn from SWC, DFAIT, CIDA, and Human Resources Development

(i.e., the Women's Program) – the four key departments on the interdepartmental committee. On the NGO side, the committee's membership consisted of representatives not only from women's groups but also from labour, development, and human rights organizations.[76] The decision to expand the NGO membership to include labour, development, and human rights groups was done to ensure that a broad spectrum of Canadian society was represented on the committee and to provide access to these groups that clearly had specific interest related to the *PFA*.[77] But the decision to include these other groups may also have been prompted by the fact that these groups enjoyed better working relations with their respective departments than those that existed between the women's groups and SWC.[78]

The six women's groups represented on the committee were nominated by the CBFC,[79] whereas the list of other groups to be included was compiled by IDC '95. Since the government provided no travel funds, most of the groups represented on the CPC were Ottawa-based. Groups with membership on the committee were given an explicit responsibility to share the information gained through membership with other groups working in the same issue area. The International Centre for Human Rights and Democratic Development, for instance, was expected to share information with other human rights groups. There was, however, no monitoring to ensure that such consultations actually took place.

On December 15, 1993, the CPC held its first meeting to discuss the roles and functions of the committee, the *PFA*, Canada's preparations for the Intersessional Meeting of the UN Commission on the Status of Women, which was at that time less than one month away, and approaches to preparing *Canada's National Report to the Fourth World Conference on Women*. In 1994, the CPC met after each of the major international negotiations pertaining to the Beijing conference (e.g., the meetings of the UN Commission on the Status of Women and the Vienna Regional Meetings). By 1995, the CPC was meeting before, as well as following, the international negotiating sessions.

The CPC meetings, which generally lasted about three hours, began with reports by government officials on developments within the UN and within Canada pertaining to the Beijing conference. These reports were followed by questions from the NGO representatives, who tended to focus on concerns about financing, about provisions to assist NGOs in attending the UN negotiations (i.e., the preparatory meetings as well as those in China), and about facilities in China.[80] Overall, relatively little time was spent discussing the substantive issues in the *PFA*.

None of the NGO representatives on the CPC who were interviewed thought that they had exerted any significant influence over the direction or substance of Canada's official policies. One NGO representative described the CPC meetings as "somewhat painful": government officials and NGOs reflected "two solitudes."[81] Another NGO observer described feeling "manipulated" by these meetings:

> The government's attitude towards women's organizations was quite patronizing. At the meetings, government officials said how nice it was that everyone was there and provided information – a lot of which was rather superficial – but they did not really let the NGOs into Canada's strategy or Canada's thinking on specific policy issues. The NGO presented their concerns – sometimes gently and sometimes forcefully. In response, minor adjustments might be made to the peripheral issues, but changes were not made to the big or central issues.[82]

Yet another NGO member on the CPC complained that "the government still has the attitude that NGOs are naïve and that it needs to educate NGOs, which is patronizing; as a result NGOs don't feel like partners in the process."[83] The CPC served first and foremost as a venue in which government officials could provide information to the NGOs. Although it facilitated the presentation of NGO views to government, the NGO representatives did not perceive it to be a forum where partners sat down to hammer out policy together.

Assessing the Government-Sponsored Mechanisms

On the positive side, the mechanisms facilitated a two-way communication between the federal government and NGOs and ensured that the government received input from NGOs from across Canada. The CBFC did achieve considerable heterogeneity in its membership. It reflected regional diversity, including anglophones, and francophones from Quebec as well as from other parts of the country. Among its members were Inuit, Aboriginal, and Métis women; visible minorities; lesbians; handicapped women; and seniors. As a result, the CBFC provided a useful focal point for government contact with diverse women's groups: "The government relied on the CBFC for information and to serve as our link to the NGOs."[84] The CBFC provided feedback on the types of materials NGOs found useful. It also did an excellent job of producing an informative newsletter and circulating it and other relevant materials to those on its distribution list. The only major disappointment here was the relatively small size of its distribution list. The CBFC had a database containing the names of just over 2,000 people. Some of those on the list were contacts for groups, who no doubt shared the information with their respective memberships, while others were individuals seeking the information for personal edification. One would have expected the CBFC to have ended up with a considerably larger database. After all, 2,000 was the number of groups – not individuals –

contacted initially by SWC when the CBFC was being established. In light of the interest generated by the conference and the high quality of the information distributed by the CBFC, the small circulation was regrettable.

The CBFC mechanism facilitated NGO networking within Canada and enabled NGOs to conduct a detailed analysis of the negotiating texts. As a result, a wider range of groups was able to enjoy more meaningful participation in the policy-making process than would have been possible if there had not been a government-sponsored mechanism. In addition, the groups collectively were better able to present their priorities and positions clearly and succinctly to government than would otherwise have been possible. But the key question remains: How useful were the preparatory process and the documents it engendered? The process was very useful in terms of clarifying NGO positions. Having produced a coordinated response to the *Draft Platform for Action*, Canadian NGOs were among the best prepared groups at the 1995 New York Preparatory Meetings. As such, they were able to exercise lead roles in the international NGO caucuses. This level of preparation would not have been possible without government funding.

In terms of influencing policy, the NGO texts had little impact on specific Canadian positions.[85] Two factors in particular undermined the NGOs ability to exert influence: the timing and the format of their input. By the time the NGOs had produced a focused, coordinated document, the conference agenda and the government's objectives were already clearly established. As one government official noted, "the summer of 1995 was too late to be introducing new issues."[86] To be fair, the late release of the official text did not facilitate the preparation of either government positions or NGO positions. Nonetheless, the NGOs would have been in a better position to cope with time constraints if they had been able to establish clear priorities within each issue area early in the process. These priorities could then have served as the conceptual framework for conducting in-depth analysis of the negotiating texts when they were issued.

A second problem related to format. It would have been more effective if the NGOs had not only established their priorities but also provided line-by-line analysis for each priority. Yet to produce line-by-line analysis, one needs to know UN language and the specifics of provisions previously agreed to at other recent conferences. Few NGOs have the experience and expertise necessary to do this. Even if the NGOs had presented their priorities and provided concrete language for changes to carefully selected priorities, there is still the question of receptivity on the part of government decision makers. As most students of Canadian foreign policy agree, government decision makers are generally remarkably impervious to input from NGOs.[87]

On the NGO side, the most important shortcoming with the process was that some of the key leaders lacked UN experience. In essence, the time required to master an in-depth understanding of the structures, rules, procedures, and terminologies of UN negotiations, and, hence, of the parameters within which government delegates operate in such settings, exceeded the preordained lifespan of the CBFC. To have operated at maximum efficiency, the organization would have had to have more leaders with long-standing expertise in Canadian foreign policy at UN conferences.

Government officials did little to convey this vital knowledge to NGO leaders. To be fair, there were some functional barriers to educating groups. Those who had the strongest long-term links with the groups and who maintained regular contacts with CBFC were those in the Women's Program who administered the funds that are so vital in facilitating the participation of groups in the policy-making process. This made it awkward to advise NGOs on lobbying tactics because such advice could be misconstrued as coercive or threatening. For example, a suggestion that groups would do better by working cooperatively could be interpreted to mean: cooperate or you will lose your funding! Those who worked most closely with the groups felt constrained in what they could say and in offering advice.[88] The situation became all the more awkward when the Women's Program became part of SWC and an internal contradiction was created. There was no longer a structural separation between the government unit funding the NGOs and the government unit with primary policy-making responsibility regarding the status of women. Within SWC, one had the Women's Program funding groups to monitor government policies as well as other public servants spearheading the formation of government policies. Funding one's critics was not always seen as desirable by the policy makers within SWC.[89] For all these reasons, the officials in the Women's Program took a "hands-off" approach when it came to advising on lobbying strategies.[90]

In addition to the question of whether government officials should have advised NGOs on lobbying strategies, there is the question of how receptive the groups would have been to advice from government officials. Mutual distrust was a key element in the relationship between the women's groups and government officials, and this distrust undermined the former's ability to exert influence.

NGO leaders are frequently leery of cooperating too closely with government for two reasons. First, there is the fear that cooperation will result in co-option. Second, there is a worry that leaders who do cooperate closely with government will be seen by their memberships as having been co-opted. These are important concerns. There are opportunity costs in foregoing potentially fruitful alliances to achieve specific goals, for fear of co-option. It is not an easy task for NGO leaders to reach a satisfactory balance between those two apparently contradictory sets of concerns. The quest to find the balance is explored in greater depth in the concluding chapter.

The way the government set the parameters within which the CBFC was created and operated was seen by several of the key NGO actors as a carefully crafted ploy to ensure that the NAC did not assume the lead.[91] Although the NAC had been a member of the Manitoba UN End of Decade Committee, the former expected that SWC would work out the details for a CBFC with the Group of Twenty-Three which represented the vast majority of the major feminist groups in Canada and of which the NAC was a prominent member.[92] If this approach had been adopted, the NAC would have been on the CBFC and might well have ended up chairing it. According to the president of the NAC, "this outcome would not have been acceptable to Minister Finestone. The reliance on the Manitoba UN End of the Decade Committee was a bid to keep NAC out."[93] Relations between SWC and the NAC were not good during the Beijing process. This was because of differences in approaches, which were exacerbated by personal animosities between the secretary of state for the status of women and the NAC executive. The NAC criticized SWC for its lack of advocacy, especially for failing to apply strong pressure on the Canadian government for a substantial financial base to work for the equality of women.[94] In the case of the Beijing process, this translated into disapproval of the ministers' decision not to allocate additional funds to facilitate the participation of NGOs: "SWC acted as if women's rights had already been achieved instead of advocating strongly the need for more money to provide a strong financial basis to promote women's equality. The SWC budget had been eroded over the past three years and this is unacceptable. Canada may be a rich country but poverty among women and children is increasing, as noted by the UN. As long as the Canadian government is doing little to advance women, there will always be tension with the NAC."[95] The NAC criticized the way in which the CBFC had been organized and constituted, and it criticized SWC for not advocating more strenuously within the federal government for increased funding and more effective programs to benefit women.

NAC representatives also differed with government officials over the degree of openness expected of the latter. When the NAC asked for the official government positions, the request was refused. This was obviously vexing for the NAC: "It was very frustrating and annoying that we could get the positions of some of the Group of Seventy-Seven countries and the United States from our contacts with NGOs in these countries but we could not get Canada's positions from our own government. This confirmed our view that we could not work cooperatively with government officials."[96] This conclusion has significant repercussions in terms of choice of tactics. As discussed in Chapter 6, the NAC chose to "go public" during the Beijing conference. Rather than trying to cooperate quietly with the Canadian negotiators behind the scenes, it released a paper highly critical of the Canadian government's record on women's rights.

Overall, the Canadian government's policies on the *PFA* were moving in the same direction as those of the NAC, though the NAC sought to go further faster. Nonetheless, there were some areas of conflict, especially when the welfare of women was seen as being sacrificed in favour of other interests. The NAC was, for instance, outraged when Canadian negotiators succeeded in having brackets placed around provisions to have health regarded as a basic human right presumably because of a fear that strong language might open the door to litigation within Canada.[97]

These differences in approach were exacerbated by interpersonal frictions which, in turn, further soured relations between SWC and the NAC. As the former president of NAC comments, "the bad blood goes back a way. Sheila Finestone had been on the executive of NAC but left under unpleasant circumstances. When she became minister for SWC, NAC feared it would be in for a rough ride, and we did feel a backlash once she became minister. Relations with the bureaucrats in SWC went downhill when Finestone became minister. From early on in the Beijing process, the NAC executive felt that their concerns were not being taken seriously."[98]

The NAC was by no means the only NGO distrustful of government. REAL Women saw the government officials involved in formulating Canada's policies on the *PFA* and in negotiating on behalf of Canada as inherently biased against its interests. According to that organization's national vice-president, "they were all strong, radical, entrenched feminists. Minister Finestone, as a former executive member of the NAC, was hardly receptive to us, to say the least."[99] Although REAL Women is at the opposite end of the ideological spectrum from the NAC, there were nonetheless some similarities in their perceptions that government officials were not sufficiently receptive to their demands, as well as in their choice of tactics. In objective terms, Canada's official policies were much more reflective of the NAC concerns than they were of the positions of REAL Women. Nonetheless, the NAC was dissatisfied that the Canadian positions did not go further in advancing women's equality, particularly in promoting the economic interests of women. REAL Women rejected feminist notions of equality and vehemently opposed most of Canada's positions, particularly those on sexual and reproductive rights and the rights of lesbians.

Like the NAC, REAL Women chose to go public with its concerns in an attempt to embarrass the Canadian government. REAL Women never lost an opportunity to denounce Canada's positions as being unreflective of the views of most Canadians.[100] At the New York meeting, representatives of REAL Women handed out flyers claiming that the Canadian delegation was not speaking for Canadians. At the Fourth World Conference on Women, REAL Women sought to discredit publicly both the *PFA* and the Canadian delegation. The *PFA* was described as a "racist" document which "deals only with the demands of radical feminist/lesbian women in the western cultures and ignores the genuine needs of women in developing nations."[101] The Canadian delegation was accused of pursuing "extremist policies" and of "attacking its own country's values."[102]

The public servants resented the aggressive tactics employed by some of the Canadian NGOs. As one Canadian negotiator remarks, "We are human beings with feelings, too. One can only take so much verbal abuse before it begins to taint how receptive one is to a group, how much energy one is willing to devote to it, and how much assistance one is willing to offer. I continue to provide basic assistance but I am just not willing to go the extra mile for those who continually subject me to a barrage of personal insults."[103] This view was echoed by many of the Canadian negotiators in off-the-record discussions. Some government officials questioned the motivation behind certain NGO activities. For example, to some government officials, the late release of the NGO document was not so much the result of inexperience and inefficiencies as it was a deliberate attempt to discredit the government's positions.

This element of distrust and hostility that existed on both sides undermined the efficacy of women's groups. It must be noted, however, that not all government-NGO relations were strained. Quite to the contrary, Adèle Dion was extremely positive in her description of relations between the DFAIT and human rights groups: "Of all the UN conferences and commissions that I have been involved in, the NGO input for this conference had the most direct and comprehensive impact on Canada's positions. Never have I been exposed to a process that was so interactive and that had such an impact on policy development."[104] Likewise, CIDA enjoyed constructive working relations with the Canadian NGOs involved with women and development, including the Association québécoise des organismes de coopération internationale, the Canadian Council for International Cooperation, the North-South Institute, and Match. In addition to hosting consultations with these groups, CIDA sponsored a speaking tour for Bella Abzug, a founder of the Women's Environment and Development Organization, who spoke in several cities across the country during International Development Week. While CIDA recognized NGOs to be important sources of information as well as partners in implementing its programs, they were not considered partners in the development of policies: CIDA's responses to the *PFA* were determined by its own officers.

As well as the problems of inexperience and mutual distrust that existed between at least some of the NGOs and government officials, there were different understandings among the members and staff of the CBFC as to its role. Although the mandate for the CBFC clearly specified that it was to lobby on behalf of Canadian NGOs as well as to facilitate their participation in the policy-making process, its members differed as to the relative priority to be given to these two functions. For example, according to

Madeleine Gilchrist (VOW) and Lise Martin (coordinator of the CBFC and CRIAW staff member), the CBFC was primarily a facilitating committee rather than a committee designed to lobby directly. In contrast, Shelagh Day (who had represented the NAC on the CBFC) criticized the committee for not exercising sufficient leadership: "Overall, the CBFC facilitated but it did not lead. More time should have been devoted to developing strategies to exert influence."[105]

Different understandings of the CBFC's role no doubt made it harder for the committee to be focused. They also resulted in different evaluations of the CBFC's success. In Madeleine Gilchrist's assessment, "Overall, the CBFC did an outstanding job given its very limited financial resources and staff."[106] The president of the NAC was more critical: "The CBFC never had an arms-length relationship from government. It did not want to make government uncomfortable or to pressure it to deal with tough issues. It never developed a macro framework, that is, a women's perspective, at the beginning from which to conduct its analysis. Even when the CBFC released its final report, it was still reluctant to hold government accountable."[107] The NAC expected the CBFC to develop and implement effective lobbying strategies.

The government-sponsored mechanisms get mixed reviews. They facilitated contact and dialogue between government officials and Canadian NGOs. They served as efficient channels for circulating information about the conference to the attentive public. They facilitated and encouraged networking among a diverse range of Canadian NGOs, in general, and of women's groups, in particular. Furthermore, the process of selecting the composition of the CBFC was democratic: its members were elected. In comparison with the NGO coordinating committees established for the 1995 Copenhagen Summit for Social Development and the 1993 Vienna Conference on Human Rights, the CBFC scores both positively and negatively. On the positive side, the process of selecting membership was democratic, whereas in the case of the other committees, leading groups in the field began the process and gravitated into the lead positions. On the negative side, most of the key individuals in the CBFC lacked experience with international negotiations, whereas the leaders of the NGO facilitating committees for the Copenhagen Summit for Social Development and the Vienna Conference on Human Rights had extensive international experience. Inexperience was a major cause of the problems encountered by the CBFC as it sought to develop effective strategies for seeking policy input.

The government-sponsored mechanisms did not result in the NGOs having significant influence over Canada's positions for several reasons. Most importantly, government officials developed policies with a great deal of autonomy from civil society and, as exemplified by developments in the CPC meetings, they were reluctant to engage in in-depth analysis of the issues with the NGOs, let alone to make major changes to the positions they had already agreed to in the interdepartmental discussions. The NGOs, for their parts, were slow to capitalize on opportunities for access largely because of problems of inexperience but also because of externally imposed time constraints.

It is important to remember that the Beijing Conference on Women was part of an ongoing process and that the success of the government-sponsored mechanisms should not be assessed solely in terms of the conference itself. In fact, the long-term benefits are perhaps the most important considerations. The most significant long-term gain has been the growth and development of the network of women's groups in Canada. In preparing for and participating at the Beijing Conference on Women, groups have gained greater knowledge of the workings and the demands of UN negotiations, as well as significant experience in working together to analyze an international text and in lobbying cooperatively to influence policy.

After the 1985 Nairobi Conference on Women, there was only one group in Canada – the Manitoba UN End of the Decade Committee – that was meeting regularly to assess Canada's progress in implementing the Nairobi *Forward-looking Strategies*. Such was not the case after Beijing. There now exists a well-informed constituency to monitor the government's progress. These groups have invested too much time and energy and too many of their scarce resources to let the issues drop now, and they expect action! The CBCF's final issue of *Onward from Beijing* concludes with six pages of information to facilitate taking action on the *PFA*. Action at the international level means ensuring that future international conferences and meetings reflect and build on the provisions in the *PFA*. At the domestic level, action means holding the Canadian government responsible for the commitments it made in Beijing. In order to facilitate actions at both the domestic and international level, the CBFC newsletter provides information on upcoming UN conferences and additional reference materials. It also lists the addresses and contact persons for each of the lead groups that had agreed to coordinate future actions pertaining to the *PFA* as well as to their specific issue of concern. In the spring of 1996, the CBFC produced its final publication: *Take Action for Equality, Development and Peace: A Canadian Follow-up Guide to Beijing '95*. The 184-page document explains the key provisions for each of the issues discussed in the *PFA*. Each section concluded with recommendations to bring about change within one's local community as well as strategies for lobbying federal and provincial and territorial governments. The final pages of the monograph are devoted to outlining five basic steps for effective lobbying. A questionnaire was also provided to assist groups in assessing a government's performance in each of the twelve critical areas of concern.

Canadian NGOs have taken up the challenge to hold the Canadian government and provincial and territorial governments accountable to the commitments made in Beijing. They continue to monitor governments' performances and to lobby for greater compliance. In its highly critical review of Canada's policies on women, *Women in Canada After Beijing: Left Out, Left Over, Left Behind!,*[108] the NAC uses the provisions in the *PFA* as benchmarks for judging the governments' performances. In publicizing the deficiencies in government policies, it seeks to engender public support in its efforts to hold government accountable. Numerous groups across the country that were involved with the Beijing process continue to hold regular meetings to assess progress made since Beijing and to develop strategies for pressuring government to move ahead in fulfilling its obligations. Many were involved in activities relating to the "Beijing +5" conference, which the UN convened in June 2000 to assess the achievements realized during the five years since the Fourth World Conference on Women. Canadian NGOs, for example, were active participants in a series of Internet working groups entitled "Beijing +5 Global Forum," organized by the United Nations' Women Watch website. The workshops examined areas where progress has been made in order to identify factors promoting success. They also identified obstacles to progress and developed strategies for overcoming these barriers. In short, the networks among Canadian women's groups, and between them and other NGOs, that were forged and strengthened during the Beijing process continue to flourish. The government-sponsored mechanisms in the Beijing case played a significant role in facilitating the development of valuable expertise and of more effective lobbying networks, which continue to assist women's groups in their struggle to hold the government responsible to the commitments it made at the Fourth World Conference on Women.

Before closing the discussion of the NGO activities in Canada, it is necessary to say a word about the expense of the government-sponsored mechanisms. Although the CBFC was a lean organization, the consultative mechanisms were considered a significant expense at a time of fiscal restraint. Such criticisms were issued most often by those opposed to the direction and substance of Canada's positions, but they were also heard within government circles. Not only did the mechanisms involve a significant expense but their very existence generated requests for funds early in the planning process and continuing through to the conference itself. This concern for cost must, however, be weighed carefully against the democratic imperative to provide funding to ensure that a broad spectrum of NGOs – not merely those with the greatest resources – are able to gain access to the policy-making process.

5
Canadian Delegation

Assessing the effectiveness of the Canadian delegation at the Beijing Conference on Women is the focus of this chapter. Yet, in keeping with a dominant theme in this book – that the conference and Canada's participation at it were parts of an ongoing process – the discussion begins by examining the work of the Canadian delegation at the two principal sets of substantive negotiations leading up to the Beijing conference: the October 1994 Vienna Regional Meetings for Europe and North America; and the March 1995 CSW Meetings in New York. A brief overview is provided of the final, and much smaller, set of informal consultations that was conducted in New York for five days in late July and early August to try to remove at least some of the remaining brackets in the *PFA* before the Beijing conference was convened.

After examining Canada's participation at the key sets of negotiations leading up to the 1995 World Conference on Women, the remainder of the chapter is devoted to an examination of the Canadian delegation at the conference itself. Here the discussion is divided into two main sections. The first addresses the controversial issue of the composition of the Canadian delegation. The second section assesses the contributions made by the Canadian delegation.

The Negotiations Leading to Beijing

Vienna Regional Meetings (October 17 to 21, 1994)
As discussed in Chapter 2, the UN's five regional commissions each held a meeting at which its member countries identified key issues for women, assessed the principal impediments to women's advancement, identified regional needs and priorities, and recommended actions to advance women in their respective regions. Canada was an active participant at the Vienna Regional Meetings, which were convened by the Economic Commission for Europe (ECE) from October 17 to 21, 1994. Membership in the Commission

consists of fifty-two European countries as well as Canada and the United States. Overall, the debates at the Vienna Regional meetings were less confrontational than were the CSW negotiations, since the participants at the former were relatively like-minded compared to the diversity evident among the 189 states participating at UN meetings.[1] On the other hand, the ECE had not traditionally addressed women's issues, and it was, therefore, a challenge to try to get agreement among Canada, the United States, and fifty-two European countries. Furthermore, the initial negotiating text was weak and had to be reworked to incorporate more progressive language from other UN documents, including the *Convention on the Elimination of All Forms of Discrimination Against Women* and the *Vienna Declaration and Programme of Action*[2] that had been adopted at the 1993 Conference on Human Rights. After much hard work, the Canadian negotiators managed to have structural adjustment policies included in the text and, in cooperation with Belgium and Sweden, to have unpaid work considered in calculations of work done in such sectors as agriculture, food production, and the home.[3] On the other hand, Canadian efforts to reinsert a provision for reducing military spending were vetoed by Germany, Holland, and the United Kingdom.[4] In the end, the intergovernmental meetings did adopt an *ECE Regional Platform for Action* – the first major document on women that the commission had ever negotiated. Nonetheless, its provisions pertaining to violence, peace, health, and the environment were considerably weaker than those in the NGOs *Call to Action*.[5]

Canada was one of only eight countries to have a NGO representative on its delegation to the Vienna Regional Meetings.[6] Prior to these meetings it had been decided that the NGOs on the CPC would choose a representative to sit on the Canadian delegation to all the subsequent negotiations leading up to, and including, the Fourth World Conference on Women. The NGOs nominated Madeleine Gilchrist, and the nomination was accepted. She was an active, long-time member of Canadian Voice of Women for Peace, with extensive experience lobbying on behalf of the peace movement at UN negotiations in New York and Geneva, at meetings of the North Atlantic Treaty Organization in Brussels, and at sessions of the Warsaw Pact Treaty Organization in Bulgaria. Gilchrist proved to be a hardworking, dedicated representative of the Canadian NGOs. To attend both the Vienna Regional Meetings and the New York Preparatory Meetings, she absented herself without pay from her job at Women's College Hospital in Toronto.

In Vienna, Gilchrist both participated in the work of the international NGOs to prepare a composite NGO text and attended the intergovernmental negotiations. The latter were, for two days, closed to the NGOs, which put enormous pressure on the few nongovernmental observers on state delegations. In particular, Gilchrist faced two problems.[7] One was the exhaustion of running back and forth between the closed official negotiations and the NGO meetings to keep the latter informed of developments in the former and to present government negotiators with highlighted sections from the international NGO composite document. Each trip between the NGO meetings and the official negotiations took fifteen minutes,[8] even for a fast, energetic walker like Gilchrist. Second, there was the problem of expertise. No one person could be expected to have an in-depth knowledge of all the issues under discussion. Yet only those with expertise in a particular issue could fully analyze developments in the negotiations on that issue and thereby facilitate the input of NGOs.

Gilchrist drew two major lessons from her experience in Vienna.[9] First, to participate in drafting, one needs specific language, which in turn requires prior preparation of line-by-line analysis. Second, although she realized that the government would be unlikely to fund this initiative, Gilchrist recommended that future Canadian delegations include one NGO representative with expertise in each of the critical areas of concern.[10] In the end, the Canadian delegation to Beijing did include twelve nongovernmental observers, but they were chosen as individuals rather than as representatives of NGOs in each of the twelve areas. On the other hand, the CBFC's decision to designate lead groups to produce line-by-line analyses in each of the key issue areas reflected lessons learnt in Vienna. In Vienna, the Canadian delegation began to provide daily briefings for Canadian NGOs in response to a request from the latter.[11] These briefings not only provided NGOs with information important to their work and daily access to the negotiators but they also seemed to ease tension between the NGOs and government.[12]

New York Preparatory Meetings (March 15 to April 7, 1995)

The main preparatory negotiations for the Beijing conference took place at the 39th session of the UN Commission on the Status of Women, held in New York from March 15 to April 7, 1995. As discussed in Chapter 2, delegates to the New York Preparatory Meetings faced several problems. The *Draft Platform for Action* had been circulated to governments only a month before the meetings; hence, textual analysis had been rushed. Since the text under discussion at the 1995 New York Preparatory Meetings was radically different from the previous text, much of the negotiations were spent with delegates trying to introduce and reintroduce clauses, particularly those agreed on at the regional meetings. Often the negotiators were spread too thinly, the result of inadequate numbers to handle the quantity of work. In addition, many negotiators were weary, having attended the Copenhagen Summit for Social Development just before being sent to the negotiations in New York.[13] The Group of Seventy-Seven, in particular, only began preparing a coordinated position for its 130-plus members at the preparatory meetings themselves. Meetings were repeatedly postponed as the Group of Seventy-Seven struggled to reach a unified position. The conference secretariat, for its part, suffered from poor organization, inadequate resources, and the difficulties inherent in being part of a relatively small division within a large organization in which women's issues were generally marginalized.[14] Tensions at the preparatory meetings were further heightened by the increased presence of right-wing actors, who were more numerous and more outspoken than they had been at the previous meetings.

The conservative states were small in number but very vocal. In a venue where consensus is the basis for decision making, a vocal minority can exercise considerable influence. Conservative forces posed particular problems for the Canadian delegation. For instance, REAL Women circulated press releases condemning Canada's delegation for its stands: "The Canadian delegation, composed of representatives from the radical feminist agency of Status of Women and Sympathetic Non-Governmental Organizations (NGOs), has launched an all out war against the traditional family in its proposals at the meeting ... Canada has embarrassed itself by taking such extreme positions at this conference."[15] This and similarly critical statements were circulated widely at the preparatory meetings, both in the open negotiating sessions and in meetings of NGOs from around the world, in an effort to discredit Canada's positions. But the diatribes from antifeminist NGOs extended beyond Canada's official positions. "We came under personal attack as well as under attack for Canada's policies. To make matters worse, the UN secretariat was not providing adequate support. These meetings were terrible,"[16] recalls Rhonda Ferderber. The attacks were at times so vicious that the Canadian delegation consulted the Department of Justice in Ottawa.[17] As a result of these factors, the negotiations were stressful and chaotic. In an effort to inject order into the chaos, the UN secretariat announced during the first week of negotiations that all states had to submit their revisions to the *PFA* by Friday evening of that week, thereby increasing pressure in an already tense atmosphere.

Instructions to the Canadian delegation, like those for all states, had been prepared at short notice; they were "never processed into a coherent whole."[18] Nonetheless, Canada went to the Third Preparatory Meetings with several broad priorities: "eliminating violence against women; addressing economic inequality and the feminization of poverty; promoting and protecting the human rights of all women including reproductive rights; reconceptualizing women's health in the context of socio-economic factors; sharing power, responsibility and decision-making in public life and within families; recognizing the importance of literacy and education to all areas of critical concern; and enabling women to network and communicate their own reality through alternative and mass media."[19] The instructions had to be broad to facilitate responding to an evolving text.

The Canadian negotiators were few in numbers relative to the quantity of work that confronted them. As a result, they were "run ragged" during the long days of negotiations. Just as there had been perceptions of inner and outer circles among some members of IDC '95, there was a perception among some of its members that the delegation consisted of "the ins" (those from SWC, DFAIT, and CIDA) and "the outs" (those from other departments).[20] There was ongoing tension, which at times erupted into "unpleasant confrontations" between Abby Hoffman and the alternate representative for the delegation, Valerie Raymond, over relations with NGOs, the appropriateness of adding new wording to the Canadian briefing positions at the conference itself, and who should do the actual negotiating of the health section.[21]

Nevertheless, the Canadian negotiators realized some appreciable gains in the negotiations. Before the New York Preparatory Meetings, Kerry Buck (DFAIT) had organized JUSCANZ – an informal negotiating group comprising Japan, the United States, Canada, Australia, the Netherlands, Norway, and New Zealand. Various incarnations of JUSCANZ already existed in other venues, such as the international negotiations on the environment, though the exact composition of each JUSCANZ group varied with the conference or summit. Before the 1995 preparatory meetings, there had, however, never been a JUSCANZ operating in the areas of human rights or women's rights. As the founder of the group in this context, Kerry Buck was nicknamed the "Gaia of JUSCANZ." Canada remained particularly active in this group of relatively like-minded states, which sought to move the agenda ahead and which frequently worked to bridge the gap between the two principal negotiating blocs: the European Union and the Group of Seventy-Seven.

Abby Hoffman, in collaboration with delegates from other JUSCANZ countries, developed the JUSCANZ health proposals. These progressive proposals broadened the concept of health in the text[22] and encompassed a new way of thinking about the issues that recognized that health is not just a matter of physical wellness but also involves emotional and social well-being. They took account of the fact that a woman's ability to enjoy good health in all its dimensions is determined not just by biology but also by the political, economic, and social realities in which she lives. Much of Hoffman's work in this area was incorporated into the *PFA*.

Canada also took the lead to ensure that the language on violence in the *PFA* was consistent with that contained in the UN *Declaration on the Elimination of Violence Against Women*. By addressing the three levels on which violence against women occurs (violence occurring within the family and within society, as well as that condoned and perpetrated by the state), the *Declaration* had broken new ground. At the New York Preparatory Meetings,

Canada successfully led the campaign to ensure that all three levels on which violence against women occurs were addressed in the *PFA*.

In addition to its successes in the areas of health and violence, the Canadian delegation took the lead on several other prominent issues, all of which remained bracketed in spite of Canada's efforts to move the agenda ahead. The Canadian delegation worked to have gender analysis and a diversity clause incorporated into the text. In its publication, *Beijing Update,* SWC called attention to these priorities: "Canada highlighted the need for gender analysis in policy making as a central approach to achieving gender equality. Canada also promoted the importance of valuing women's diversity while recognizing different factors that maintain barriers to equality for many women."[23] The Canadian negotiators also led the campaigns to get acceptance of gender-based persecution as grounds for claiming refugee status and the war crimes provision, both of which were brought to successful resolution in Beijing. The prominent roles played by the Canadian delegates in New York and the successes they achieved made them key targets for the conservative backlash.

Canada included two nongovernmental observers on its delegation to New York: Madeleine Gilchrist, who had been on the Canadian delegation to Vienna, and Gulzar Samji, who was new to the UN process.[24] As in Vienna, being a nongovernmental observer on the Canadian delegation was a challenging task. As Samji points out, "there was no list of expectations, to define the role of an NGO representative on the delegation."[25] Once again there were the problems of being spread too thinly and of having to cover too many issue areas. Most of the substantial negotiations were conducted in "informal informals" accessible only to official state delegates. The negotiating sessions began in the mornings and often ran late into the night. As a result, Gilchrist, as well as the Canadian negotiators, worked eighteen to twenty hours a day.[26]

The Canadian NGOs were fairly well organized in New York and would wait outside the room where the closed negotiations were being held on issues of particular interest to them. Gilchrist would step out of the meetings to brief the NGOs on developments in the negotiations, and the NGOs would feed her highlighted text they wanted conveyed to the Canadian negotiators. As in Vienna, Gilchrist was still left to monitor a wide range of issues on behalf of the NGOs but, at least this time, the NGOs with expertise in the particular issues under negotiation were standing by to provide expert advice.

As members of the Canadian delegation, Gilchrist and Samji received the official government position, but they were given strict instructions not to share it with the NGOs.[27] For someone like Gilchrist, who was on the board of the CBFC and had been chosen by the NGOs to represent them, this injunction presented a moral dilemma: to obey the instructions given to the Canadian delegation and thereby not to assist fully the NGOs or to disregard the instructions by providing the NGOs with information that would enhance the effectiveness of their lobbying efforts.

The NGOs requested that the Canadian delegation release to them its negotiating positions and the revised text it had submitted to the UN secretariat on the Friday of the first week (i.e., Canada's formal positions). Clearly the delegation was unwilling to make its negotiating positions public. Furthermore, there are understandable reasons for withholding the official Canadian positions: the fear that the material could get into the wrong hands and be used both by other states to undermine Canada's bargaining position and by Canadian NGOs, both right-wing opponents and feminist groups intent on embarrassing the Canadian government to discredit the work of the Canadian delegation. On the other hand, it would have been fairer to have told the NGOs from the outset that the briefing notes for the Canadian delegation were not to be made public, rather than releasing a few positions over time on an ad hoc basis and resorting to platitudes such as, "The document is not ready," "There are not enough copies" and "We are awaiting confirmation from Ottawa." All these statements may at one time or other have been true, but it is unlikely that any one was the real reason. The ensuing "cat and mouse" game resulted in frustrations and anger.[28]

In response to requests from the Canadian NGOs, the Canadian negotiators provided daily substantive briefings. The Canadian negotiators deserve accolades for making time in their frantic schedules to provide in-depth briefings for the Canadian NGOs. This is commendable in absolute terms but even more so when one compares the efforts of the Canadian delegation with those of most other states. According to Lise Martin, the CBFC coordinator, "the briefings were very useful. The Canadian delegates were well prepared and knowledgeable. They gave us an idea of what was going on in that complex process, and they allowed us to hold the members of our delegation accountable for Canada's positions."[29] It must be noted, however, that not all NGO representatives were equally appreciative of the efforts made by the Canadian delegates.

The one Canadian negotiator who did receive accolades from the NGOs for her openness was Abby Hoffman. As Gilchrist noted, "Health was the only area where NGOs had any real input, and this input was possible only because of Abby's openness."[30] In a similar vein, Lise Martin commented: "Abby was the most open. She would sit down with you and go over the NGO language and she would listen. She would also take NGO recommendations back to the delegation."[31] No doubt Hoffman was particularly receptive to the NGOs. However, other Canadian negotiators also went to considerable lengths to brief the NGOs. In addition to their daily briefings, Raymond and several of her colleagues agreed, when asked by NGO representatives, to a second meeting during the day to discuss specific issues and sections of the *PFA*. Again, these meetings represented significant allocations of time in the negotiators' frantic schedules. The government delegates, for their part, felt unsupported by the NAC and several other Canadian feminist groups, particularly when they came under attack from REAL Women and other conservative groups.[32]

In an effort to finalize the draft document, the preparatory meetings were extended by three days. By April 7, 1995, 65 percent of the text had been agreed on and so was not in brackets. Nonetheless, a daunting 35 percent remained in brackets. In light of the number of items left to negotiate and the amount of controversy generated among conference participants, the UN Economic and Social Council authorized the CSW to convene open-ended informal consultations from July 31 to August 4, 1995, in New York.

Informal Consultations (July 31 to August 4, 1995)

The objective of the informal consultations was to remove as many of the remaining brackets as possible.[33] In keeping with the CSW understanding that the bulk of these negotiations would be done by diplomats already posted to New York and that only issues within their competencies would be addressed, only four Canadian negotiators represented Canada at the consultations: Valerie Raymond, Sheila Regehr, Kerry Buck, and Karine Asselin (Bureau of Legal Affairs, DFAIT). As mentioned in Chapter 2, the discussions were successful in removing a further 10 percent of the brackets in the *PFA*. Headway was particularly notable in the areas of human rights and economic structures. For Canada, a main achievement at the informal consultations was getting references to indigenous women mainstreamed throughout the *PFA*.[34] Significant progress also was made towards getting agreement for Canada's language pertaining to gender-based persecution as grounds for claiming refugee status. The results of the consultations were compiled in a nonpaper submitted to the Fourth World Conference on Women in Beijing.[35]

Fourth World Conference on Women

The Canadian delegation to the Beijing Conference on Women, along with the delegations from all other participating states, faced the daunting task of having to negotiate the removal of the brackets which remained in some 25 percent of the *PFA*.[36] When the conference began, brackets remained around language pertaining to such controversial subjects as sexual and reproductive rights, the primacy to be given to religion, cultural and ethnic values, and the mandates and structures of the main UN bodies charged with advancing women, including the Commission on the Status of Women, the UN Development Fund for Women, the International

Research and Training Institute for the Advancement of Women, and the Committee on the Elimination of Discrimination Against Women. In addition to all the work remaining to be done on the *PFA*, the *Declaration*[37] had to be negotiated in its entirely.

This discussion of Canada's delegation to the Fourth World Conference on Women begins with an examination of its composition. Who were sent to Beijing to represent Canada? How were they selected? Why did some of the appointments cause controversy? After answering these questions, the discussion focuses on the contributions of the Canadian delegates. Who contributed a great deal? Were there categories of delegates who could have contributed more? Why? What was the relationship between appointment decisions and levels of contributions?

Composition of the Canadian Delegation
Membership on the Canadian delegation conferred significant privileges. In keeping with standard regulations for all government travel, members of the Canadian delegation were entitled to travel in business class to Beijing, to have their hotel accommodations paid, and to receive a per diem of $69.80.[38] Official delegates also had access to the intergovernmental negotiations, most of which were conducted in "informal informals" (i.e., sessions open only to official state delegates). This meant that the few nongovernmental observers on state delegations had tremendous advantages not enjoyed by any other Canadian NGO representatives attending the conference.

In times of economic restraint, government is concerned about the visual image presented by large numbers of officials travelling to international meetings.[39] All delegations to international conferences need the approval of the minister of foreign affairs, and rigorous selection criteria are applied.[40] Yet the pertinence of the criteria used in this case was called into question on several scores.

Canada sent a delegation of forty-five to Beijing. At its head was the Honourable Sheila Finestone, secretary of state for the status of women, who was assisted by the Honourable Ethel Blondin-Andrew, secretary of state for training and youth. Its membership also included ten parliamentary observers, six provincial/territorial observers, eleven public servants (those who did the actual negotiating), twelve nongovernmental observers, and two academic advisors.

In keeping with standard procedures, the minister of foreign affairs wrote to the whips of each of the political parties represented in the House of Commons, inviting each to nominate a representative to serve on the Canadian delegation. As is usually the case, the government took advantage of the fact that these prominent Canadians were going to be in China to further bilateral objectives. Thus, during the course of the conference, most of the Members of Parliament spent several days developing links with Chinese leaders.

In the selection of public servants for the delegation, the principal criterion was the relevance of a person's specific expertise to the upcoming negotiations on the *PFA*: only those deemed to be vital to the negotiations were accorded membership.[41] Once the decisions had been made as to which issues were the highest priorities for Canada and which issues were likely to be most difficult to resolve, the expertise and credentials of those working on these issues were assessed in terms of the established needs. This is why it is so important to coordinate government positions in advance; negotiators on Canadian delegations are quite often carrying instructions from two or even three departments not represented on the delegation.

One of the casualties of this streamlining was Abby Hoffman, director general of the Women's Health Bureau (Health Canada), who had played such a pivotal role in New York in expanding and strengthening the provisions in the Health section. By the time of the Beijing conference, most of the Health issues she had been working on were considered to have been resolved; hence, she was not included on the delegation in spite of a request for her inclusion by the deputy minister of health to the minister of foreign affairs. Her absence was considered regrettable by several of the government negotiators. Ruth Archibald, director of the Refugees, Population and Migration Division (DFAIT), voices a common opinion: "Abby understood the issues and the politics. She also had established contacts with some of the key international NGOs. She would have been helpful."[42] Outside government circles, Hoffman's exclusion was decried by many NGO representatives.

All but two of the Canadian negotiators at the World Conference on Women had participated in at least some of the multilateral meetings leading up to Beijing. Ruth Archibald and Ross Hynes (DFAIT) were added to the team for Beijing for two reasons: their positions as directors of key policy divisions and their expertise. Ross Hynes was director of Human Rights, Women's Equality and Social Affairs Division. It is usual practice to include senior personnel responsible for areas where issues are outstanding and where the negotiations are evolving so that they can provide on-the-spot approval and policy guidance for last-minute changes that must be made. With a twelve-hour time difference between Ottawa and Beijing, it was not always feasible to telephone home when instructions were needed.

It is customary for the government to put additional senior experts on a delegation once the key issues are identified and the negotiations are focused on specific and/or technical provisions. It was clear that reproductive and sexual rights would be key issues at Beijing and that the negotiations would be focused on specifics. Archibald, a recognized expert on population who had negotiated sexual and reproductive rights in Cairo, was brought in to handle the negotiations in Beijing.[43] Hynes was an expert both on human rights and on UN procedures and was very involved with the "Chapeau" in the *Beijing Declaration*.

Each province and territory was invited in the spring of 1995 to nominate two observers to the Canadian delegation to Beijing.[44] Manitoba, the Northwest Territories, and Quebec each sent two observers. The expenses for provincial and territorial observers were paid by their respective governments. The fact that women's bureaus in the other provinces and territories were unable to send delegates did not reflect a lack of interest on their parts; instead it reflected a lack of financial resources.[45]

The selection of nongovernmental observers for the Canadian delegation stirred up the greatest controversy. When Gilchrist had first been chosen as the sole nongovernmental observer on the Canadian delegation to the Vienna Regional Meetings, it had been on the understanding that she would also serve on the Canadian delegations to the New York Preparatory Meetings and the Beijing conference. As discussed earlier, she did attend both sets of preparatory meetings, but she never went to Beijing.

In early April 1995, following the New York Preparatory Meetings, Gilchrist decided to resign from the Canadian delegation to Beijing:

> It was not an easy decision but four factors lead me to take this position. The first was the lack of openness of the government's part vis-à-vis membership on its delegation. The government had asked the CBFC for guidelines for choosing nongovernmental observers for the Canadian delegation which it promptly chose to ignore in working out a deal with *Homemakers Magazine*. Second, the government had sponsored the creation of the CBFC but had subsequently ignored the recommendations contained in the NGOs' line-by-line analysis which made all the work we had done appear to be for nought. Third, as an advocate of disarmament, I could not in conscience be part of the delegation of a country whose government was selling arms and Candu reactors to China. And finally, I resigned to draw attention to a flawed process in which the NGOs were treated with condescension and not as equal partners.[46]

With Gilchrist's resignation, the CBFC lost its voice of experience on the Canadian delegation. The CBFC nominated eleven women for membership on the Canadian delegation to Beijing, expecting that two or three of these candidates would be selected.[47] Of the nominations, only Pat Beck was appointed.[48] Although Beck had not attended the negotiations leading up to Beijing, she had been involved with the Manitoba UN End of Decade Committee as well as with the CBFC since its inception.

In both Vienna and New York, Gilchrist had made an informal recommendation on behalf of the CBFC to Raymond and Ferderber that lead groups – those with expertise on each of the key issues in the *PFA* – be included on the delegation to Beijing.[49] This recommendation was never acted on. Nonetheless, efforts were made to ensure that the nongovernmental observers chosen for the delegation represented a wide spectrum of sectors and interest.[50] SWC compiled an initial list consisting of those proposed by the NGOs on the CPC as well as those who had applied directly for delegation membership. The list was narrowed down to thirty women, who were chosen on the basis of their expertise in the outstanding issues, as well as to reflect regional balance and to represent diverse categories of women.[51] The list was adjudicated by public servants in SWC and DFAIT before being submitted to the minister of foreign affairs who, in keeping with his prerogative, made the final selection.[52] The most controversial aspect of this process was the decision to appoint individuals, instead of representatives of particular groups.[53] The wisdom of appointing youth to the delegation was also questioned.

At her first meeting with the Canadian delegation, Minister Finestone said explicitly that the nongovernmental observers had been chosen as individuals rather than as representatives of specific NGOs or sectors of the NGO community.[54] One casualty of this decision was the NAC – the largest umbrella group of feminist organizations in Canada – which was not represented on the Canadian delegation. The NAC had formally recommended a candidate for membership on the delegation, but its recommendation had not been accepted. Once Lorraine Michael had been chosen to serve as a nongovernmental observer on the delegation, she was asked by Louise Bergeron-de Villiers whether her affiliations could appear on the list of Canadian delegates not only as the Ecumenical Coalition for Economic Justice – her place of employment – but also as the NAC, since she had been on its board.[55] Michael declined, saying that the NAC had made a formal recommendation which had been rejected, that she had not been recommended by the NAC and that she did not have a mandate from the NAC to represent it.[56] On the list sent to the Chinese government, Michael's sole affiliation appeared as the Ecumenical Coalition for Economic Justice,but in the delegation's *Briefing Book* she was listed as having two affiliations: the NAC as well as the Ecumenical Coalition for Economic Justice. Why was Michael listed as representing the NAC when she had explicitly said that this was not the case? The answer is assumed to be that the NAC affiliation was included for political reasons: to create the appearance of representation on the delegation when in fact none existed.

This selectivity in listing the affiliations of the nongovernmental observers was extended to at least one other person. Pat Beck, the one nongovernmental observer on the delegation who was also on the board of the CBFC, was listed only as representing the National Council of Women. Why was the representative of the CBFC not identified as such? The lack of clarity in identifying the affiliations of certain nongovernmental observers and, most particularly, the decision to appoint individuals rather than representatives of key NGOs had negative consequences for fulfiling one of the key roles assigned to the nongovernmental observers in the delegation's *Briefing Book:* to liaise with NGO representatives.

A second aspect of the selection process that caused some consternation among NGO representatives in Beijing was the decision to reserve two of the twelve places on the official delegation that were allocated to nongovernmental observers for youth. SWC, in partnership with Telemedia Communications, publisher of *Homemaker Magazine* and *Madame au Foyer*, ran a "Write Your Way to China" contest to select the two youth delegates. Young Canadians were asked to answer, in 250 words or less: "If you could address the 1995 United Nations World Conference on Women in Beijing, China, what would you say?"[57] Contestants were asked to explain their reasons for wanting to attend the conference and the contributions they hoped to make while there. The contest was to ensure that capable "grassroots" youth were selected rather than members of elite organizations.[58] The compositions "came from all over the country: from students, young mothers, assembly line workers and budding professionals."[59] Panels consisting of journalists, as well as officials from SWC and Telemedia, judged the 1,500 entries.[60] The English-speaking Canadian and the French-speaking Canadian whose responses were deemed best were given places on the delegation.

Many in the NGO community questioned the wisdom of allocating two of the highly sought-after twelve places reserved for nongovernmental observers to youth who had not had – nor could they be expected to have had – years of experience working with women's issues or at UN negotiations. As one highly experienced woman, who has devoted most of her adult years to advancing women's issues, comments, "Was a life's work for the cause worth less than 250 words of prose?"[61] Overall there was feeling within the NGO community that some funding should have been provided to allow youth to attend the NGO forum but that places on the Canadian delegation should have been reserved for those with strong and extensive records of working to advance the status of women – for those who knew the issues and could provide valuable links between the NGO community and the government negotiators.

At the ministerial level, however, it was considered important to have "grassroots" youth represented on the delegation[62] and ministerial preference prevailed. The two young women selected, Marjolaine Bélair and Susan Dowse, were very active in the youth caucus and reported back faithfully to the delegation on developments in the caucus.

There was, nonetheless, considerable discontent in the NGO community over the composition of the Canadian delegation. As one nongovernmental observer says, "The way observers were chosen for the delegation to Beijing was a slap in the face to the women's movement in Canada."[63] This is not to say that the nongovernmental observers on the delegation did not have good credentials. Individually and collectively, they had extensive experience working to advance the status of women. For example, Glenda Simms had served for five-and-a-half years as president of the Canadian Advisory Council on the Status of Women, Lucie Pépin was the commissioner of the National Parole Board, Madeleine Dion Stout was the director of the Centre for Aboriginal Education at Carleton University and Gisèle Côté-Harper was the chair of the board of directors for the International Centre for Human Rights and Democratic Development. In her own way, each of the nongovernmental observers made significant contributions to the work of the delegation. The question that is addressed later in the chapter is: Could they collectively have contributed more to the effectiveness of the Canadian delegation?

Contributions Made by the Canadian Delegation

Work at the Fourth World Conference on Women took place in four settings.[64] The plenary initially approved the rules, the agenda, and the organization of the conference work and elected its officials. Thereafter, it was the site of general debate on documents, such as the *Second Review and Appraisal for the Implementation of the Nairobi Forward-looking Strategies for the Advancement of Women to the Year 2000* and the reports of the regional meetings. It was also the venue in which the leaders of the official state delegations outlined the priorities and commitments of their respective countries.

The negotiation of the *Beijing Declaration* and *PFA* was the responsibility of the Main Committee, which worked through the text on a chapter-by-chapter basis. Yet the task of negotiating the *Declaration* and removing brackets in 25 percent of the *PFA* in two short weeks was beyond the capability of any one body. Two working groups were established.[65] The toughest, most controversial issues were referred to contact groups set up specifically to facilitate resolution of each. Once a contact group managed to reach general agreement on the designated issue or set of issues, it reported back to the appropriate working group. The working groups, in turn, reported to the Main Committee, which received their recommendations, negotiated any remaining brackets in the text, and ultimately submitted the negotiated documents to the conference for adoption.

Members of the Canadian delegation were active in all the organizational venues mentioned above, as well as at the NGO Forum on Women '95. But before examining their various contributions, it is important to recognize the conditions in which they had to function. Holding the conference in China posed logistical problems for all in attendance. The most serious

problem was the 42 kilometre separation of the intergovernmental conference in Beijing from the NGO forum. The geographic separation posed
particularly acute problems for Jackie Claxton and Duy Ai Kien, who were
expected to attend the daily 8 a.m. delegation meetings at the Hotel
Kempinski and then to travel out to Huairou to liaise with, and facilitate
the participation of, Canadian NGOs at the forum. While there, Claxton
and Kien participated in the daily briefings for the Canadian NGOs at the
forum and gathered intelligence for the delegation on relevant developments at key workshops and on the thoughts of the NGOs. Much of their
time was taken up with arranging logistics. For example, space had to be
found and arrangements made for the days when the secretary of state for
the status of women went to the forum to meet with Canadian NGOs. Kien
was saddled with the unenviable task of delivering 200 invitations for a
reception at the Canadian embassy in Beijing to Canadian NGO representatives spread out in hotels all over Huairou. Claxton and Kien also spent
time listening to the NGOs' problems and, where possible, they tried to
find solutions. It was a difficult and demanding task as many of the NGOs'
complaints pertained to regulations and arrangements that Canada did not
have direct jurisdiction over, such as the problems associated with holding
the conference in China and the decision to exclude the NGOs from the
work of the contact groups.[66]

The geographic separation of the conference and the forum also made it
more difficult for the CIDA representatives to carry out two diverse sets of
objectives.[67] Their primary objective was to advance the government's negotiating objectives and to ensure that the positive gains enshrined in the
language that had been adopted at the Cairo Conference on Population
and Development, as well as at the Vienna Conference on Human Rights
and the Copenhagen Summit for Social Development, was included in the
Beijing Declaration and *PFA*. In addition to their negotiating objectives,
CIDA delegates were expected to liaise with their Southern partners (i.e.,
the Southern NGOs with which CIDA had development projects).

The NGO forum brought together NGO representatives from all over
the developing world, offering opportunities for hearing Southern views
and for finding out about emerging issues and trends. It was through similar types of contact that CIDA had first come to recognize that violence
against women is a development issue. It was Southern women who asked,
"Why should I go out and try to get a better education? Why should I try
to take the training programs that you offer when I'm getting beaten up in
my home or when I can't go out in the streets to attend classes for fear of
being attacked?"[68] Clearly violence, and the fear thereof, are major impediments to the empowerment of women, which in turn is critical for human
development. CIDA had sponsored representatives of the Southern groups
to attend so that the latter would have the opportunity to share views with

women from other Southern countries. But the attendance of Southern women also offered CIDA representatives important opportunities for making and further developing valuable contacts with a wide range of Southern NGOs. Unfortunately, to take advantage of these opportunities, they had to take time out from the negotiations to make the trek to Huairou.

In contrast to the large distance between the Beijing conference and its NGO forum, the 1995 Copenhagen Summit for Social Development and its NGO forum had been located twenty minutes apart in the same city, and frequent shuttle buses had been provided. As a result, those accredited to the summit had been able to take short breaks from the negotiations in order to brief their sisters at the NGO forum.[69] The 1994 Cairo Conference on Population and Development had been located in even closer proximity to its NGO forum: "In Cairo, Diana Rivington could leave the official conference and walk down the street to the NGO forum, present a film for CIDA and then walk back."[70] To perform the same activity in Huairou required a time commitment of half a day, at the very least.

Problems of geographic separation were exacerbated by inadequate transportation and communications. Each morning, members of the Canadian delegation would receive notes under their bedroom doors announcing the latest changes to the transportation arrangements for that day. For Rhonda Ferderber, who was in charge of logistics for the Canadian delegation, "it was a nightmare trying to ensure that delegates got to where they needed to go, when they needed to be there ... [given the] constant changes in arrangements by the Chinese officials."[71] It was also frustrating for delegates who woke up thinking their day was planned, only to find that the arrangements had been changed.

Canadian officials had cellular telephones to facilitate maintaining contact with their colleagues at the Beijing International Convention Centre, the office of the Canadian delegation at the Hotel Kempinski, the Canadian embassy in Beijing, and the NGO forum in Huairou. But while they had the telephones, the infrastructure to enable them to function effectively was lacking. Calls were often cut off after only thirty seconds. As Ferderber relates, "On a particular rainy day, I had to get a message to Jackie Claxton, who was struggling through mud at the NGO site in Huairou. I began the conversation by telling her that I was not even going to ask her how she was but instead would go directly to the business at hand. In other words, we had to dispense with the pleasantries because the channels of communication were so uncertain."[72] So the inadequate telephone system in addition to transportation and other logistical problems made staying in contact much more problematic, more stressful, and less pleasant than it should have been.

The office for the Canadian delegation consisted of a hotel suite with two small rooms and a bathroom. Working space for the staff was crowded.

Several times their office was used by the Canadian negotiators for meetings with their counterparts from other countries. There they struggled to reach compromises and strategies squeezed into a tiny room amongst the photocopier and the refrigerator. While such meetings were being conducted, the support staff and other members of the Canadian delegation were shut out of the office. This arrangement was inconvenient for all but especially hard on the support staff who were already overworked. Furthermore, no one could accurately predict when such a meeting would be over; the staff had to stay outside, waiting to return to their office.

These were just some of many logistical problems encountered. There were others. For example, the Hotel Kempinski issued only four cards to access the Canadian office – clearly far too few to allow a card for each staff member and delegate. As a result, Rhonda Ferderber had to keep track of the four cards, in addition to all her other duties, to ensure that those who needed access were indeed able to get into the office when they needed to be there.

Then there was the problems of hygiene – of trying to ensure that everyone stayed healthy. Since the support staff and negotiators were working at full capacity, they could not afford to have anyone succumb to illness. Rhonda Ferderber instructed her staff: "Don't eat anything that has not been commercially packaged."[73] She later recounted the ramifications of her warning for at least one staff member: "Cathy McRae was having to rush back and forth between Huairou and Beijing. As a result, she had missed lunch and was ravenous. So she purchased a sandwich and was just about to bite into it when she recalled my warning and thought 'Rhonda will kill me if I eat this sandwich and get sick.' So she decided to forego lunch."[74]

In a context where finding time to eat was often at a premium, and where food that would not cause gastrointestinal problems was not always immediately obtainable, attending to health concerns was far from easy: "We ate a lot of spaghetti; it was a comfort food, it was readily available, and it was relatively safe. Nonetheless, it seemed strange to be eating spaghetti in China!"[75]

In addition to the prospect of having to face the logistical problems inherent in meeting in China, the Canadian negotiators set off for Beijing with memories fresh in their minds of the extremely active and vocal conservative forces they had encountered at the New York Preparatory Meetings and of the verbal and written attacks they had endured at the hands of these conservative governments and NGOs. Similar opposition was expected at the conference in China. "The fact that the UN secretariat had failed to provide us with adequate support when we had been faced with attacks not only on Canada's policies but also on our characters did not leave us feeling confident about the arrangements for Beijing,"[76] comments Ferderber.

Fortunately for the Canadian delegation, the conservative backlash that had been so strong and vocal in New York was more muted in Beijing, where the gathering was far larger and the conservative forces made up a proportionally smaller minority. Nonetheless, Valerie Raymond, Kerry Buck, and Ruth Archibald all came under personal attack from right-wing groups at the Fourth World Conference on Women.[77] Yet, in spite of the opposition and challenges involved in holding an international women's conference in China, the Canadian government officials persevered with their objectives. They knew their priorities, they had a clear sense of what had been accomplished at previous sets of international negotiations, and they sought to build on past progress.

The Canadian negotiators put in long days, beginning with their 7 a.m. strategy meeting, followed by briefings to the whole Canadian delegation. Immediately thereafter, they set off for JUSCANZ's morning strategy meeting. At 1 p.m., they provided briefings to the Canadian NGOs at the intergovernmental conference. They met again each evening to review their progress and to develop strategies for the next phases of their work.[78] The rest of the day and often late into the night, they were fully engaged in the negotiations.

In Beijing, as at the New York Preparatory Meetings, the Canadian delegation was an active member of JUSCANZ and often worked as a broker between the Group of Seventy-Seven and the European Union. As a broker, it needed to promote compromise wording that would get the approval of both sides without sacrificing principles that were of importance to Canada. While each negotiator had an area(s) of expertise, he or she was frequently called upon to handle additional areas when the person responsible for that set of issues was engaged in another set of negotiations.[79] The negotiators had to be sufficiently flexible and versatile to be able to cover areas in addition to their primary responsibilities. At various points, Kerry Buck, Adèle Dion, and Ross Hynes all worked on human rights, armed conflict, and violence against women. Sheila Regehr focused on poverty and economic issues, but when she was not involved with these issues, she negotiated decision making. When she was not available to handle decision making, another negotiator dealt with this set of issues. The coordination of evolving positions and the allocation of negotiating responsibility was usually done at the negotiators' daily 7 a.m. strategy meeting. But when the issues were evolving quickly, the coordination process could not always wait until the next strategy meeting; instead, responsibilities were settled on the spot, often in the corridors.[80]

The Canadian negotiators functioned well as a team under Raymond's capable direction. Each negotiator knew his or her issues and objectives well. In addition, their diplomacy and skills in negotiation were widely recognized, as exemplified by the facts that Canadians were often called upon to provide leadership and that the majority of the contact groups were chaired by them. When CNN (the Cable News Network) decided to do a documentary on the "Bracket Busters" at the Beijing Conference on Women, it was the Canadian delegation that it chose to feature. Being asked to chair the contact groups was a tribute to the Canadian negotiators but it also taxed their resources yet further and meant that they were spread even more thinly. While Canada's overall success in achieving its negotiating objectives is assessed in Chapter 7, it is important to recognize here some of the major accomplishments of Canada's negotiators.

As alternate representative for the delegation, Raymond was, in the eyes of her colleagues, "superlative – there is no other word to describe her. She was an inspiration!"[81] Raymond's hard work, commitment, and sensitivity to others were in evidence as she juggled her many responsibilities. She was responsible for the overall planning for the conference and played key roles in the management of the delegation and the coordination of policy for the delegation, in what proved to be a complex and multifaceted set of negotiations. She successfully put together an excellent negotiating team, which involved identifying individuals capable of making major contributions in the negotiations and then securing ministerial approval for their participation. She handled many of the media interviews, and she was the major point of liaison between the secretary of state for the status of women, Sheila Finestone, and the SWC coordinator, Louise Bergeron-de Villiers, on one hand, and the Canadian negotiators, on the other. Just as Raymond's colleagues were highly laudatory of her leadership, she had high praise for the Canadian negotiators, who she described as being an "absolutely first class negotiating team."[82]

Ruth Archibald, a "brilliant negotiator,"[83] realized two major successes. First she chaired the contact group on parental rights – an issue that had the Vatican and its allies and the Islamic fundamentalist countries pitted against the Western countries and the advocates of children's rights. The former asserted the rights of parents to prevent their children from gaining access to information on contraception and other related matters whereas the latter advocated the child's right to such information even in cases of parental opposition. Archibald was chosen to chair the contact group both because Canada was seen as holding a middle – rather than an extremist – position and because she had managed to work out mutually acceptable language in Cairo with the delegate from the Holy See and the chief negotiator for Iran. It took seventy delegates more than seventy hours to negotiate the forty references to parental rights in the text.[84] The compromise reached recognized the right of the child "to information, privacy, confidentiality, respect and informed consent while respecting the rights of parents and legal guardians to provide direction and guidance in a manner consistent with the evolving capacities of the child."[85] The compromise was applauded by the international NGOs who commended Archibald for her work.

After the contact group on parental rights had successfully completed its task, Archibald was then asked to chair the contact group on women's sexual rights. The issue had been negotiated previously but it re-emerged in the section on human rights and needed to be revisited. The fundamentalist Islamic states were keen to roll back progress made in previous negotiations, whereas the European Union, in particular, was eager not to lose ground and in fact to push beyond what was in the text. It was a major triumph in these highly political negotiations when agreement was finally reached at 11:30 of the last evening.[86] As another Canadian negotiator comments, "We had hoped to hold the line on Cairo language. Thanks to Ruth, the *PFA* goes beyond Cairo in its provisions for sexual and reproductive rights."[87] As is discussed below, Ross Hynes also played an important and constructive role in these negotiations.

Hynes chaired the contact group on the *Beijing Declaration*. This was a complex set of negotiations because he had to ensure that the *Declaration* moved the agenda ahead and that there were no clauses in the *Declaration* that weakened the provisions in the *PFA*. Once these objectives were met and the *Declaration* was approved, Hynes joined Archibald in the negotiations on reproductive rights. Together they constituted a formidable team, with Archibald chairing the contact group and Hynes strongly advocating Canada's position.

The contact group established to tackle the issues of the girl child was chaired by Diana Rivington, who was described by her director as being an "experienced negotiator who was excellent in drafting text."[88] These skills were vital to the work of her contact group, which succeeded in reaffirming the human rights of girls and recognizing the need to address "son preference" and other forms of violence against girls. The group also tackled the highly contentious issue of inheritance, which remains a controversial debate, particularly within the South. It was finally agreed that girls and women have equal rights to inherit and equal rights to succession with boys and men. Having equal rights to inherit is not, however, the same as having the right to inherit equally. Thus, the contact group definitely moved the agenda ahead on the issue of inheritance, though there is still considerable distance to go before it will be fully resolved.

The financial and institutional arrangements were handled by Adèle Dion. In this area, the Holy See and its allied states, as well as the fundamentalist Islamic states, sought to narrow and weaken the mandates of, and reduce the resources allocated to, two key UN bodies existing to advance the status of women: the Commission on the Status of Women and the Division for the Advancement of Women. In these negotiations, Dion made several important contributions. She proposed language both to review and strengthen the mandate of the CSW and to request that the UN secretary-general provide adequate resources from the regular UN budget to enable the Division for the Advancement of Women to function effectively. In each case, Dion was successful in gaining the support of the European Union, the United States, and the Group of Seventy-Seven for her compromise proposals. The wording was adopted, albeit in the case of the Divisions' funding, not before 3 a.m.[89]

On the issue of unpaid work, Canada took the lead, with Sheila Regehr chairing the contact group.[90] The issue was highly complex and was approached very cautiously by some, both because of its newness and because of its implications. Delegates to the Copenhagen Summit for Social Development had struggled with this controversial issue. The South was committed to gaining recognition for women's unpaid work, whereas the United States and the European Union were opposed. The group met for two solid days before achieving a breakthrough. In the end, the United States and the European Union yielded to the adamant demands for recognition. The negotiations were aided by the participation of some individual state delegates with significant expertise and experience. There were, moreover, expert representatives of relevant UN organizations who could be called upon when points of facts needed clarification. Regehr did a "brilliant job of chairing," for which she received accolades from the international community.[91] The agreement negotiated by her contact group was subsequently accepted by the conference.

Kerry Buck negotiated the sections on the human rights of women, violence against women, and women and armed conflict. The reaffirmation in the *PFA* that rape is a war crime and a crime against humanity and the introduction, for the first time in a UN document, of the concept that, under certain conditions, rape constitutes an act of genocide, was due in large measure to Buck's effective negotiating skills.[92] She was also successful in having sexual violence and gender-related persecution recognized, for the first time in a UN document, as grounds for refugee status. Furthermore, Buck proposed the language on cultural relativism that finally gained acceptance at 2 a.m. of the final day of the conference, thereby breaking the deadlock that had previously persisted over whether deference to culture was to take precedence over the promotion and protection of women's human rights. The adoption of Buck's language ensured that women's rights are given highest priority. Buck received the Professional Association of Foreign Service Officers' Award for her work in Beijing. This is the highest award given by the DFAIT annually in recognition of outstanding performance.[93]

Behind the scenes, Rhonda Ferderber and her team of support staff handled the logistics for the delegation. She coordinated its meetings; arranging who would meet whom, when, and where, ensured that the delegation was represented at all the official receptions to which it was invited, and attended to the needs of the nongovernmental observers. Just as the Canadian negotiators held a daily 7 a.m. breakfast meeting to discuss their strategies for the day, Ferderber convened a daily 7 a.m. breakfast "prayer" meeting with her staff to work out the logistical arrangements. Before the meeting, she would have received the Canadian Press' reporting of the conference to determine the type of coverage the delegation was getting and what response was required. Every evening around 9:30, she would call Ottawa to report on the press coverage and on other relevant matters, such as the response that the minister's speech had elicited.

Beginning on the eighth day of the conference, Rhonda Ferderber and Cathy McRae started producing updates on developments in the negotiations. Canada was the only country to issue such updates, and their production was possible only because the Canadians were playing such central roles in the negotiations, enabling them to report back daily on the specific developments in their respective meetings. Before issuing the updates, Ferderber and McRae would check their accuracy with the individual negotiators at their 7 a.m. breakfast meeting. These almost daily reports provided concise "road maps" of where the negotiators had been and were going, as well as of Canada's roles and positions in the process. The updates were given to the media. Unfortunately, the quality of media coverage did not improve appreciably in spite of these efforts, as Ferderber notes with disappointment: "I had hoped that the updates would encourage the media to report more substantially on the negotiations but such was not the case. There was not much improvement in the media's coverage of the substance of the negotiations."[94] The updates were also given to the UN secretariat so it would have a detailed record of the negotiations and of the conference's achievements.

In addition to their successes in the negotiations, the government officials are to be commended for their in-depth daily briefings to the NGOs. Few – if any – other countries devoted more time and energy to keeping their NGOs informed. The daily briefings for the NGOs were organized by the Women's Program of SWC in cooperation with the CBFC. The briefings were chaired by Charlotte Thibault and Marge Friedel, the two co-chairs of the CBFC. The sessions were held at roughly the same time each day, though their exact location in the International Convention Centre changed depending on the availability of space. News of each day's location spread by word of mouth, which caused some frustration. In addition, the meetings were often held in noisy corridors or at the back of a negotiating chamber. There were some complaints that the organizers should have worked harder to procure a more adequate and more permanent meeting place but, to be fair, space at the Beijing International Convention Centre was at a premium.

Most importantly, the briefings provided by the Canadian negotiators were in-depth – virtually identical in content to those they gave to the Canadian delegation at its daily 8 a.m. meetings – with each of the key government negotiators reporting on developments in his or her issue area. The NGOs never appeared to have worked out a coherent lobbying strategy in advance of these meetings. Some individual NGO representatives raised questions in response to the briefings, to which the Canadian negotiators replied. Then the briefing would end and everyone drifted away.

Before the beginning of the NGO forum in Huairou, two orientation briefings were held at the Canadian embassy in Beijing on August 29 and 30. During the Fourth World Conference on Women, daily briefings were also held at the NGO forum in the North American/European Tent. Between forty and fifty people attended each of these briefing sessions.[95]

The briefings represented a considerable allocation of time, given that there were relatively few negotiators to participate in the many ongoing meetings, and that these people were already putting in extremely long days, beginning with the 7 a.m. delegation meetings, and participating in negotiations that often went late into the night. This willingness to allocate scarce time reflected a personal commitment to ensure NGO participation on the part of Valerie Raymond and her colleagues.[96] The negotiators realized the utility of a daily two-way dialogue: NGO representatives, particularly those familiar with the UN environment, provided useful feedback on what positions Canadian and other NGOs were taking; some useful intelligence on developments in the NGO caucuses and the NGO community at large; and informal feedback on the positions of other government delegations.[97] The briefings were seen as offering symbiotic benefits.

While the Canadian negotiators deserve high scores for their leadership and for their many successes, an assessment of the contributions of the nongovernmental observers produces more mixed conclusions. Collectively, they definitely contributed to the effectiveness of the Canadian delegation and some individuals made major contributions. But not all were equally willing or able to contribute; and their overall effectiveness was not as great as one might have wished. Early in the first week of the conference, many NGO representatives, especially those who had experience at previous UN negotiations, were asking who the nongovernmental observers were and which sets of negotiations each was observing so they would know who their key liaisons were in each issue area. Lorraine Michael raised this matter in the delegation meeting on Wednesday morning of the first week. That evening, SWC organized a special meeting of the nongovernmental observers to discuss the latter's role. The government officials reiterated the "Roles of a Non-Governmental Observer" listed in the *Briefing Book*:

- Liaise with other Canadian representatives of NGOs and representatives of NGOs from other countries;
- Provide input to negotiators on matters being addressed at the Conference/in *Platform for Action;*
- Report on the activities of NGOs at Forum '95 and at the Beijing International Conference Centre (Beijing International Convention Centre), youth caucuses, etc.;
- Represent the Canadian delegation at events/official functions as required;
- Attend negotiating sessions and Canadian delegation meetings.[98]

The nongovernmental observers were then told to choose from this list the activities they "felt comfortable" pursuing.[99] The question then is: How effective were the nongovernmental observers in fulfiling these tasks?

All the nongovernmental observers on the delegation acted, at least to some extent, as two-way links between the delegation and the NGO community. As such, each contributed information to the delegation from time to time on developments within the NGO caucuses and on intelligence gained from other NGOs about the positions of other countries and negotiating groups. In addition, they shared knowledge they had gained from delegation membership with other NGOs. For example, Glenda Simms conferred widely with women, particularly those from Africa and the Caribbean, and she was a useful source of intelligence for the Canadian delegation.[100] Madeleine Dion Stout, along with Ethel Blondin-Andrew (secretary of state for training and youth) and Sue Heron-Herbert (Northwest Territories), was active in the indigenous caucus. So the nongovernmental observers, as well as other members of the Canadian delegation, did interact with Canadian NGOs and those from other countries. But the whole process of gathering and sharing information was done on an ad hoc basis. Few nongovernmental observers provided two-way communications on a systematic basis (i.e., systematically reporting, on at least a daily basis, the views of their respective constituencies to the government negotiators, and carrying information back to their NGO constituencies to facilitate the latter's lobbying efforts). According to Lorraine Michael, part – but only part – of the problem was that the term "nongovernmental observer" was "somewhat ambiguous": "First of all, not all delegates under this title were strictly non-governmental. Second, while the name hinted at the notion of nongovernmental organizations (NGO), in actual fact it did not mean NGO. This ambiguity caused confusion for me personally, for some of the delegates and for the NGO sector that was accredited at the Conference. Based on past experience we expected NGO observers on the Canadian delegation who would be there representing specific organizations of the NGO sector."[101] The minister's reiterations of the fact that the nongovernmental

observers had been appointed as individuals rather than as NGO representatives did little to encourage the liaison function.

Systematic liaison work with the Canadian NGO community was perhaps best exemplified by Lorraine Michael and Nancy Riche, both of whom
had served on previous Canadian delegations where nongovernmental
observers had provided effective ongoing contact between the NGO community and government negotiators.[102] When it became clear early in the
first week that no formal direct lines of responsibility had been established
between the nongovernmental observers and the NGO community, Michael
became, in practice, the principal conduit for the Canadian NGO community at the daily delegation meetings. She met regularly daily with representatives of the NAC executive and its committees, as well as with members
of some of the key international NGO caucuses (e.g., those concerned with
human rights, lesbian rights, economic justice, and labour), both at the
Convention Centre and at the Grace Hotel, where many of these NGO
delegates were staying.[103] On several occasions, NGO representatives sent
urgent messages to Michael in the economic negotiations, asking her to
attend other sets of negotiations from which they were excluded because
they were worried that the negotiations had taken a turn for the worse. As
executive vice-president of the Canadian Labour Congress, Nancy Riche's
loyalty was to organized labour. She spent most of her time networking
with the international labour network and ensuring that language from the
international trade union movement was conveyed to the appropriate
Canadian negotiators. Here were examples of using one's observer status to
facilitate the work of NGOs.

It must be noted that the two youth delegates, Marjolaine Bélair and
Susan Dowse, also provided systematic representation of their constituency. They had been appointed to the delegation specifically to bring the
voice of youth, and they were regularly asked at the 8 a.m. delegation
meeting to report on the work of the youth caucus. Although they did not
have prior UN experience, both took their responsibilities seriously and
were active and effective members of the caucus. Thus, they systematically
liaised with their particular sector of the NGO community on an ongoing
basis and kept the delegation apprised of the activities and general concerns of the caucus. In short, "they did what was expected of them, and
they did it well."[104] Their activities were not, however, policy focused as
was the work of some of the more experienced nongovernmental observers,
who had long established relations with their NGO constituencies, understood UN negotiations, and directed their energies to affecting the content
of the negotiating documents.

The nongovernmental observers who saw their primary role being that
of intermediary between the Canadian delegation and the NGO community were frustrated that they were shouldering the lion's share of these

extensive responsibilities.[105] As indicated earlier, this frustration was shared by many in the NGO community who felt deprived of systematic representation on the Canadian delegation and in the negotiations and of valuable information that could come only from those attending the closed negotiating sessions. One cannot lobby effectively without understanding the evolving dynamics of the negotiations and without knowing the specific position of the country or countries one seeks to influence. Naturally, specific wording must be developed with direct reference to the language under discussion. In addition, receptivity to proposed wording is likely to increase when it provides a way of surmounting barriers to reaching agreement, and one cannot understand the nature of a stalemate without having insider information.

The CBFC did little in advance or at the conference to coordinate the activities of the observers and the NGO community. Unlike the Canadian NGO Organizing Committee for the World Summit for Social Development, which had contacted all the NGO observers on the Canadian delegation before the preparatory meetings and the summit, the CBFC did not contact most of the nongovernmental observers on the delegation to Beijing in advance. The opportunity to develop valuable contacts with the only Canadian nongovernmental actors able to attend both the delegation meetings and the closed negotiations was lost.

While the list of roles for nongovernmental observers included providing input to the negotiators and attending negotiating sessions, it did not specify assisting the government negotiators in the negotiations. Furthermore, at the first meeting of the full Canadian delegation, one got the distinct impression that the nongovernmental observers were not expected to be following the negotiations closely, since there was no substantive reporting on the issues to be discussed. Instead, to the consternation of several delegates, the secretary of state for the status of women focused her remarks on social events, which prompted their demands for substantive briefings by the Canadian negotiators.[106] This request was granted and thereafter the Canadian negotiators provided substantive briefings and answered questions at the daily 8 a.m. delegation meetings.

On the other hand, few of the nongovernmental observers had read the *PFA* prior to the conference, let alone done any line-by-line analysis of any of its sections. Moreover, few regularly attended the negotiating sessions or worked consistently on the wording in the *PFA*. None of the nongovernmental observers contacted Madeleine Gilchrist to gain insights from her experience as a nongovernmental observer on the Canadian delegations to the two key preparatory conferences in which Canada participated: the 1994 Vienna Regional Meetings and the 1995 New York Preparatory Meetings.[107]

Yet in the areas where nongovernmental observers were actively attending

negotiations and working on the text, their contributions were significant. In the area of unpaid work, Canada's negotiator, Sheila Regehr, spoke
highly of the contributions made by Michael and Riche.[108] Regehr had
negotiated unpaid work for Canada at the preparatory meetings leading
up to the UN Summit for Social Development as well as at the Copenhagen
Summit itself. In the course of this process, she had developed good
working relations with Michael and Riche.[109] Riche provided useful, precise
wording from the international trade union movement, while Michael consistently attended the negotiations and supplied analysis and precise wording developed by the International Women Count Network. Since the
government was committed to gaining recognition for women's unpaid
work, this was an area where there were good opportunities for NGO input.
Regehr, for her part, was described as "an excellent model of how a government official can both represent the elected government and be receptive to the views of the NGO community."[110] When a breakthrough was
achieved on this issue, both Michael and Regehr were given personal
recognition by the international community for their valuable work.

In the area of women's human rights, the contributions of Rebecca
Cook, an academic advisor on the delegation, and Gisèle Côté-Harper, were
particularly noteworthy. Both were professors of law and internationally
recognized experts in the field. They each attended the negotiations and
provided valuable advice and support to Adèle Dion and Kerry Buck.[111]
Audrey McLaughlin (member of Parliament) was knowledgeable and helpful on issues pertaining to women and the economy, while Caroline
Anawak attended the sessions on women and health and was effective in
reporting back on relevant developments in this issue area.[112] There were,
therefore, some nongovernmental observers who attended the negotiations
and offered concrete, valuable support to Canada's negotiators.

All the nongovernmental observers attended delegation meetings on a
regular basis and represented the delegation at official functions. Some,
such as Pat Beck, provided the short-staffed government delegates with
administrative assistance, including staffing the Canada Desk. There was
an expectation on the part of the minister and other government officials
that the nongovernmental observers would sit at the Canada Desk in the
plenary to be a point of contact for any Canadians in need of assistance.
Yet, not all nongovernmental observers were willing to perform administrative or public relations functions. One nongovernmental observer described
staffing the Canada Desk as "a waste of my time."[113]

Each member of the Canadian delegation made a unique contribution,
though the degree to which they were willing and/or able to assist the
negotiators varied considerably. While there were some notable exceptions,
the nongovernmental observers were not as effective overall as they could
have been either in developing fruitful, substantive working relations with

the Canadian negotiators or in providing a systematic liaison between the delegation and the NGO community. Several factors produced this suboptimal outcome. Most important was the decision to appoint individuals rather than representatives of NGOs, which resulted in frustration and in the lack of systematic liaison between the delegation and the NGO sector.

Timing also posed a problem. The selections of nongovernmental observers were only announced in August, allowing little opportunity for individuals to prepare for delegation membership.[114] Inexperience was a further impediment to efficacy. Many of the observers were attending UN negotiations for the first time and had little idea of how to play useful roles. Some of the ensuing frustration was the natural result of experiencing, for the first time, the confusion and unfamiliar structures and procedures of UN negotiations. But the level of frustration could have been lessened if the CBFC and government officials had been more proactive. Most importantly, the CBFC should have met with the nongovernmental observers either prior to – or at least at the very start of – the conference to establish priorities and procedures to facilitate liaison. This was its responsibility, and the opportunity was missed.

Government officials should have explained more thoroughly right at the beginning, with use of examples, the ways in which nongovernmental observers could have contributed. Not all the nongovernmental observers would have been receptive to such briefings, but some would have been.[115] When the frustration felt by several nongovernmental observers who wanted to contribute more but who were unsure of how to do so was brought to the attention of government officials, no steps were taken to remedy the situation. Instead, the frustration was attributed to the fact that the nongovernmental observers were dynamic women used to taking charge in their daily lives, who therefore found the slow and somewhat chaotic nature of UN negotiations difficult.[116] It is regrettable that, for a variety of reasons – the late ministerial decisions about delegation membership, a shortage of time, inadequate resources and, in some cases, poor organization[117] – government officials did not provide in-depth briefings for the nongovernmental observers. Such briefings would have assisted those unfamiliar with UN negotiations, in general, and the Fourth World Conference on women, in particular, to develop their own strategies for ensuring that they performed their roles as effectively as possible.

In discussing the interaction between government and nongovernmental actors, several of the Canadian delegates – both nongovernmental and governmental – negatively compared relations between nongovernmental observers and government officials on the Beijing delegation to the types of relationships that had existed at other conferences. One government negotiator commented that at the Cairo Conference on Population and Development, there had been only six Canadian government negotiators and eight working groups to cover; hence, some of the negotiations were delegated to the nongovernmental observers on the Canadian delegation.[118] Here, the working relationships between the government negotiators and the nongovernmental observers were based on mutual trust and respect: the latter respected the government's positions and the government officials respected the nongovernmental observers' abilities to handle the negotiations.[119]

Two nongovernmental observers contrasted the deep frustration and alienation they felt as members of the Canadian delegation to the Beijing conference with their "wonderful" experiences as members of the Canadian delegations to the Copenhagen Summit for Social Development and to its Third Preparatory Conference, respectively.[120] It is clear from these comments that, for a variety of reasons, the contributions of the nongovernmental observers were suboptimal and that this was a concern for both government officials and nongovernmental observers.

Conclusion

After reviewing the work of Canada's delegation to the Fourth World Conference on Women as well as that of its delegations to the 1994 Vienna Regional Meetings and the 1995 New York Preparatory Meetings, several conclusions are evident. First, the Canadian delegation, like those of all participating states, faced some formidable challenges, including the breadth of the negotiating agenda, the number of contentious issues to be addressed, and the logistical problems associated both with holding a conference in China and with geographically separating the intergovernmental meetings from the NGO forum. In addition to these problems, the Canadian negotiators faced harassment by conservative forces that were particularly vocal and aggressive in New York.

Second, in spite of the challenges faced, Canada's delegations made major contributions to each set of negotiations. In Beijing, the Canadian negotiators demonstrated effective leadership both in drafting and in cultivating support for key provisions in the *PFA*, including the recognition of the universality of women's human rights, the agreement to mainstream women's human rights and a gender perspective throughout the UN system, the declaration that rape is a war crime, the decision to measure and value unpaid work, the recognition that sexual violence and gender-related persecution are legitimate grounds for claiming refugee status, and the broadening and strengthening of women's sexual and reproductive rights.

Third, the decision to appoint individuals and to allow each to choose the activities from the prescribed list of roles that she felt comfortable in pursuing had two consequences: frustration in various quarters, and the suboptimal use of nongovernmental observers. From the point of view of empowering Canadian NGOs, it would have been preferable to have chosen nongovernmental observers, each of whom directly represented a specific constituency in the NGO community. From the point of view of assisting the Canadian negotiators, it would have been desirable to have selected nongovernmental observers who had UN experience, who had expertise in at least one of the twelve critical issues of concern in the *PFA* and who had analyzed the *PFA* provisions in their respective area(s) of expertise before going to the conference. Although each of the nongovernmental observers made her own unique contribution to the work of the Canadian delegation, collectively their contributions could have been enhanced by a selection process that paid greater attention to ensuring that those appointed were those best able to perform the roles prescribed for nongovernmental observers in the *Briefing Book*. Furthermore, the nongovernmental observers would have been better positioned to monitor the negotiations and to assist the negotiators if government officers had provided in-depth briefings on the dynamics of the negotiations before the start of the conference. In light of the cost of sending observers on a Canadian delegation and the privilege conferred on those who are selected, it is critical that the problems outlined in this case be addressed. On the other hand, it must also be recognized that, although most of the nongovernmental observers contributed little to the development of the conference documents, their membership on the Canadian delegation did produce some positive, longer term benefits, such as raising the profile of the issues under negotiation with the people back home and generating domestic support for the *PFA*.

It is important that the shortcomings outlined above are not allowed to obscure the many contributions made by Canada's delegation to the Fourth World Conference on Women, as well as those made by its delegations to the preparatory meetings. Their successes are explored further in Chapter 7, which evaluates the extent to which Canada realized its negotiating objectives vis-à-vis the *PFA*.

6
Canadian NGOs at the International Negotiations

In addition to the members of the official Canadian delegation, 500 Canadian women travelled to China in late August and early September 1995 to participate in the Fourth UN Conference on Women and the NGO Forum on Women '95.[1] This chapter examines the activities and contributions of Canadian NGO representatives at the negotiations leading to Beijing as well as at the Fourth World Conference on Women and the NGO Forum on Women '95. It begins by identifying the barriers to NGO participation: restrictions on which groups were accredited to attend the official conference, inadequate funds to cover the costs of attending, the closed nature of many of the key negotiations, problems securing visas to enter China, and the geographic separation of the NGO forum and the intergovernmental conference. The first three barriers impeded participation at the preparatory negotiations as well as at the conference, while the last two were specific to the Beijing conference itself.

Having discussed a range of obstacles impeding NGO participation, consideration is given to two ways in which Canada supported its NGOs that were not discussed in previous chapters: funding forty women to attend the international meetings, and disseminating important briefing materials to those on the CBFC distribution list.

The chapter then examines the contributions made by Canadian NGOs at the international negotiations. The section begins with brief overviews of their participation at the 1994 Vienna Regional Meetings and at the 1995 New York Preparatory Meetings. NGOs were not given access to the informal consultations held in the summer of 1995; therefore, these meetings are not included in the discussions. After considering the work of Canadian NGOs at the preparatory meetings, the chapter then examines their participation at the Beijing conference where the NGOs concentrated their final lobbying efforts. The chapter concludes with a brief look at the work of the Canadian NGOs at the forum. The latter was not a venue for seeking direct input into the policy-making process, but it did enable NGOs to come together to work out lobbying strategies before, and during the first week of, the conference. It enabled those not accredited to the conference to meet with those who were accredited. Furthermore, the activities and networking that took place at the forum have significant implications for the future, both in terms of enabling NGOs to better hold governments responsible for promises made in Beijing and to better coordinate their lobbying efforts for subsequent conferences.

Barriers to Participation

Accreditation

As has been the norm with all recent UN world conferences and summits, there were two distinct classes of NGOs: those accredited to attend the intergovernmental conference, as well as the NGO forum, and those accredited to attend only the NGO forum. Registration for the conference and for the NGO forum involved entirely separate processes. Any interested person was eligible to register for the forum, whereas the process of accreditation for the conference was much more selective. Accreditation to the intergovernmental conference allowed NGO representatives access to the Beijing International Convention Centre where the official conference was held. Once inside the centre, they could attend plenary sessions, and at least some of the negotiations; participate directly in the ongoing lobbying efforts of the international NGO caucuses; and seek access to government negotiators. Yet, of the 30,000 who attended the NGO Forum on Women '95, only 4,035 were accredited to the intergovernmental conference. The demographics of Canadian participation were consistent with the international trend. Of the 831 Canadian NGOs that registered for the NGO forum, only 85 were accredited to the intergovernmental conference.[2] Not all those attending the forum sought accreditation to the official conference but access to the latter was, nonetheless, reserved for a relatively small, select set of NGOs.

Three categories of NGO representatives were accredited to attend the Fourth World Conference on Women:

1 members of government delegations
2 representatives of NGOs having consultative status with the UN Economic and Social Council
3 those who satisfied the criteria set out by the secretary-general of the World Conference.

Of these three categories, nongovernmental observers on state delegations had most privileges as they alone were able to attend all the negotiating sessions. In most cases, their travel expenses were paid by their respective governments. Yet relatively few states included nongovernmental observers on their delegations, and offers of delegation membership were entirely at the government's discretion.

Most NGO representatives at the intergovernmental conference were members of NGOs that had consultative status with the UN Economic and Social Council (ECOSOC).[3] As had been the case at previous gatherings, including the Cairo Conference on Population and Development and the Copenhagen Summit for Social Development, international NGOs having accreditation with ECOSOC could each send five delegates, whereas their national counterparts were each allowed to send two delegates. Even for these NGOs accreditation was not automatic; they had to register their intent to send representatives. Those which had already sent delegates to the CSW preparatory meetings were automatically accredited to the Beijing conference.

The third category of NGO participants was composed of those accredited by the Secretariat of the Fourth World Conference on Women. The selection process here was politically charged and controversial. The secretariat drew up objective criteria for determining accreditation. A NGO received accreditation if

- it could prove itself to be a bonafide NGO
- its purpose and objectives were clearly relevant to the conference and within the scope of the conference
- it functioned at the national and/or the international level
- it submitted its fully completed application by January 13, 1995.[4]

As is true throughout the UN system, states remain the gatekeepers for NGO participation. The issue of NGO accreditation was hotly debated at the 1995 preparatory meetings. At the time of those meetings, 500 of the 1,326 NGOs that had applied for accreditation had had their applications denied.[5] Those denied accreditation included Armenian, Iranian, Tibetan, and Taiwanese groups, prochoice groups, and groups promoting lesbian rights. Some states sought to restrict access to NGOs whose objectives conflicted with their own. For example, both the Chinese government and the Vatican sought to silence their respective critics by pressing the UN not to provide accreditation to such groups. In particular, China sought to exclude Taiwanese NGOs and Tibetan groups that it did not sanction. Like China, the Vatican sought to deny access to lesbians. It also exerted pressure to have accreditation denied to religious groups that did not share its perspectives, such as Catholics for a Free Choice and similar prochoice organizations in Brazil, Mexico, and Uruguay. Moves to restrict the participation of NGOs already approved by the conference secretariat were protested by Canada, Australia, Japan, the European Union, Norway, and the

United States on the grounds that the secretariat had compiled its list fairly and objectively, whereas those seeking to limit participation were motivated by political considerations.[6] The thorny issue of accreditation was finally resolved at the July meeting of ECOSOC. In the end, most, but not all, of the NGOs on the secretariat's list of groups recommended for accreditation were accredited.[7] Western states registered their disapproval of the exclusions,[8] but the decision of the council was final. The geographic representation among the accredited NGOs was good.

Visas

Once group representatives had been accredited to attend the official conference or registered to participate in the NGO Forum on Women, they still had to secure visas to enter China. When the UN had accepted China's offer to host the Fourth World Conference on Women, China had promised to grant visas to anyone accredited to the conference or the NGO forum by the April 30, 1995, deadline. In June, China announced that visas would be granted only to those who had received confirmations of both their registration at the NGO forum and their hotel accommodations. The announcement triggered renewed concern among the NGOs, since confirmations of hotel reservations were slow in coming,[9] and a renewed flurry of media activity. Yet, the media overstated the extent of the problem, as Canadian broadcaster Judy Rebick explained in her account of her experiences attending the NGO Forum on Women: "I apply for my visa three days before I leave. The problems with visas are, like many other issues the media chose to dwell on throughout the conference, greatly exaggerated. Almost everyone I know who wanted a visa got one, although it might have been on the day before departure."[10] Similar views were expressed by Sunera Thobani, president of the NAC:

> Just three days before I left Canada to attend the United Nations Fourth World Conference on Women in Beijing, a reporter phoned asking if I had received my visa. When I said yes, she asked if I knew anybody who had been denied a visa. The newspapers had carried a number of stories about the Chinese government allegedly denying women visas to attend the conference. I said sorry, I couldn't give her any names, everybody I knew had got a visa. No conspiracy here by the Chinese government to stop Canadian women from attending, I laughed to the reporter. She did not call me back![11]

Problems securing visas were experienced most by Tibetan and Taiwanese women. One week before the start of the NGO forum, only nine of eighty Tibetan women living outside China and who had been registered for the forum had received a visa.[12] For most participants worldwide, the visas did arrive, though they came only shortly before the individuals were scheduled to leave for China. These late arrivals generated considerable anxiety because most participants had already purchased nonrefundable airplane tickets in order to minimize the cost of their travel.

Cost

In addition to problems of accreditation and visas, cost was a serious barrier to participation. With advance booking, economy airfare from London, Ontario, to Beijing was $2,030. Then one had to pay $50 for a visa and $137.40 to register for the NGO forum. Accommodation in Huairou was relatively inexpensive but hotel prices in Beijing were exorbitant – far in excess of what one would pay for a comparable hotel in any of Canada's major cities. Through booking early and shopping carefully for the lowest prices, the CBFC arranged to send Canadian women to the conference for an average cost of $4,500 – a figure considered modest by government officials.[13] Nonetheless, paying $4,500 for a trip is beyond the means of a great many Canadian women, and it would be unthinkable for most Southern women. Thus, cost was a serious obstacle to broader – especially grassroots – participation.

In addition to financial expenses there were other costs to attending the conference that cannot be overlooked. Attending the Fourth World Conference on Women or the NGO Forum on Women also involved major commitments of time and energy. Juggling family, work, and other responsibilities to travel to China is not a minor undertaking for most women. Quite to the contrary, such responsibilities often preclude participation at international meetings. Who will take care of a single mother's children in her absence? Who will ensure that the needs of elderly or sick relatives are addressed? In an age when so many of those employed face daunting workloads, employers may be reluctant to grant a two- or three-week leave of absence, and employees may feel too overwhelmed with work-related responsibilities to justify taking time off. In many cases, the social as well as the economic costs involved in attending a world conference or NGO forum preclude participation.

Access to Meetings

After surmounting the challenges of getting accreditation, of generating sufficient funds to attend, and of making suitable arrangements for other responsibilities while they were away, NGO representatives faced a further barrier to participation at the intergovernmental negotiations. At the 1994 Vienna Regional Meetings, the 1995 New York Preparatory Meetings, and the Fourth World Conference on Women, much of the negotiating was carried out behind closed doors. NGOs were allowed in the plenary sessions and in some of the committee meetings, but they were excluded from the "informal informals," where most of the tough negotiations on the specific provisions were carried out. Such negotiations were accessible only to official state delegates. States justified the exclusion of NGOs from these key negotiations on grounds of insufficient space. However, there would have been other means of facilitating access, such as allowing the negotiations to be televised so that the NGO representatives could watch the proceedings on monitors. Such alternatives were not adopted, which suggests that for most states, the real reason for excluding NGOs was a reluctance to allow NGOs to monitor their performance in the negotiations. In discussing the exclusion of NGOs from the key negotiating rooms in New York, Gertrude Mongella, secretary-general of the Fourth World Conference, "characterized the situation as one where the delegates, as hosts, invited the NGOs into their sitting room, but then disappeared to the kitchen to cook, keeping their guests waiting and hungry."[14]

The closed nature of most of the in-depth negotiations negatively affected the lobbying efforts of Canadian NGOs in several ways. The nongovernmental observers on the Canadian delegation had access to these important negotiations, but the rest of the nongovernmental participants from Canada did not. The latter had no direct knowledge of what was taking place behind closed doors. Effective lobbying requires not only a clear understanding of the issues and of developments in past negotiations but also an intimate understanding of how the debates are evolving, of who one's allies are, of the alignments on a particular issue and of the specific positions each side is taking. Only then is one in a position to present compromise wording that has a chance of being accepted by the contending parties and also reflects the negotiating objectives of the group.

When negotiations are closed, nongovernmental observers on official delegations are under increased pressure to keep their excluded colleagues informed of developments. As mentioned in Chapter 5, Madeleine Gilchrist, the only nongovernmental observer on the Canada delegation to the Vienna Regional Meetings and one of two observers on the Canadian delegation to the New York Preparatory Meetings, was run ragged trying to monitor multiple sets of closed negotiations and to keep each of the NGO representatives waiting outside apprised of developments. It must also be remembered that the pressure on official Canadian nongovernmental observers does not come solely from the Canadian NGO community. Because Canada is one of the few countries to include nongovernmental observers on its delegation, NGOs from other countries as well as the international NGOs frequently seek out Canadian nongovernmental observers. It was the International Women Count Network that first initiated contact with Lorraine Michael when she was a nongovernmental observer on the Canadian delegation to the Third Preparatory Commission for the Copenhagen Summit for Social Development. The network is a well-organized coalition of 1,200 feminist groups from around the world committed to getting women's unwaged work recognized and valued. The network contacted Lorraine Michael again shortly after her appointment to the Canadian delegation to the Fourth World Conference on Women was announced.[15] Michael, the Canadian government, and the International Women Count Network all shared the objective of having women's unpaid work recognized and valued; the relationship between Michael and the network was mutually beneficial. As a member of an official delegation, Michael had access to all the negotiations. She understood the issues well, and she was dedicated to observing the intergovernmental debates. The International Women Count Network did not have access to the closed negotiations but it did have tremendous expertise. During its almost twenty years of existence, the network had established an effective infrastructure which produced briefs, information sheets and packages, petitions, and analysis. For example, it provided information packages and analysis to each official delegate entering the negotiations on unpaid work. Moreover, it had the expertise to be able to propose compromise language to help break the logjam on this issue. The International Women Count Network provided the nongovernmental observer with credible data and analysis and specific wording, while the latter kept the network apprised of developments in the negotiations and served as a conduit to state negotiators. The network recognized the importance of having contacts who knew the issues and who could be monitoring the negotiations first-hand. It had done the homework necessary to identify the nongovernmental observer with expertise on unpaid work and then contacted her. Of course, it is not always possible to find nongovernmental observers willing and able to do this kind of liaison work. There is, moreover, no substitute for being able to monitor the negotiations first-hand.

Location of the NGO Forum
On April 4, China publicly announced without warning that the NGO forum was being moved from the Workers' Sports Service Centre in Beijing to Huairou. The UN secretariat of the NGO Forum on Women '95 had been advised of the change of location only four days earlier, on March 31, 1995. Chinese officials justified the move on the grounds that the Workers' Gymnasium at the Sports Service Centre had been found to have structural flaws. No explanation was given for the late discovery of these flaws. To be fair to China, few cities in the world are equipped to host a NGO forum attracting over 30,000 participants as well as a major UN conference.[16] On the other hand, the allegations of faulty structures seemed suspect, especially since the Chinese continued to use the site after the announcement was made to host major events, including large sporting competitions[17] and the opening ceremonies for the NGO forum. Throughout the NGO community and in many other quarters as well, there was a widely held

belief that China's real reason for moving the forum out of Beijing was to limit the contact between its population and NGO activists and feminists, and to reduce the latter's opportunities for holding potentially embarrassing demonstrations in Tiananmen Square. Relocating the forum was "perceived as a deliberate attempt to keep the 30,000 women expected to attend the NGO Forum, many of them seasoned political activists, far from ordinary Beijingers and from the official United Nations conference, dominated by hand-picked government delegates."[18] NGOs, UN officials organizing the NGO forum, and several Western countries responded quickly and angrily to China's announcement. As mentioned in Chapter 2, the office of the UN secretary-general was deluged with letters and signed petitions from all over the world protesting the move. Irene Santiago, executive director of the NGO Forum on Women '95, expressed her concerns directly to the Chinese officials: "We've told them we have a very big problem with the fact that it is far away. A good site means we have to be close to the UN conference."[19] The chorus of protesters was joined by several Western countries, including Canada, Australia, and New Zealand, which made high-level representations to China's foreign ministry.[20]

The Secretariat of the NGO Forum on Women '95, as well as numerous NGOs, asked Boutros Boutros-Ghali either to postpone the conference or to move it out of China if the latter refused to locate the forum in Beijing. The threat of moving the conference – had it been made by the secretary-general – would have been significant because the Fourth World Conference on Women was the first major UN conference ever scheduled to be held on Chinese soil. Holding a major, high-profile international event was seen as positive recognition by the international community; it was a matter of national pride to host the conference. In spite of pressure from the secretariat and numerous NGOs, the threat was never made. Boutros Boutros-Ghali did, however, conduct what he termed "quiet diplomacy"[21] with Chinese officials, and on June 8, 1995, final agreement was reached between the NGO Forum on Women '95 Secretariat and the China Organizing Committee. In keeping with China's wishes, the forum was held in Huairou. China promised to dedicate a 42 hectare site to the forum rather than spreading its events around various locations in Huairou; to grant visas to all those registered for the forum; to provide free and regular bus service between Huairou and Beijing; to install sufficient IDD lines to meet the requirements of the NGOs and the press; and to establish a base in Beijing that could be used by NGOs, both those accredited to the official conference and those without such accreditation.[22] Having finally settled the issue of location, there remained the enormous task of getting the new site ready by the end of August to host over 30,000 people.

There were some advantages to holding the NGO forum in Huairou. As Chinese officials had promised, accommodation was much more affordable than it was in Beijing, where prices had been jacked up just before the conference. My clean – if rudimentary – room in Huairou cost $14 per night. In contrast, a room at the Hotel Kempinski in Beijing cost $320 per night. The countryside around Huairou was picturesque, the air was far superior to that in Beijing, and the facilities in Huairou were better able to handle the huge numbers of participants and activities. Workers' Sports Service Centre in Beijing had seventy meeting rooms and a stadium capable of seating 13,000.[23] The NGO forum frequently had over 120 workshops, panels, and seminars being conducted at any one time.

Nonetheless, the disadvantages of locating the NGO forum far from the conference greatly outweighed the advantages. As Sarah Burd-Sharps, a UN special adviser to the Fourth World Conference on Women, says, "The whole point of holding parallel events to official UN conferences is to allow delegates from both sessions to consult and mingle with each other."[24] As China had promised when it first announced its decision to move the forum, transportation between Huairou and Beijing was free, and it was fairly frequent and reliable. But there were several major drawbacks to the service. To find sufficient vehicles for the transit, city buses were pressed into service. These buses were unsuited to highway speeds. As a result, they rattled, shook, and belched smoke as they struggled up and down the highway between Huairou and Beijing. The trip took one-and-a-half hours by bus but only one hour in the embassy car. Yet in spite of the discomfort and the noise, most women on the buses remained cheerful and determined to use the travel time to get to know their sisters from others parts of the world. Their perseverance in reaching out to others and in sharing with each other was inspirational.

The practical difficulties did not end upon reaching Beijing. The buses did not go to the International Convention Centre. Instead, they dropped off their passengers at Workers' Stadium, part of the Workers' Sports Service Centre (the original choice of site for the forum), which was at least twenty minutes away from the conference. There was free bus service between Workers' Stadium and the International Convention Centre, but it was extremely erratic and unreliable. Bus drivers, happily chatting and playing a form of checkers with each other, were very reluctant to leave their comrades in order to drive the buses. In frustration, many women gave up waiting and hailed taxis, but the latter were expensive and clearly not an option open to all.

Commuting between the NGO forum and the intergovernmental conference was a long, laborious process. It clearly served to further isolate those without accreditation to the Fourth World Conference on Women from both the negotiations and the conference participants. Once the negotiations were underway, conference participants had little time to spare. Travelling back and forth to Huairou to brief, and share concerns with,

NGO representatives not accredited to the conference had significant opportunity costs; it meant missing at least half a day of the negotiations and possibly losing important opportunities to influence provisions in the *Beijing Declaration* and *PFA*.

NGOs without accreditation to the conference were not allowed into the International Convention Centre. The Beijing Recreation Centre, separated from the Convention Centre only by a hotel, was designated as a place where NGO representatives could meet each other and where those without accreditation could meet with state delegates and NGOs accredited to the conference. Yet, in practice, such meetings were problematic. They required NGO representatives to travel from Huairou to the Workers' Sports Service Centre and then on to the recreation centre. They required that state delegates take time from important negotiations to walk to the recreation centre. State delegates and NGO representatives attending the intergovernmental conference were unlikely to wander over to the recreation centre unless formal meetings were scheduled in advance; the chance of nonaccredited NGO representatives having impromptu chats with those accredited was remote. Nonetheless, the centre did provide NGOs without accreditation with a base from which to operate in Beijing and a place to arrange meetings. For example, indigenous women on the Canadian delegation attended a prearranged meeting at the recreation centre with other indigenous women, some of whom were accredited and some of whom were not. Yet, the centre was not a place where conference delegates congregated, so the opportunities for contact with them were extremely limited unless appointments had been made.

The problem of the geographic isolation of the NGO forum from Beijing was compounded by infrastructure problems. As discussed in Chapter 5, telephone (particularly cellular telephone) linkages were very unreliable, making it even more difficult to maintain contact between Beijing and Huairou.

The site of the NGO forum posed particular problems for women with disabilities. One woman recalls, "Everyone who attended the NGO Forum was frustrated by the logistics but as a woman who is multiply-disabled, I found the Forum to be a constant challenge. The site was very large and the paths were paved with uncured concrete pavers that crumbled and became loose in the heavy rain. The uneven surfaces and many stairs, combined with the lack of elevators and ramps, made being autonomous an impossibility for many women with disabilities."[25] Many of the paths were unpaved, and wheelchairs would become bogged down in the mud. The women in the wheelchairs were dependent on other women to lift the wheelchairs onto dryer ground, which they were quick to do. Thus, women with disabilities faced yet another set of limitations to their access, in addition to the restrictions faced by all participants.

Government Support of Canadian NGOs

The Canadian government facilitated the participation of Canadian NGOs at the international negotiations in four ways: it included nongovernmental observers on its delegations, its delegations briefed NGOs at the international negotiations, it funded some NGO representatives to attend the preparatory negotiations as well as the conference and NGO forum, and it prepared comprehensive information kits about the Beijing conference and arranged for their distribution to all those on the circulation list of CBFC. The first two of these contributions were discussed in the previous chapter. The latter two are discussed below.

Information Kits

Government officials had provided significant information to the NGOs throughout the Beijing process. In addition to the materials already discussed in Chapter 4, two excellent briefing packages were sent out in the summer of 1995 to those of the CBFC distribution list. The first, prepared by SWC with the assistance of CIDA, included a 25-page discussion of the problems facing women, both in Canada and around the world, in each of the twelve critical areas of concern. Most importantly, the package included the Canadian government's negotiating objectives for each of the twelve areas of concern in the *PFA* as well as for five issue areas that had been designated as Canada's highest priorities.[26] It is highly significant that this information about Canada's priorities and negotiating positions was identical to that provided to the nongovernmental observers on the Canadian delegation. As is typical of instructions to Canadian delegations, the positions were phrased in broad terms, such as the need for gender analysis in all policy and decision making. They did not give specific measurements for what exact wording would be needed to satisfy each requirement. But instructions to Canadian delegations are usually phrased in general terms so as to allow Canadian negotiators the leverage necessary to bargain effectively as negotiations evolve. In short, government officials shared their objectives with the NGOs – something that had not occurred during the preparatory negotiations. This degree of openness on the part of government officials facilitated NGO lobbying at the conference.

In addition to the package provided by SWC, those on the CBFC distribution list received a separate information kit from Health Canada. Again, the material provided was substantial. It explained Canada's macro-level objective to broaden the concept of health by placing "more emphasis on the gender and social, cultural and economic factors which affect health, rather than focusing on a purely physical, biological or medical model."[27] To assist the NGOs in focusing their lobbying efforts, Health Canada distributed a concise, user-friendly compendium of the major health provisions to be negotiated in Beijing. Most of the 102 paragraphs included in the compendium contained bracketed text that had been clearly highlighted. Health Canada kits also contained important background information, including reviews of the health provisions in the *Nairobi Forward-looking Strategies* and of the *Draft Declaration on Women and Health Security* being developed by the World Health Organization/Global Commission on Women's Health.

The briefing kits provided useful background information as well as clear indications of the Canadian government's negotiating priorities and objectives. Canadian NGOs did not have to guess where their government stood; instead, they could compare their own positions with Canada's stated objectives and plan their lobbying strategies accordingly. Government officials need to be given full credit for these efforts to inform the NGOs. The only major concern here was timing: it would have been helpful to have received the packages earlier in the summer. On the other hand, the informal consultations convened by the CSW were not completed before August 4, 1995 and their progress had to be reflected in the disseminated information.

Funding

The Canadian government funded thirteen NGO representatives to attend the Vienna Regional meetings (October 1994), sixteen to attend the preparatory meetings in New York (March 1995), and forty to attend the NGO forum in China, ten of whom were also accredited at the intergovernmental conference.[28] Although forty was substantially less than the sixty who had been funded to attend the Third UN Conference on Women in Nairobi ten years earlier, securing funding for forty women to attend the Beijing conference was a significant achievement in times of fiscal restraint. The director of the Women's Program, Jackie Claxton, did an outstanding job of persuading various government departments to sponsor one or more women from NGOs involved in their issue areas to attend the Beijing conference.[29]

For the previous World Conferences on Women, decisions on who received funding to attend had been made by the secretary of state for foreign affairs, who had chosen from a list of potential recipients drawn up by the public servants. By 1995, women's groups had gained a lot of experience and expected to play a larger role in decision making; the process devised for Nairobi would not have been acceptable to them.[30] As a prominent member of the CBFC comments, "The CBFC was eager to ensure that the actual selection of individuals to receive funding was made by those active in the Canadian women's movement rather than by government officials."[31] Similar views were voiced by NAC leaders: "We were eager to ensure that decisions on who got funding were made by women with connections to the feminist movement and not by government officials."[32] Government officials recognized that decisions on who would be funded to attend the Fourth World Conference on Women would have to be made by nongovernmental actors and at arms-length from government.[33]

The selection process for determining which groups would receive funding for Beijing began with the Interdepartmental Committee, in consultation with the CBFC, developing a list of criteria to ensure that the selection would be sufficiently representative of diversities within Canada. Those chosen had to reflect regional diversity and to include English- and French-speaking women, groups from the various issue areas (e.g., health, development, and business), and from various constituencies (e.g., young, old, disabled, and indigenous). Together, the CBFC and Women's Program brainstormed and agreed that decisions on who would receive funding to attend the NGO forum would best be made by five "Wise Women." Nominees for these five positions had to be women who

- possessed in-depth knowledge of and experience in the women's movement;
- were not expected to request funding for Beijing;
- were not government employees; and
- were not actively involved with any women's organizations.[34]

Collectively, the Wise Women were charged with ensuring that "selected representatives of women's organizations and other NGOs attending the NGO Forum in Beijing reflect Canada's diversity and expertise on the issues to be discussed in Beijing, based on the guidelines developed by the Women's Program."[35] The five Wise Women chosen were Judy Rebick, a prominent broadcaster and past president of the NAC; Madeleine Dion Stout, director of the Centre for Aboriginal Education, Research and Culture at Carleton University and past president of the Aboriginal Nurses Association; Gerry Rogers, a filmmaker from Newfoundland; Madeleine Parent, an activist for women's rights and labour rights in Quebec and a former member of the NAC executive; and Carol Anne Soong, a retired public servant who had worked in the Women's Program.

A letter was then sent out jointly by the Women's Program and the CBFC to all on the latter's mailing list, inviting applications for funding from those who met certain criteria:

- selected individuals should demonstrate experience/expertise in one or more areas of concern to be discussed at the Conference notably poverty, violence, media, peace, political participation, globalization of the economy, human rights, health, education and training, environment & housing;

- selected individuals must have demonstrated commitment/experience in promoting women's equality in Canada;
- selected individuals must also represent a non profit organization which addresses issues related to women's equality. The organization must be supported or recognized by the community that it claims to represent;
- selected individuals must also provide an information dissemination plan or a follow-up plan regarding the results of the conference.
- selected individuals must be available for the full time period of the Forum. Allowing for travelling and briefing sessions, this means *Aug. 27 to Sept. 10.*[36]

Of the over 1,300 NGOs on the CBFC's list, some 280 sent in applications for funding.[37]

The five Wise Women spent two days cloistered in a hotel room evaluating the applications. They were given a set amount of money and instructed to decide, taking due account of the representational criteria outlined above, which applicants were to receive funding. The NGOs to which the nominees belonged were asked to contribute funds, where possible, to assist with the travel costs. Many groups responded positively, which increased the pool of available money and permitted funding several extra people.[38] Through this process, forty women received travel funds.[39]

Once the forty women had been chosen, the CBFC handled the travel arrangements. Through careful shopping, they were able to book inexpensive airline tickets and to send each woman to China for the two-week conference for a total cost on average of $4,500 – a major triumph in light of the distance flown and the inflated costs of hotel rooms in Beijing during the conference period. Furthermore, ten of the forty women selected were Aboriginal women who were active in a range of women's NGOs. This was significant in light of the fact that Aboriginal women had felt somewhat excluded earlier in the process.[40]

While there were some rumblings, especially among right-wing groups, about the choice of those to be funded, and about the process itself, most of the key participants were pleased with both the process and the outcome. Madeleine Gilchrist comments, "Choosing who would get funding was a tough job but somebody had to do it. The NGOs did not want the government to make the decision. The Wise Women did their job well."[41] According to Joanna Kerr, the process was a creative solution to a difficult problem and definitely the best attainable option.[42] Jackie Claxton commented that the Wise Women process had worked well and that the forty women selected were good choices for funding.[43] The women selected all had extensive experience working in the women's movement to advance the status of women in Canada, and together they were representative of the diversity specified by SWC.

NGO Contributions at the Intergovernmental Negotiations

The Canadian NGO representatives accredited to the official conference contributed to the process in several ways: they chaired, as well as participated in, the international NGO caucuses; they played key roles in the development of the composite document prepared by the NGO caucuses; and they lobbied governments, individually and in cooperation with NGOs from other states, in order to influence the agenda and substance of the *Beijing Declaration* and *PFA*. NGO forums were held just before the 1994 Vienna Regional Meetings and the 1995 New York Preparatory Meetings, as well as in conjunction with the Beijing conference. Canadian NGOs participated in all these venues.

Before examining the contributions made by Canadian NGOs, it is important to recognize some of the parameters within which they have to operate. The problem of access to key negotiations has already been discussed earlier in the chapter. The nature of the environment poses another set of challenges. Attending a major UN conference can be quite overwhelming, even for those with previous experience in such venues. For those without prior experience, they can be totally baffling. NGO representatives attending UN negotiations for the first time are often taken aback – at least initially – by how chaotic the conferences appear, by how difficult it is to get information, by the number of meetings being convened at any one time, by the number of people bustling about, and by the challenge of trying to figure out how to play creative roles. A lot of learning must take place before one can function effectively at UN negotiations. They are not venues for the faint-hearted nor are they kind to the inexperienced.

Seeking Input into the *Beijing Declaration* and *Platform for Action*

A key component of an effective lobbying strategy for NGOs attending UN conferences is to prepare a composite NGO line-by-line analysis of the documents under negotiation. Such analysis enables government delegations to readily compare the wording being proposed by the NGOs with the existing text. For Canadian NGOs, the process of developing such texts in cooperation with NGOs from other states began at the Vienna Regional Meetings. Just before the intergovernmental meetings, 1,200 people – 36 of them Canadians – attended the NGO forum, held in Vienna from October 13 to 15, 1994.[44] There NGOs from participating countries produced their response – the *Vienna NGO Forum Call to Action* – to the formal text of the Economic Commission of Europe – the *ECE Regional Platform for Action*. The *Call to Action* was the first NGO text ever to be included among the official documents for an ECE meeting.[45] The UN supplied the conference text on diskette, which facilitated producing a line-by-line analysis within a short period. NGOs in each of the key issue areas tried to reach consensus on their section of the text. Much of the work was done in an apartment in the Centre for Women, where working conditions were less than ideal.[46] As Madeleine Gilchrist, the only nongovernmental observer on the Canadian delegation to Vienna and an active member of the peace caucus, comments, "All the lead people of the workshops sat together and worked day and night. There were not enough chairs, so some were sitting on the floor, some were working on laptop computers, and women with printers were greatly sought after. We worked over the weekend when all the shops and businesses were closed. You could not get anything. No photocopies, no supplies, no food."[47] Kerr (North-South Institute) was one of the eight women, mostly from the Women's Environment and Development Organization and the NGO forum secretariat, who sat in the hotel room compiling a composite text from the analyses submitted for each of the issue areas. From these submissions, she and her coworkers drafted the NGO composite text, which was then sent back to the NGOs for comment. Once the comments were received, the group stayed up for three nights in a row redrafting the text.[48]

By Monday morning – the very morning when the negotiations began – the NGOs had a line-by-line analysis[49] which they circulated to all countries on the drafting committee. Although some countries did refer to the NGO document when preparing their positions, the text came too late in the process.[50] Since the NGO text had been produced at short notice, there had been no time to prepare preambles explaining why changes were being proposed and why they were deemed necessary. Furthermore, since the text was circulated only on the morning when the negotiations began, NGOs had not had time to lobby their governments in advance. With no written preambles and no opportunities to explain the rationales behind the proposed changes before the onset of negotiations, the potential impact of the document was undermined. The best NGO representatives could do was to highlight their highest priorities in the text relevant to the particular sections of the formal document that was under negotiation. Nonetheless, the document did present NGO demands in a consolidated and relatively "user-friendly" format, and NGO representatives had precise wording to offer when lobbying their governments. The problems of timing were apparent to those centrally involved in the drafting process and were lessons carried forward in preparing for the New York Preparatory Meetings.[51]

In New York, the NGOs again produced a composite text. The Canadian NGOs that participated in the CBFC were particularly well prepared to participate in the process since they already had a composite NGO document and knew where they stood on particular issues. In New York, some 1,400 women participated as the international NGO caucuses drafted line-by-line responses to the draft *PFA* in two days.[52] Again, the process advantaged the English-speaking participants as both the document and the NGO negotiations were in English and no translation services were available.

In addition to time constraints and language barriers for those not proficient in English, there was the problem of space. As the coordinator of the CBFC notes, "we only had three rooms in which to work so we had to divide the issues between the three rooms and deal sequentially with each set of issues. It was a very fast process, but it was a process that brought a lot of satisfaction because we were accomplishing what seemed like an unreachable goal – producing a very user-friendly NGO document which could be used to lobby governments and which could provide precise language to which government delegations could refer in the official UN negotiations."[53] The NGOs used their composite text as a lobbying tool at the New York Preparatory Meetings.

Both in New York and in Beijing, much of the work of developing NGO texts and of developing lobbying strategies in specific issue areas was orchestrated by the large array of NGO caucuses. There were caucuses for each of the major regions of the globe. There were caucuses set up to deal with specific issue areas, such as health, human rights, human settlement, economic justice, grassroots organizations, the environment, count women's work, and peace. There were also caucuses that focused on particular categories of women, including youth, seniors, girls, lesbians, women with disabilities, and women of colour. The Women's Linkage caucus, which served as a caucus for the caucuses – or an umbrella caucus – continued its work following the preparatory meetings. At the start of the NGO Forum on Women, it issued two useful documents to inform state delegates of the composite NGO positions and to serve as tools for NGO lobbying. *Recommendations on Bracketed Text in the WCW Draft Platform for Action (A/Conf. 177/L.1 and A/Conf.177/L.3)* presented a clear and concise line-by-line analysis of the provisions in the *PFA* that remained bracketed after the informal consultations in the summer of 1995.[54] The second document, *Take the Brackets Off Women's Lives! Women's Linkage Caucus Advocacy Chart,* provided excellent background information for lobbyists. For each of the bracketed paragraphs, it not only summarized the Linkage caucus' position but also provided relevant language agreed to at previous UN conferences and summits.

Canadian NGOs continued to be active in drafting texts at the Beijing conference, where they participated in the work of the NGO caucuses and also led several international NGO caucuses. For example, NAC representatives chaired the caucus on the globalization of the economy and the caucus on women of colour, while the lesbian caucus was chaired by Canadian human rights activist, Shelagh Day. Mary Silletts, a representative of Pauktuutit, a Canadian group of Inuit women, and other indigenous women from Canada, and some thirty other countries worked within the indigenous caucus to produce the *Beijing Declaration of Indigenous Women.* As leaders of and participants in the international NGO caucuses, Canadian

NGO representatives developed NGO positions and coordinated lobbying strategies. In particular, they assumed lead roles in the drafting of the *Alternative NGO Beijing Declaration,* which was announced and distributed at the end of the conference. As usual, the NGOs' document was more specific and went further in its commitments than did the official *Beijing Declaration.*

By Beijing, negotiations focused on removing the remaining brackets in the *PFA*; it was much too late to introduce new issues or discuss matters on which consensus had already been reached. Most of the serious lobbying of government officials and UN officials had been carried out well in advance of the actual conference. Yet, what had been true at earlier negotiations was all the more evident in Beijing. Those NGOs best able to exert influence at this advanced stage in the negotiations were those which not only had access to the negotiations but also could provide specific wording that would break a stalemate in the negotiations, that would meet with widespread support from the conference participants and that would, at the same time, realize the objective of the NGO.

NGOs attended the Fourth World Conference on Women for a variety of reasons, including the desires to influence the *Beijing Declaration* and *PFA,* to develop and expand relations with NGOs from around the world that would facilitate future lobbying efforts, and to use the international setting as a means of drawing attention to deficiencies in government policies and their implementation back home. The relative importance of each of these reasons varied from group to group; however, influencing the conference documents was at least one of the motivations – if not the primary motivation – for most of the NGOs in attendance. The key determinant of such influence was a group's effectiveness in convincing state delegates of the merits of its positions. Valerie Raymond attributed the positive outcome of the Fourth World Conference on Women first and foremost to the fact that "the vast majority of countries genuinely wanted a strong and forward-looking document"; she also credited the intensive lobbying efforts by thousands of NGO representatives who sought to ensure that real progress was made as being further reasons for the advances contained in the *PFA*.[55] In the case of Canadian NGOs, one would expect the Canadian delegation to be their initial and principal point of contact, especially since the vast majority of the Canadian NGOs involved in the Beijing process shared the overall objectives of the Canadian negotiators: to build on the language advancing women that had been agreed to at previous conferences and summits and to move the agenda ahead. The major macro-level difference in their objectives was that the NGOs wanted to go further faster than the government officials were authorized to go. In spite of sharing many of the same macro-level objectives, there was not a strong sense of trust between government officials and many of the NGO representatives. The former felt that they did not receive adequate support and cooperation from the

Canadian NGOs, especially when the Canadian negotiators came under personal attack from right-wing groups for pursuing policies that were in keeping with the objectives of the majority of the Canadian NGOs. Such personal attacks were most severe at the New York Preparatory Meetings, where they were primarily targeted against Valerie Raymond and Kerry Buck. Although the personal attacks were less vehement in Beijing, they still continued, with Valerie Raymond, Kerry Buck, and Ruth Archibald being the key targets.

Some Canadian NGO representatives did demonstrate support. As Madeleine Gilchrist comments, "When the Canadian delegation was under siege from REAL Women and other right-wing groups, Canadian NGOs circulated a petition among women from all over the world, which I gave to Rhonda Ferderber so the Canadian negotiators would have evidence of our support."[56] If nothing else, there was clearly a difference in perceptions of how much support was necessary and of where it was expected to come from. The Canadian delegation received international kudos for its achievements in the negotiations, both in the preparatory meetings and especially in Beijing, yet it did not receive any accolades from the NAC; "this did not go unnoticed in government circles."[57] Several government negotiators contrasted the constructive relationships they had enjoyed with some international NGOs with the less than satisfactory relations that had existed between them and the Canadian NGOs in Beijing. In Beijing, Archibald "worked closely" with international NGOs such as the Women's Health Committee of the Commonwealth Medical Association and Family Care International, the lead groups on the health issues in Beijing, and the International Women's Health Coalition, which had also been very active in Cairo.[58] "These groups were well organized, they understood the process, and they had extensive contacts among Southern as well as Northern states; thus they were able to float ideas and to ascertain what was likely to achieve consensus,"[59] Archibald recalls. The ability of these international NGOs to propose specific wording likely to gain the support of at least a large number – if not all – of the state delegations enabled these groups to facilitate the negotiations and to exercise considerable influence. In contrast, Canadian groups frequently seemed to be "working outside rather than inside the process, and resorting to public relations stunts aimed at embarrassing the government instead of seeking to establish constructive working relations."[60] Government officials were not the only ones to negatively compare the attitude and behaviour of some Canadian NGOs with those of the international NGOs. Such assessments were also made by members of the NGO community:

> One of the things that surprised me was the comparison between the highly effective organizing strategies of the international NGOs and the

relative lack of group strategies among the Canadian NGOs. There were no Canadian NGOs in the sexual and reproductive health field, although those working on economic and human rights issues were effective (I think in particular of Shelagh Day and DAWN members such as Linda Christiansen-Ruffman). The "silo" effect of having twelve critical areas of concern meant that we could not work, strategize, and lobby effectively as a Canadian group, especially in light of the right-wing conservative Canadian groups being present at every government briefing. As a consequence, I allied myself with the international NGOs working on sexual and reproductive rights, which proved to be an excellent and productive strategy where I learned a good deal.[61]

Many of the representatives of Canadian women's groups were attending UN negotiations for the first time. They had developed strategies for confronting the government at home, but these strategies were not always well suited to the international environment. At home, one can focus solely on the Canadian government's record, whereas at international negotiations, one must recognize where Canada stands relative to other countries and the parameters within which it must operate – an environment in which most states are less progressive in recognizing and promoting women's rights than is Canada.[62]

Of course, not all government-NGO relations were confrontational. For instance, Vuyiswa Keyi of Women's Health in Women's Hands worked well with Abby Hoffman at the 1995 New York Preparatory Meetings. Kerry Buck enjoyed constructive working relations with a number of Canadian NGOs, including the Montreal-based International Centre for Human Rights and Democratic Development, the North-South Institute, and Voice of Women.[63] Adèle Dion spoke highly of the contributions of the human rights groups throughout the Beijing process, and CIDA officials had good working relationships with the North-South Institute and Canadian development groups.[64] In addition to expertise, some Canadian NGO representatives contributed logistical support for the Canadian delegation. For example, members of VOW brought much-needed food to hungry Canadian negotiators who were unable to leave the negotiations long enough to find meals. Yet in spite of these examples of collegial relations, there was overall a prevailing sense of tension and distrust between the government officials and the Canadian NGOs, in general, and the women's groups, in particular. It is not possible to outline in detail all the major lobbying activities of the Canadian NGOs. The few cases outlined below illustrate some of their activities.

The Canadian Labour Congress (CLC) carried out most of its preparations for the Fourth World Conference on Women and its work at the conference in the context of the International Confederation of Free Trade

Unions (ICFTU). Since many states, including Canada, had trade union representatives on their delegations, the international labour movement was well positioned to seek input. The CLC (and the ICFTU) had two sets of objectives in Beijing.[65] The first related directly to the *PFA*. All the issues being negotiated at Beijing were within the mandates of both the CLC Department of Women's and Human Rights and the Women's Committee of the ICFTU. As such, they sought to build on the progress achieved at the Copenhagen Summit for Social Development. In particular, they advocated increasing the visibility of unions in the *PFA* and sought to have all states adhere to at least minimal labour standards (e.g., freedom of association, collective bargaining, no forced labour) and to support the *Convention on the Elimination of All Forms of Discrimination Against Women*. The CLC's second objective in attending the Beijing conference was to expose the problems confronting labour, generally, and female workers, in particular. The ICFTU had connections with the Free Labour Unions of China – a group operating in exile from its headquarters in Hong Kong. The Free Labour Unions of China published a booklet on conditions confronting working women in China, which was launched at the NGO forum in Huairou by the Women's Committee of the ICFTU, in cooperation with Education International. In Beijing, the Women's Committee of the ICFTU organized a press conference to announce the book. The book launchings happened to take place the same week that twenty Chinese women were burned to death in a cigarette lighter factory. Thus, the workshop in Huairou and the press conference in Beijing offered good opportunities for publicizing this tragedy. The tragedy, for its part, exemplified the problems outlined in the booklet. Beijing was considered a success by the trade union movement on several scores.[66] The trade union caucus functioned well and grew larger at each day's meeting. Contacts between the trade unions, on one hand, and international and national NGOs, on the other, which had not been strong in the past, flourished. Furthermore, the *PFA* promoted international labour rights, including freedom of association and the right to organize, which were cherished by both the CLC and the ICFTU.

Although its involvement with international negotiations does not date as far back as that of the CLC, the NAC had participated at the Third World Conference on Women in Nairobi and had attended subsequent UN conferences and summits dealing the women's rights. The NAC had domestic as well as international objectives at the Beijing conference. In an effort to further domestic objectives, it used the conference, and the public attention it drew, to publicize the deficiencies it saw in the Canadian government's policies and programs to advance women. During the Beijing conference, for example, the NAC called a press conference, where it presented "A Decade of Deterioration in the Status of Women in Canada." The report gave Canada failing grades in living up to the commitments it had made at the Third World Conference on Women. It vehemently chastised the Canadian government for its poor performance in many of the issue areas under negotiation in Beijing. Among the many criticisms, the government was accused of failing to provide adequate antipoverty programs and social safety nets, to uphold the rights of women migrants, to ensure food security for women and their children, to support female-headed households, and to allocate additional financial resources to tackle the root problems faced by women living in poverty. Calling a press conference during the conference generated greater media coverage than it would usually have on an average day in Canada. Therefore, the NAC's choice of timing to release its report was effective in generating greater publicity in Canada than would normally have been the case. It also had repercussions at the conference. The release of the report and the media attention it received detracted from the efforts being made by Canadian government officials in general and by the secretary of state for the status of women in particular, to portray Canada as a progressive country that was making good progress.

On the international front, the NAC sought to ensure that the provisions in the *Beijing Declaration* and *PFA* were consistent with its own objectives. It was particularly interested in ensuring that the highly detrimental effects that global restructuring and the globalization of the economy were having on women were recognized. One of the complaints it voiced about the Canadian delegation as well as about the conference in general was the latter's failure to address the trends associated with globalization that are exacerbating the marginalization of women and increasing the feminization of poverty around the world. Sunera Thobani, president of the NAC, writes:

> The *PFA* is seriously flawed in its approach to women's economic rights. There is no recognition that the existing global economic system is increasing women's inequalities. There is no acknowledgement that the current model for economic growth and globalization, based as it is on "free" market principles and reducing the role of government in re-distributing wealth, devastates the lives of women. Because the document does not address the causes of women's poverty, it is unable to address how to end it. The power of international financial institutions, of corporations and multinationals, remains unchallenged. No questions are raised about the accountability of these institutions to the women of the world.[67]

The NAC representatives felt angry and frustrated at the Canadian government's refusal to address the structural root causes of women's inferior political, economic, and social status, as well as by the deficiencies in its record of advancing women at home. Although Lorraine Michael, a

nongovernmental observer on the Canadian delegation and a former board
member of the NAC, made time each day to brief the NAC representatives
at their hotel, the NAC's relations with the Canadian delegation as a whole
were more confrontational than cooperative. There was no NAC representative on the delegation, which was seen as a slap in the face to Canada's
largest feminist umbrella group. The NAC representatives negatively contrasted what they considered to be the unhelpful, guarded attitude of the
Canadian government officials with the openness that they witnessed
between Caribbean women's groups and their governments.[68] Government
officials, for their part, found the NAC approach aggressive and, at times,
embarrassing.

The NAC saw the conference and the forum as venues for strengthening
its linkages with other NGOs. In addition to chairing two international
NGO caucuses, the NAC worked with international groups with which it
already had good, ongoing relations, such as the Global Economic Alliance,
Women's Environment and Development Organization, and other feminist
groups in the United States.[69] In the four years preceding the conference,
the NAC had given higher priority to linkages with women's groups in
the South: "NAC has lots of Southern women on its board which facilitates making contacts with, and building alliances with, Southern women's
groups."[70] The NAC's participation at the Fourth World Conference on
Women and NGO forum assisted it in drawing public attention back home
to the shortcomings of the Canadian government. It also enabled the
NAC to build and strengthen its international network. The interactions
between the NAC and Canadian government officials, however, did nothing to improve already strained relations.

At the other end of the ideological spectrum, REAL Women also chose to
"go public," since it perceived Canadian government officials to be unsym-
pathetic to its concerns: "Why would we waste our time on the Canadian
delegation, or the American delegation for that matter, since we know
they are hard-core feminists?"[71] Through participation in workshops and
through the distribution of leaflets, it sought to draw attention to perceived
deficiencies in Canada's positions. In particular, REAL Women sought to
court allies among Southern women; hence, it appropriated terminology
widely used by Southern leaders and scholars. The *PFA*, for example, was
described as *"a racist document"* and *"another example of colonialism."*[72] As
such, REAL Women sought to embarrass the Canadian delegation and to
engender opposition to many of its key positions as well as to the overall
orientation of the *PFA*.

The examples discussed above involve Canadian NGOs that sent their
own members to represent their concerns. There were other Canadian nongovernmental actors who went as representatives of international, rather
than national, NGOs. For example, Katherine McDonald was accredited to

the New York Preparatory Meetings and the Beijing conference because of her position as a board member of International Planned Parenthood, which has consultative status with the UN Economic and Social Council. International Planned Parenthood sought to build on and move beyond the gains made at the Cairo Conference on Population and Development, where the link had been firmly established between population issues and the education, socioeconomic status, and empowerment of women. International Planned Parenthood participated actively in the work of the sexual and reproductive health caucus, whose membership comprised large numbers of Southern as well as Northern women. The caucus was confronted by two serious, externally generated problems: the closed nature of the negotiations – an impediment that was faced by all the NGO caucuses – and intense harassment by antichoice groups – a problem that was not unique to the sexual and reproductive health caucus, though the latter was undoubtedly a primary target for such assaults. McDonald recalls that "the anti-choice groups did whatever they could to obstruct and in-convenience us. They would not hesitate to rifle through a briefcase or the papers that you had placed on the chair beside you even while you were sitting there talking to the person on the other side of you. In response to such harassment, the caucus became incredibly strong and closely knit. Members were dedicated. We never missed a meeting, and we stayed up half the night preparing lobbying documents."[73] The harassment they experienced at the 1995 New York Preparatory Meetings prompted the caucus members to begin to hold their meetings in secret – a practice that continued at the Beijing conference. In between the negotiations, key members of the caucus convened meetings to plan for the next round of intergovernmental negotiations. They were also active in developing lob-bying materials and in encouraging their national affiliates to lobby their respective governments.[74]

Although McDonald had extensive experience with the issues, she was a relative newcomer to UN negotiations. Nonetheless, she was quickly pro-pelled into active liaison work on behalf of the international caucus. Canada was taking a lead role in the negotiations on sexual and reproduc-tive rights, and it was logical to have a Canadian – rather than a national of a foreign country – presenting caucus positions to the Canadian nego-tiators. It must be noted that good working relations already existed between the key Canadian negotiators involved with issues of sexual and reproductive rights and the leading international NGOs in the caucus. Ruth Archibald, Diana Rivington, and international NGOs such as the Commonwealth Medical Association, Family Care International, Interna-tional Women's Health Coalition, and International Planned Parenthood had all attended the Cairo Conference on Population and Development, where they had shared similar objectives.

Although these examples of NGO activities and strategies are few and the discussions of them are brief, they tend to substantiate conventional wisdom about NGO tactics. Groups enjoying access to and good relations with key government decision makers do not generally embarrass the latter publicly. In this case, the CLC had a designated representative on the Canadian delegation and Nancy Riche, as vice-president of the CLC, was active in presenting her views in delegation meetings. Overall, Canada's positions accorded with CLC objectives at the conference, so there was no need to embarrass the Canadian government. However, the CLC, through the ICFTU, did publicize the deficiencies in the Chinese government's record regarding women's rights.

Although radically different in their orientations and their understandings of the issues, both the NAC and REAL Women felt – albeit in varying degrees – alienated from the Canadian delegation. In response, both chose to go public to engender support for their respective positions and thereby to exert indirect influence on the Canadian government. The primary channel for going public was the media.

Media Liaison

UN conferences attract a great deal of media attention, providing NGOs with opportunities to gain access to audiences worldwide as well as to audiences back home.[75] There is the chance that such coverage may encourage a groundswell of support for the NGO's position that might, if sufficiently strong and well focused, exert some pressure on government leaders to adopt (or continue to support) positions consistent with the NGO's interests. Most importantly, media coverage offers the opportunity for educating large audiences about an issue, in the hope that such outreach will result in the long-term benefit of building a large, committed constituency whose support can be marshalled to bolster future lobbying activities.

Courting media coverage is, nevertheless, time-consuming, not equally available to all participants, and uncertain of outcome. First, it requires securing media coverage favourable to the NGO's position. Second, the coverage must not only reach the targeted audiences but must also motivate them to exert pressure on the key decision makers to make the desired change. Third, the decision makers must be receptive to the demands being made and be willing and able to adopt the positions being promoted. Media personnel are most receptive to those who can provide them with what they need: concise, credible stories that will be of interest to their audiences and that can be delivered within the tight time frames within which they operate. Knowing how to present the media with a story that meets these criteria requires expertise about the parameters within which the media operate as well as about the issue being discussed. Not all issues are equally amenable to media coverage. Graphic pictures of environmentalists braving the ocean swells in tiny dinghies in order to save beleaguered whales from the massive, heavily armed fishing trawlers convey a message quickly and play on the audience's emotions, engendering widespread support. Other issues, such as the use of nuclear energy, are far less amenable to media coverage because a catchy picture or a quick news-bite are insufficient to argue one's point; instead, the advantages and disadvantages must be carefully weighed. The media tend to focus on conflict and on that which they consider exciting rather than on substantive issues. So most of the coverage of the Beijing conference focused on problems with visas, excessive Chinese security, the mud at Huairou. Relatively little examined the substance of the provisions under negotiation. As Canadian broadcaster Judy Rebick writes, "I have never before experienced such a total media distortion of an event in which I was involved. I tell my audience: if you want to stop the media covering mud, visas and security men, just start a fight. A rip-roaring battle among feminists is sure to finally draw their attention away from the Chinese and onto us."[76] Rebick's tongue-in-cheek remarks highlight a serious problem facing all UN conferences, summits, and forums, as well as the women's movement: how to get the media to take the issues seriously and to educate the broader public on their significance.

Even groups with media expertise have no guarantee that the coverage they receive will be favourable, let alone that it will be sufficient to engender strong, widespread public support so that government decision makers will be receptive to public pressure if it is exerted. Once governments have publicly announced positions, they are extremely reluctant to make changes that could make them appear weak or indecisive. By the time a conference is taking place, the likelihood of seeing any significant change in government positions is extremely small.

Courting media, and in turn public, support is problematic, but it can nonetheless serve as a useful adjunct to other ways of seeking influence. Many of the Canadian NGOs accredited to the conference had extensive experience, both with the issues under negotiation and with the dynamics of UN conferences. In addition to working with the UN caucuses and lobbying governments, they worked with the media. Nancy Riche recalls her experience convening a press conference in Beijing: "Since NGOs were not allowed to convene press conferences at the Beijing International Convention Centre, another site had to be procured. The site allocated by the Chinese authorities to the ICFTU was at least a fifteen-minute walk from the Beijing Convention Centre, down alleys, and up stairs: access was not made easy. Nonetheless, it was attended by ten members of the press, and the ICFTU considered it a success to have managed to hold the press conference at all."[77] Calling press conferences was not the only tactic for gaining media attention. Several of the Canadian NGO representatives remained in active contact with the media back home. For example, local radio stations in Halifax called Katherine McDonald daily for updates on the conference.[78] Joanna Kerr gave interviews to the Canadian media, including the *Globe and Mail* and *Toronto Star* newspapers and the Canadian Broadcasting Corporation.[79] Canadian NGO representatives attending the conference also conveyed daily updates to colleagues in Canada via e-mail, where the latter fed the stories to the local media. Although Madeleine Gilchrist had declined membership on the Canadian delegation to the Fourth World Conference on Women, she was sought out by the Canadian media prior to the conference. During the conference, she assumed the role of media contact-person for both the CBFC and VOW.[80] E-mail enabled her to keep in close touch with members of both organizations who were accredited to the Fourth World Conference on Women. Through these ongoing contacts, she kept abreast of developments in Beijing and was able to provide up-to-date reports to the Canadian media. In contrast to the experiences of some of the government officials and other members of the NGO community that have been cited earlier, Madeleine Gilchrist thought that the quality of media coverage improved during the course of the conference: "As time went on, the headlines in the newspapers changed from 'Half-naked activists China's worst nightmare' and 'The world's biggest estrogen bomb,' to 'Voices that won't be silenced' and 'Revolution has begun.'"[81] An examination of Canadian newspaper coverage during the conference shows that the coverage did become somewhat more substantial, though it is difficult to say whether this is because of the efforts of Canadian government officials and NGO representatives or because there were more issues of substance to report, as particularly contentious issues were resolved in the negotiations. What is clear is that Canadian NGOs recognized the media opportunities presented by the conference and NGO forum and they were active in courting the media to disseminate their concerns to as wide an audience as possible.

Participating at the NGO Forum on Women '95

The NGO Forum on Women '95 was held from August 30 to September 8 in Huairou, a beautiful resort town 42 kilometres north of Beijing. There, the 30,000 participants attended "the largest NGO Forum as well as the largest international gathering on women ever."[82] The theme for the forum was "Look at the World Through Women's Eyes." During the ten-day period, over 5,000 workshops, panels, plenaries, and cultural events were convened.[83] There were five regional tents – corresponding with the UN's five regional economic commissions – where women from each region could meet to discuss and to strengthen their networks. The tents also served as bases for sharing regional perspectives and cultural activities with women from around the globe. They featured exhibits, films, singing, dancing, and even the cuisine of the region. There were also seven diversity tents for particular categories of women: older women, youth, lesbians, women with disabilities, indigenous women, refugee and stateless women, and grassroots women. An additional three tents were devoted to peace, healing, and quiet. Some of the panels and workshops were held in school classrooms and rooms in administrative buildings, while others were in tents. Up to 126 workshops and seminars of varying sizes could be run simultaneously in fifty-seven rooms and sixty-nine tents.[84] An additional six large rooms had facilities to provide simultaneous translation into the six official UN languages;[85] these were used for the major plenary meetings. A very large tent housed the Global Pavilion, where participants could get maps and information on a wide range of matters, from updates on scheduled events and bus timetables to details on visits to Chinese women's projects and tourist attractions. Since many women had brought goods from home to sell, the area in and around the Global Pavilion was always colourful, intriguing, and bustling.

While activities at the forum had far less relevance for policy making, especially for the short term, than did the NGO participation at the conference, the significance of the forum cannot be overlooked. It enabled women from almost every country, from vastly different walks of life, and from diverse ethnic backgrounds, to learn about each other's concerns and to strategize together for common advancement. For many NGOs, a key reason for attending the forum was to seek to broaden the constituency of support for their concerns. As a representative of the Voice of Women says, "Peace education is a high priority for VOW. We see our greatest strength in building networks among women in the international women's movement. For us, a major goal in participating at the forum was to educate other NGOs about peace issues, generally, and about the need for disarmament, in particular."[86] It was not only NGO representatives who benefited from the diverse contacts made possible by the convening of the NGO forum. For certain government officials, it provided an important venue for reaching their attentive public. For instance, Canada's secretary of state for the status of women travelled from Beijing to the NGO forum to meet with Canadian NGOs. The contact was seen as being of sufficient political importance to warrant the minister's trip to Huairou. As discussed in Chapter 5, the forum also provided important opportunities for CIDA officials to meet with their Southern partners.

Canadians participated in many of the activities that took place at the NGO forum in Huairou. They were active in the regional tent for Europe and North America, as well as in the work that was carried out in the diversity tents. Quebec groups got La Francophonie movement started and were instrumental in its work. Canadians not only attended panels, plenaries, workshops, and seminars but also were active as presenters and moderators.

These contributions are far too numerous to mention in detail, but some illustrative examples of panels organized by Canadian NGOs are outlined in Figure 2. The list gives an example of the range of workshops Canadian NGOs offered. In addition to sponsoring workshops, Canadian NGO representatives participated on many more panels and in the group discussions that followed.

Canadian NGOs and government officials had a key contact in the Secretariat of the NGO Forum on Women. Chandra Budhu had been the co-chair of the CBFC before moving to New York to take up her position as program of plenaries coordinator in the secretariat. She was well known and respected by the key players in the CBFC process and, more broadly, in the Canadian women's movement. She was also an important access point and source of information for the Canadian delegation.[87]

Figure 2

Examples of panels organized by Canadian NGOs at the NGO forum

Canadian NGO sponsor	Title of workshop
Canadian Indigenous Women's Resource Institute	Aboriginal Women and the Struggle for Recognition of Hereditary Rights
Canadian Voice of Women for Peace	Don't Give Us Military Solutions
General Union Palestinian-Canadian Women	The Difficulties Immigrant Women Face in Canada
Immigrant Women of Saskatchewan	Speaking Out: Sharing Our Stories of Struggles and Strength
Jamaican Self-Help Organization of Canada	South-North Women's Links for Progress
Korean Canadian Women's Association	Sexual Slavery – Korean Comfort Women
National Association of Women and the Law	Women's Human Rights and the Med-Liberal Economic Project
North-South Institute	Global Economic Reform and Women in China
REAL Women	The Family as the Cornerstone of Society
Réseau québécois des chercheuses féministes	Contribution de la recherche féminine à la société québécoise
United Nations Association in Canada	Peace Agreement
Women's Health in Women's Hands	Female Genital Mutilation (FGM) in Canada

Media reports of the forum – or of the official conference, for that matter – did not begin to do justice to their importance: "The Western press has been writing about the death of feminism since the early '80s, and they're now managing to report on an international conference of 30,000 feminists without acknowledging that the women's movement not only has life left in it, but is probably the most vibrant and powerful social movement in the world today."[88] The forum not only facilitated sharing, learning, and strategizing but also had an energizing effect: "The energy generated by being in the midst of women from all over the world working on a multiplicity of issues had a spill-over effect. We carried that energy back to Canada with us to renew our efforts at home to advance women."[89] The sharing, consciousness-raising, and networking that went on both at the NGO forum in Huairou and the Fourth World Conference on Women were highly valued by the participants. As a prominent human rights activist observes, "perhaps the most important thing gained from the NGO Forum and UN Conference is the realization of just how connected we are. Working in a national women's movement, we can make the mistake of believing that our struggles are particular to our social, political and economic climate; in part they are. But listening to women from other parts of the world demonstrates that ... [our struggles] are also similar to and connected to the struggles of women everywhere."[90] The solidarity fostered and the networks built and strengthened are critical foundations from which women from around the world must work together to combat discrimination against women wherever and whenever it arises.

Conclusion

As discussed in this chapter, a series of daunting hurdles impeded NGO participation at the international negotiations. Nonetheless, a significant number of Canadian NGOs persevered and overcame the barriers. Overall, the Canadian NGOs' representatives contributed to the international gatherings in important and diverse ways. They were active in the international caucuses, where they frequently took lead roles. They were instrumental in the development of the NGO texts and in lobbying in support of these documents. They cooperated with others to foster better and more extensive relations among NGOs from around the world. Furthermore, their many contributions added significantly to the offering at the NGO forum. Not surprisingly, there were enormous variations in the extent to which individual NGO representatives were able to contribute, particularly at the intergovernmental negotiations. The key determinant of efficacy at the official negotiations was the extent of one's previous experience in such forums. Several other factors, however, played roles, including a person's innate ability, dedication to the process and, in the case of the novices, the success in finding a mentor to guide him or her through the process.

Katherine McDonald had never attended a UN negotiation before the New York Preparatory Meetings, yet she already had close working relations with leaders from International Planned Parenthood, who had extensive experience and who guided her through the process. As a result, she was active and effective in both New York and Beijing. A further factor to consider is the NGO's primary motivation for attending. It would be unfair, for example, to criticize a NGO for contributing little to the development of the NGO texts or for not conducting an effective lobbying campaign apropos the *PFA* if its primary objective was to elicit widespread publicity and support for its goals back home. The contribution each NGO representative was able to make depended on a variety of factors, including personal experience, the amount of support received, personal dedication and ability, and the objectives of his or her group.

The efficacy of the Canadian NGOs was undoubtedly enhanced by government support. Government funding of the development of the CBFC composite texts enabled Canadian NGOs to go to the New York Preparatory Meetings and the Fourth World Conference on Women not only with a clear idea of their own priorities but also with a written text, which in New York was used as a basis for drafting the international NGO texts. Government funding also facilitated NGO attendance at the 1994 Vienna Regional Meetings, the 1995 New York Preparatory Meetings, and at the Beijing conference and NGO forum, ensuring that diverse women with demonstrated commitment to the advancement of women were able to participate. The women, for their part, worked hard to maximize these opportunities and to build links with others from diverse parts of the globe to assist in their crusades to advance the status of women. In addition to its participation in funding and development of NGO positions, the government is to be commended for its efforts to keep the NGOs apprised of developments before and during the negotiations. Through the CBFC network, the attentive public received relevant information on an ongoing basis, as discussed in Chapter 4. Just prior to the Beijing conference, two highly informative briefing kits were sent out. The Canadian negotiators also made time in their frantic schedules, on a daily basis, to brief the NGOs accredited to the official negotiations. During the Beijing conference, Jackie Claxton commuted daily to Huairou to brief the Canadian NGOs attending the forum. In spite of these efforts, there were certainly times when the NGOs could not get the detailed information they sought from government officials. This situation was particularly evident in the CPC meetings and at the preparatory meetings, where government officials refused to disclose the specifics of their negotiating objectives, much to the annoyance of the NGOs. While the government should be given full credit for the significant support it did provide, there were clearly limits to openness.

Canadian NGOs in general and women's groups in particular gained tremendous experience during the Beijing process and have broadened and strengthened their network both within the country and internationally. They are now far better positioned than they were earlier this decade, let alone after the Third World Conference on Women, to hold the Canadian government accountable for the commitments it made in Beijing, and to work with groups from other parts of the world to ensure the implementation of the *PFA*.

7
Canada and the *Beijing Declaration* and *Platform for Action*

The preceding chapters have traced the evolution of the *PFA* through to its adoption at the Fourth World Conference on Women and examined the ways in which Canadian government actors and NGO representatives sought to influence the focus and substance of the *PFA*. It is now time to evaluate the end products – the final conference documents – in terms of their intrinsic value and in terms of Canada's objectives. Chapter 7 begins with brief overviews of the *Beijing Declaration* and *PFA*. Thereafter, it identifies Canada's chief priorities in the negotiations and assesses the extent to which each was reflected in the conference documents that were adopted in Beijing. Through this discussion, some of the key achievements of the *Beijing Declaration* and *PFA*, as well as their shortcomings, will be explored.

Beijing Declaration and *Platform for Action*: An Overview

Beijing Declaration
The 38-paragraph *Beijing Declaration* encapsulates the core principles, issues, and strategies of the *PFA*. Although the *Declaration* was discussed in general terms at the 1995 preparatory meetings, negotiations on the *PFA* were not advanced enough at that point for delegates to feel comfortable drafting a document that would sum up the work of the *PFA*. As a result, negotiations on the *Declaration* were carried out entirely at Beijing, where they proved to be much more controversial than originally expected. Some states, particularly those on the conservative/religious right, saw the negotiations on the *Declaration* as an opportunity to reopen or to water down the provisions in the *PFA* which they opposed. Such moves were vehemently opposed by Canada and its allies from the European Union, Australia, and the Caribbean states.

As discussed in Chapter 5, it was a major credit to the contact group chaired by Canada's Ross Hynes that consensus was achieved and that the *Declaration* was adopted unanimously with no reservations. The document provides a broad overview of the issues and the commitments in the *PFA:* "The Declaration calls for elimination of all forms of violence against women and girls. Governments pledge to intensify efforts to ensure equal enjoyment of human rights and fundamental freedoms for women and girls. They commit to implement the *PFA*, ensuring that a gender perspective is reflected in all their policies and programs. They urge the United Nations system, regional and international financial institutions and all women and men to commit themselves fully to action as well."[1] On the other hand, compromises had to be made and the *Declaration* glosses over and downplays some of the conference's major advances, particularly in the area of sexual rights. Yet, overall, it contains strong, progressive language which can be cited as justification for addressing the many existing barriers to women's empowerment in the world today.

Platform for Action
The *PFA* built on the progress towards women's equality that had been achieved at recent world conferences and summits on children, the environment and development, human rights, population and development, and social development. Furthermore, the provisions in the *PFA* were much more concrete than those emanating from the other world conferences and summits that preceded it in the 1990s in outlining goals to advance women, in specifying commitments to achieve these goals, and in identifying those responsible for carrying out these commitments.

The *PFA* retained the structure of the draft *PFA*, which was adopted at the 1995 New York Preparatory Meetings. It consists of six chapters. Chapter 1 is the mission statement defining the *PFA* as "an agenda for women's empowerment."[2] It reaffirms that women's rights are "an inalienable, integral and indivisible part of universal human rights,"[3] and calls for strong commitments from governments and international organizations, at all levels, to translate the objectives and strategies outlined in the *PFA* into practice.

The global framework in which the conference is taking place is outlined in Chapter 2. It refers to previous UN conferences and notes the political, economic, social, and cultural changes that have taken place during the ten years leading up to Beijing that have profoundly affected the well-being of women around the world in both positive and negative ways. These include the end of the Cold War, the scourge of armed conflict and terrorism that is occurring in so many parts of the world, economic recessions, structural adjustment, the increasing feminization of poverty, demographic trends, the movement towards democratization, the increased strength of NGOs, and the vital contributions made by women to the economy, to society, and to the family.

The critical areas of concern are identified in Chapter 3. Reviews of the progress made in the ten years following the 1985 Nairobi Conference on

Women had identified major obstacles to women's advancements that required urgent and concrete actions. These obstacles translated into twelve critical areas of concern:

- The persistent and increasing burden of poverty on women
- Inequalities and inadequacies in and unequal access to education and training
- Inequalities and inadequacies in and unequal access to health care and related services
- Violence against women
- The effects of armed or other kinds of conflict on women, including those living under foreign occupation
- Inequality in economic structures and policies, in all forms of productive activities
- Inequality between men and women in the sharing of power and decision-making at all levels
- Insufficient mechanisms at all levels to promote the advancement of women
- Lack of respect for and inadequate promotion and protection of the human rights of women
- Stereotyping of women and inequality in women's access to and participation in all communication systems, especially in the media
- Gender inequalities in the management of natural resources and in the safeguarding of the environment
- Persistent discrimination against and violation of the rights of the girl child.[4]

Each of these issues is examined in greater depth in the subsequent chapter.

Chapter 4, "Strategic Objectives and Actions," devotes a section to each of the critical areas of concern, in which the specific problems inherent in each are discussed, the barriers to progress are identified, and concrete strategies and specific actions for overcoming them are proposed. This chapter is the core of the *PFA* and accounts for 79 percent of the text.[5]

The need for effective institutional arrangements is discussed in Chapter 5. It recognizes that governments bear the primary responsibility for implementing the *PFA* but that a wide range of institutions, drawn from the public, private, and NGO sectors and operating at the international, regional and subregional, national, and local levels have important roles to play in operationalizing the provisions in the *PFA* as well as in holding governments responsible to the commitments they made in Beijing.

Financial arrangements are addressed in Chapter 6, which notes that the financial and human resources allocated to the advancement of women have been woefully inadequate. As a result, progress in implementing the

Nairobi *Forward-looking Strategies for the Advancement of Women* was slow. To ensure the full and effective implementation of the *PFA,* the text calls for the allocation of adequate financial and human resources, including the capability to undertake gender-based analysis at the national, regional, and international levels.

Taking the six chapters together, the *PFA* is a "comprehensive action plan to enhance the social, economic and political empowerment of women, improve their health, advance their education and training, promote their marital and sexual rights and end gender-based violence."[6] It identifies barriers to women's advancement and proposes concrete strategic objectives and actions to be taken not only by governments but also by international organizations and institutions, NGOs, the private sector, and individual women and men to ensure that women are able to participate fully and equally in all spheres of life.

Canada and the *PFA*

Canada's chief reason for participating in the preparatory negotiations as well as at the Fourth World Conference on Women was to ensure that the latter adopted a document that established standards and provided concrete strategies for accelerating progress towards women's equality with men by the year 2000: "Canada has, and will continue to, work [sic] actively and constructively with other delegations on all issues in order to ensure that the platform adopted by governments at Beijing is a solid foundation for concrete action that will produce tangible results for women around the world."[7]

According to the official Canadian position, to be a solid foundation, the *PFA* had to realize two critical objectives. First, it had to incorporate and build upon the significant gains for gender equality made at recent summits and conferences.[8] As Canada's minister of foreign affairs, André Ouellet stated: "A key goal of the Conference is to bring together the agreements from previous summits and conferences into a concrete agenda for women's equality within the United Nations."[9] It was important not only to consolidate past gains but also to move the agenda ahead. As Valerie Raymond points out, "Canada sought to get the strongest language possible to protect women's equality that is consistent with Canadian domestic and foreign policy."[10] The second overarching objective was to ensure that a gender-equality perspective was used to address all the national and international political, economic, social, and cultural issues in the *Platform for Action.*[11]

The remainder of this chapter focuses primarily on assessing Canada's success in realizing its objectives in each of the twelve critical areas of concern in the *PFA*. Before beginning this discussion, it is important to recognize the major breakthrough on the issue of cultural relativism that was realized in Chapter 2 (Global Framework) of the *PFA*.[12] Here, the issue pitted the universality of women's human rights against respect for religious, cultural, and social traditions. Canada was eager to ensure that the universality of women's rights took precedence so that a state could not refer to cultural, religious, or social traditions as justification either for passing legislation that contravened its obligations to uphold international human rights or for failing to exercise due diligence in preventing and punishing violations of women's rights by nonstate actors. The issue had been the subject of heated debate at previous UN conferences and summits. While the need to consider historical, cultural, and religious backgrounds was recognized at the 1993 Vienna Conference on Human Rights, it was nonetheless agreed there that states were required to promote and protect all human rights regardless of their political, economic, and cultural systems. One year later, at the Cairo Conference on Population and Development, the balance shifted in favour of cultural relativism. The Cairo conference stressed the sovereign rights of states rather than their duties to uphold international human rights and specified that religious, cultural, and ethical values were to be given full respect. The language of the Cairo conference, which implied precedence for cultural, religious, and social backgrounds, was picked up at the 1995 Copenhagen Summit for Social Development and was included in the Beijing *PFA* as a "chapeau" to all the critical areas of concern, including health, education, and violence against women. The issue was highly controversial, as exemplified by the fact that references to cultural relativism remained bracketed until 2 a.m. of the last day of the Fourth World Conference on Women. In the end, those championing women's human rights over deference to cultural and religious values prevailed. The *PFA* not only reflects the language of the Vienna Conference on Human Rights but is stronger in promoting and protecting women's human rights, including their rights to culture and freedom of religion.[13] The wording was described by the *International Herald Tribune* as "the most far-reaching stance on human rights ever taken at a UN gathering."[14] As discussed in Chapter 5, Canadian negotiators played pivotal roles in bringing about this important breakthrough.

Government officials established specific positions on all the twelve critical areas of concern in the *PFA*. To facilitate assessing the extent to which Canada's objectives were reflected in the final conference documents, each of Canada's priorities is outlined below, as it appears in the instructions to the Canadian delegation. The key elements of these objectives are then compared with the actual provisions of the *PFA*. In the instructions to the Canadian delegation, Canada's major objectives were divided into two categories. The first encompassed Canada's top priorities, outlined under the headings of human rights, economic and social development, empowerment, gender analysis, and peace.[15] The decision to give priority to these five objectives was based on two factors.[16] Most importantly, the first four objectives reflected existing priorities for the Canadian government. The fifth objective was less directly linked to major Canadian objectives. Since Canada was not at war, Canadian women were not likely to be victims of armed conflict. Nevertheless, concern for women caught in armed conflict was a major concern of Canadian human rights groups that enjoyed constructive working relations with Adèle Dion and the Human Rights and Justice Division in DFAIT. The latter were receptive to the former's concerns about women and armed conflict; hence, this issue area became a priority.

The second category outlined Canada's objectives in each of the twelve critical areas of concern: poverty, education and training, health, violence, armed conflict, economy, power and decision making, institutional mechanisms for the advancement of women, human rights, media, environment, and the girl child. Clearly, there was significant overlap between the two categories. For example, the discussion of human rights under category one ("Canada's Priorities") is very similar to that outlined under human rights in category two, though the former is somewhat more detailed than the latter.

In addition to the overlaps between the items in categories one and two, there was considerable overlap between the coverage of issues within each of the areas of concern. For example, Canada's priorities relating to reproductive rights are referred to under the section on human rights as well as under the section on health. Violence constitutes one of the twelve critical areas of concern, and Canada outlines some broad objectives for the section; however, it also refers to violence against women in the section on human rights since violence against women constitutes a serious violation of women's rights. Referring to the same issue under a variety of headings was by no means peculiar to Canada. There is a considerable amount of overlap among the twelve critical issues of concern in the *PFA*. For example, the *PFA* discusses education not only in the education section but also in the health section's provisions to prevent the spread of HIV/AIDS and to promote family planning. Education is cited in the human rights section as a means of raising awareness of women's human rights and in the armed conflict section as a strategy for mandating a culture of peace. The needs and rights of indigenous women appear in at least five sections of the *PFA*: human rights, health, education, the media, and the environment. In light of the interconnectedness of the issue areas, a certain amount of overlap is unavoidable and is an accurate reflection of reality. For example, the facts that much of women's work, particularly in the Southern countries, is unremunerated and that many girls and women face numerous barriers to education and training are major causes of their poverty. To avoid unnecessary repetitions, the issues are discussed under the headings used in the *Briefing Book for the Canadian Delegation*, beginning with the five areas identified as Canada's top priorities (human rights, economic and social development, empowerment, gender analysis, and peace). Consideration is then given to the remaining eight critical areas of concern not addressed under Canada's top priorities (poverty, education, health, violence against women, national machinery, the media, the environment, and the girl child). Structuring the inquiry in this way should reduce the repetition. The discussion of gender, for instance, is concentrated under "gender" rather than being revisited in each of the twelve areas of critical concern. As will be seen in the discussion below, the instructions to the Canadian delegation were fairly general, allowing its negotiators considerable flexibility to determine specific wording for the *PFA*.

Human Rights

Canada's Priorities

> It is critical that the promotion and protection of all human rights and fundamental freedoms for all women are universal and are the foundation of the Platform. These include, for women and men equally, civil, political, social, economic and cultural rights and, of particular importance to women, reproductive rights, as affirmed at the International Conference on Population and Development. Canada is also working to ensure that there is action to address the causes and consequences of all forms of violence against women and girls.
>
> The Platform must reflect the common issues women face universally due to gender inequality in all societies. It must also respect and value their diversity while recognizing that many women face additional barriers to equality because of factors such as race, ethnicity, religion, sexual orientation, disability, age, family status and socio-economic class or because they are indigenous people or are migrants or refugees.[17]

Canada had two broad sets of concerns in this category: the definition of women's rights and the need to ensure that diverse categories of women were able to enjoy the broad range of their human rights.

Provisions in the PFA

Canada's objectives apropos the universality of women's rights were realized in the *PFA*, which strongly reaffirms the commitment made at the Vienna Conference on Human Rights that women's rights are human rights. The concept of women's rights as human rights provides the foundation for the entire document. The *PFA* also affirms the universal nature of women's human rights and freedoms. As a result, governments and the UN are required to promote and protect the full range of women's human rights.

The diversity clause recognized most – but by no means all – of Canada's objectives. The text identifies discrimination against women on the basis of their race, ethnicity, language, culture, religion, age, disability, and socio-economic status, as well as the discrimination faced by indigenous women, migrants, refugees, and displaced women[18] as additional barriers preventing many women from enjoying the full range of their human rights. This list of barriers appears in several places in the *PFA* and in the *Beijing Declaration*. Missing from the list are references to family status or sexual orientation. Canada, along with the European Union and several other countries including New Zealand and South Africa, campaigned actively to have sexual orientation included in the diversity clause, which identified various forms of discrimination faced by women – in addition to gender-based discrimination – that prevent them from enjoying the full range of their human rights. The inclusion of sexual orientation was vehemently opposed by such states as Egypt and Iran, which argued that it contravened their cultural and religious beliefs. At 4:30 on the morning of September 15 – the last day of the conference – after hearing the divergent views of some thirty states, Patricia Licuanan, chair of the Main Committee, declared that the bracketed references to sexual orientation would be deleted from the *PFA* on the grounds that there was no consensus on its inclusion.[19] So Canada was not successful in having sexual orientation included. Yet, its efforts were not in vain. The Beijing conference marked "the first time that the issue of sexual orientation had even been debated at any official United Nations forum,"[20] and thirty states supported its inclusion in the text. Furthermore, Canada, along with Israel, Jamaica, Latvia, New Zealand, Norway, South Africa, and the Cook Islands, issued interpretive statements on paragraph 48 (diversity) noting that they understand the term "other status" to include discrimination on the grounds of sexual orientation.[21] International negotiations are part of an ongoing process. Canada laid a foundation in Beijing, on which it can build at subsequent negotiations to ensure that future international texts will prohibit discrimination on the basis of sexual orientation.

The need to involve indigenous women and to meet their particular needs was recognized more strongly in the *PFA* than it had been in previous conference and summit documents. The *PFA* affirmed their right to participate in all levels of decision making and to gain equal access to education and health care. It also valued their traditional health care practices and their understanding of environmental management. Furthermore, the rights of indigenous women were integrated into the main text and not ghettoized at the end. Nevertheless, the text did not go as far as indigenous women had hoped. As Mary Sillet, a prominent leader and activist in the Inuit women's community, explains: "We insist on the usage of Indigenous Peoples (with an 's') because under international law, 'peoples,' not people, have the right to self-determination. Peoples have collective rights. People have individual rights."[22] From the point of view of the Canadian government, which refuses to use the term peoples for the very reasons cited above, the language in the *PFA* accords with its preference.

Economic and Social Development

Canada's Priorities

> Canada is working to ensure that the Platform is based on recognition that economic development, social development and environmental protection are interdependent and mutually reinforcing. Gender equality is at the centre of this people-centred framework. This requires an examination of a wide range of policies, including economic restructuring and adjustment measures, as well as structures and institutions themselves, from a gender perspective.
>
> We will continue to support the need for policies to protect workers' rights, to recognize the relationship between paid and unpaid work, to enable a greater sharing of family responsibilities, to assist in balancing paid work and family responsibilities, and to support more equitable investments in areas such as women's health, education and income generation. These measures not only reduce gender inequality but also improve the well-being of families and communities. They are essential to global poverty reduction and employment creation strategies.[23]

Canada's decision to title this set of objectives "Economic and Social Development" implies a need to promote such development. The titles used in the *PFA* for the critical areas of concern that deal most with the issues outlined above are "Women and the Economy" and "Poverty," both of which are more descriptive and less proactive than the title chosen for one of Canada's top priorities.

Provisions in the PFA

The *PFA*'s section on poverty recognizes that sustainable economic growth and development are predicated on the advancement of women: "Sustainable development and economic growth that is both sustained and sustainable are possible only through improving the economic, social, political, legal and cultural status of women."[24] The section on women and the economy focuses on women's unequal access to economic structures and their unequal participation in the development of these structures and institutions. The text recognizes the interrelationship among economic development, social development, and environmental protection. It advocates the integration of a gender perspective into the workings of economic institutions and into the development of economic policies and programs. It calls on governments to end discrimination in the workplace; to ensure that women have equal access to resources, markets, and trade; and to promote the equal sharing of family responsibilities between men and women. The conference accepted wording proposed by Canada on the recommendation of the trade union caucus that workers have the right to freedom of association and the right to organize. Furthermore, governments, employers, employees, trade unions, and women's organizations are urged to support nondiscriminatory labour standards to protect women and girls in the workplace.

A major achievement is the precedent set regarding women's unpaid work.[25] The very inclusion of such provisions publicizes the implicit sexism inherent in current notions of what is productive work. Examples of unpaid work include carrying water home; collecting firewood; growing, cooking, and serving food; caring for children, the sick, and the elderly; doing housework; making clothes for one's family; and performing volunteer work in one's community. Since most unpaid work is performed by women and since a great deal of the work done by women, particularly in Southern countries, is unpaid, requiring governments to measure and, most importantly, to value unremunerated work are prerequisites for recognizing the full extent of women's contributions to the economy and to society. As discussed in Chapter 5, Canadian negotiators played pivotal roles in achieving this breakthrough.

Canada's broad objectives regarding economic and social development were realized in the provisions of the *PFA*. This is not to say that the section is universally strong. The full extent of the macro-level problems are not adequately analyzed nor are their root causes fully addressed. The *PFA*'s treatments of globalization and structural adjustment programs are markedly weak, reflecting a Northern perspective. The European Union, United States, Canada, and other Western states were unreceptive to the calls by the Group of Seventy-Seven and China for in-depth analysis of the dominant economic models and for measures to rectify the existing structural inequalities in the global economy. The NAC was particularly critical of the Beijing conference's failure to address and redress the detrimental impact that globalization is having on women. The NAC's concerns were corroborated by the *NGO Beijing Declaration,* which described globalization as "a root cause of the increasing feminization of poverty everywhere."[26] The *PFA* acknowledges the negative impact globalization is having on women, though no in-depth analysis is provided nor are the macro-level problems facing women worldwide as a result of globalization addressed seriously.

In a similar vein, the *PFA* notes the negative impact structural adjustment programs are having on women in the South, but it fails to prescribe strategies and actions to address the root causes of these problems.

Empowerment

Canada's Priorities

Equality cannot be achieved without empowering women, not only to participate in existing societal structures, but also to help transform those structures to be more open, accountable and effective in meeting the needs of all members of society, male and female. This includes, for example, enabling women's own voices and realities to be portrayed in the media. The ability to participate freely and autonomously, make real choices and take decisions is critical for all women, whether it is in families and communities or in government and the private sector.[27]

Although these objectives are relevant to all twelve critical areas of concern, they relate most closely to the provisions in the section "Women in Power and Decision-making."

Provisions in the PFA
The text recognizes that women's equal participation in decision making and political life is crucial to their advancement. The barriers to full participation (e.g., gender stereotyping, child care and other family responsibilities, and the high costs of seeking and holding political office) are identified. A wide range of actors (e.g., governments, political parties, national bodies, the private sector, employers' organization, trade unions, research and academic institutions, regional and subregional bodies, NGOs, and international organizations) are urged to create gender balance in decision-making structures, to eliminate attitudes and practices that discriminate against women, to integrate women into the central decision-making structures, to ensure women get equal access to education and training to enable them to participate fully, and to encourage men to share equally in family responsibilities. Canada's broad objectives regarding empowerment are well reflected in the *PFA*.

Gender Analysis

Canada's Priorities

Gender analysis is a practical method to support equality between women and men and societal well-being. It means examining both the similarities and differences in women's and men's lives to help design fair and effective policies and programmes, with the best use of available resources. In every society there are different gender roles and expectations made of girls and boys, women and men, too often based on historic and systemic discrimination. When policy and decision-making take gender into account, unintended and discriminatory impacts can be avoided and more positive results achieved for women, and for men.[28]

Provisions in the PFA

There is no section entitled "gender" in the *PFA*; nonetheless, a gender perspective is pervasive throughout. The health section, for example, calls for the use of gender-disaggregated data, while governments and institutions are urged in the media section to encourage gender-based training. The human rights section not only reiterates the commitment made at the Vienna Conference on Human Rights to integrate women's human rights with the UN human rights mechanisms but it does so in stronger and more specific language. The section on poverty calls on governments to employ a gender perspective in the development, implementation, and assessment of all economic policies and programs, including those addressing macroeconomic stability, taxation, employment, external debt, and structural adjustment. Likewise, the section on women and the economy urges governments to develop gender-sensitive policies, while the section on education and training advocates the integration of a gender perspective into all policies and programs. The section on national machineries discusses the need to collect gender-disaggregated data and to undertake gender analysis to ensure that government bodies and programs are effective in advancing women. The text calls for the integration of a gender perspective in all plans, policies, and programs to resolve armed conflicts, as well as for gender-sensitive policies and programs to address sexually transmitted diseases, including HIV/AIDS. The importance of gender analysis is recognized and addressed in all sections of the *PFA*.

Peace

Canada's Priorities

> Women's important role in the peace process and on security issues must be reflected in the *Platform for Action*. The Platform must also be brought up to the standard of international humanitarian law. Canada will seek to address the needs of refugee, migrant and displaced women and encourage countries to develop guidelines for women refugee claimants fearing gender-related persecution.[29]

Canada's title stresses the importance of peace, whereas the corresponding section in the *PFA* is called "Armed Conflict."

Provisions in the PFA

Several important strides forward were realized in the armed conflict section, all of which were in keeping with Canada's stated objectives. On Wednesday, September 6 – only two days into the conference – Canadian negotiators realized their first major success: the Canadian proposal to recognize sexual violence and other gender-based persecutions as legitimate grounds for claiming refugee status was accepted, and the *PFA* became the first UN document to contain such provisions.[30]

One day later, on September 7, Canada realized its second major negotiating success. The strong language proposed by Canada was adopted; the text reaffirms that "rape in the conduct of armed conflict constitutes a war crime and under certain circumstances it constitutes a crime against humanity and an act of genocide as defined in the *Convention on the Prevention and Punishment of the Crime of Genocide.*"[31] This provision had been adopted at the 1993 Vienna Conference on Human Rights, but it was a Canadian initiative to have it included in the *PFA*. This wording has subsequently been adopted by other bodies, including the Executive Committee of the Commission for Refugees.

In addition to these major accomplishments, the text urges governments, intergovernmental organizations, and NGOs to uphold international humanitarian law and to protect and assist refugee and displaced women and their children. The text explicitly links peace with development and with the equality between men and women and calls for the full participation of women in all levels of decision making and conflict resolution. In each case, the provisions accord with Canada's stated objectives.

Yet, in spite of these positive achievements, the section on armed conflict is not uniformly strong. In particular, it fails to address the broader issues of war or to propose concrete strategies for disarmament. The language used in this area is highly technical. Changes to generally accepted wording or the introduction of new wording could have implications for existing norms on disarmament. None of the delegations had experts on disarmament, and they were instructed by their governments to avoid such discussions.[32] Since delegations were neither willing nor prepared to address disarmament issues in Beijing (or at the preparatory meetings), the discussions never went beyond general statements. As a result, the treatment of these issues is considered disappointing by some of the Canadian negotiators[33] and totally inadequate by Canadian peace groups such as Voice of Women.[34]

Poverty

Canada's Priorities

Canada's objective is to ensure recognition of the need for women to have access to resources, land, credit, education, health care, and to be able to attain/maintain a sustainable livelihood for themselves and their families; and to reinforce the achievements of ICPD [International Conference on Population and Development] and WSSD [World Summit for Social Development] with particular attention to the situation of women and girls living in poverty.[35]

There is some obvious overlap between the objectives Canada outlined under "Economic and Social Development" and those it discussed under "Poverty." However, overall, the former focus on macro-level considerations, such as economic development, economic restructuring, and sustainable development, as well as a broad range of issues affecting women's social and economic well-being, including workers' rights, unpaid work, and shared family responsibilities. The objectives outlined under "Poverty" focus on the more specific requirements necessary to allow women to escape the yoke of poverty, such as access to resources.

Provisions in the PFA

The *PFA*'s section on poverty addresses Canada's concerns as outlined above. It recognizes the growing feminization of poverty: "Today, more than 1 billion people live in extreme poverty; the overwhelming majority of them are women. In the past decade the number of women living in poverty has increased disproportionately to the number of men, and the risk for falling into poverty is higher for women than for men."[36] Yet, recognizing a trend is only the first step. The section also identifies the major causes of poverty and prescribes actions for government, multilateral financial institutions, and NGOs. It urges governments to review and modify their macroeconomic and social policies to ensure women's full and equal participation in economic development. It also recognizes the need for women to have full and equal access to resources (capital, land, technology, information, and inherited property), education, and health care so as to be able to achieve and maintain sustainable livelihoods for themselves and their families. Multilateral financial institutions are assigned the task of developing effective and lasting solutions to the problems of external debt. NGOs are asked to establish mechanisms for monitoring compliance with the provisions on poverty. The recommendations in the poverty section, as well as its focus on sustainable development, all reinforced and built on the achievements of previous world summits and conferences; Canada's objectives are realized.

Education

Canada's Priorities

Canada's objective is to stress that literacy and education are related to

all critical areas of concern and are fundamental to the achievement of
equality; to focus attention on the importance of training, particularly as
preparation for women's labour market participation; and to stress life-
long learning that takes women's realities into account.[37]

Provisions in the PFA

In its assessment of the major achievements in the *PFA*, SWC described
the education section as "strong."[38] It clearly recognizes literacy, education, and training as being essential prerequisites for achieving women's
equality with men and for enabling women to enjoy the full range of
their human rights. Education and training are considered fundamental
not only to a woman's ability to secure her own economic livelihood
but also to her personal development and self-esteem. The education section stresses the importance of life-long learning and focuses on the various stages of education: primary, secondary, and tertiary schooling and
job training programs. At all stages, girls and women face multiple barriers
that impede their access to education and training. These impediments
include legal prohibitions against attending school or going out alone;
culturally defined expectations about the desirability of girls marrying
early and about the appropriateness of education and training for women
and girls; culturally defined roles that prescribe responsibilities for girls
and women, such as the care of children and the sick, homemaking, sub-
sistence farming, and the collection of fuel and water, that preclude the
pursuit of education or training; inadequate financial resources to pay
tuition fees; pregnancy; and gender stereotyping that makes it much more
difficult for girls and women to pursue education and careers in certain –
usually highly valued – fields, such as mathematics, science, engineering,
and technology. In each case, the *PFA* recommends strategies for overcoming these barriers. Governments as well as employers, workers, trade
unions, international organizations, NGOs, and educational institutions
are called upon to end discrimination in education, to ensure that women
and girls have equal access to education and training, to eliminate gender
stereotyping that prevents women and girls from getting education and
training, and to promote an equal sharing of family responsibilities
between girls and boys and women and men. The text also urges government and educational bodies to respect the traditional wisdom and knowledge of indigenous cultures – a recognition important to indigenous
women.

The education section addresses Canada's chief concerns. Furthermore,
all the prescriptions noted above are important components in promoting
gender equality and women's empowerment.

Health

Canada's Priorities

Canada's objective is to ensure that women's health issues take into account the socio-economic factors that impact on women's health; to reaffirm the agreements reached at ICPD on women's reproductive health and rights; and assist in the understanding of AIDS as a gender issue.[39]

Provisions in the PFA

Negotiations on the health section were extremely controversial and, in the end, this is the section where most reservations were registered. Nonetheless, Canada's broad objectives were reflected in the text that emerged. Canadian proposals to take account of the impact of socioeconomic factors on women's health, made at the 1995 New York Preparatory Meetings, remain incorporated in the text. The need for women to access affordable, appropriate, quality health care and other social services is recognized as being essential to the central components of good health. In keeping with Canada's position, good health is defined to encompass physical, mental, and social well-being.

Language from the Cairo Conference on Population and Development was not only adopted and reinforced but also strengthened. In the area of reproductive rights, for example, the *PFA* affirms women's rights to control their own fertility and defined this right as being fundamental to their empowerment. It recognizes as basic the "right of all couples and individuals to decide freely and responsibly the number, spacing and timing of their children and to have the information and the means to do so, and the right to attain the highest standard of sexual and reproductive health."[40] This terminology represented a significant advance from the language of the Cairo conference, which had referred to women's "ability" – not "right" – to control their own fertility.[41]

Although the term "sexual rights" is not used, the text sets important precedents in this area. The Fourth World Conference on Women was the first UN conference to define women's human rights to include "their right to have control over and decide freely and responsibly on matters related to their sexuality, including sexual and reproductive health, free of coercion, discrimination and violence."[42] The text gives women the right to determine their own sexual expression – thereby setting an important precedent. Sexual relations between men and women are, moreover, to be characterized by equality, mutual respect, consent, and equally shared responsibility.

HIV/AIDS and other sexually transmitted diseases are addressed in terms of the threats they pose to the health of girls and women, and to their ability to fulfil their roles as mothers and caregivers. Governments are required to adopt policies to protect women from sociocultural practices that make girls and women particularly vulnerable to these diseases. Women are, for example, often unable to insist that their male partners practice safe and responsible sex. Governments are called upon to develop programs to educate men about safe and responsible sexual behaviour based on consent and mutual respect.

In addition to the concerns specified in Canada's objectives, the health section addresses a broad range of prerequisites necessary to ensure the physical and mental health of women and girls. They include strengthening health services to ensure they are accessible to women and responsive to their needs, promoting the health of women throughout the life cycle with special attention to the specific needs of older and indigenous women, setting targets for reducing mortality rates for mothers and infants, supporting breast feeding, urging the development of strategies for dealing with the health aspects of unsafe abortions, reiterating from the Cairo *Plan of Action* that abortion should not be considered a method of family planning while at the same time urging governments to review laws that prescribe punishment for women who have had illegal abortions, calling for adequate mental health services, and providing services for victims of domestic violence and sexual assault.

Violence against Women
In contrast to the health section, which had sparked heated debates over sexual and reproductive rights and abortion, the section on violence against women proved to be far less controversial.

Canada's Priorities

> Canada's objective is to ensure that the Platform for Action addresses the causes and consequences of all forms of violence against women and girls, and reflects the Canadian-initiated UN Declaration on the Elimination of Violence Against Women.[43]

Provisions in the PFA
The section addresses the diverse forms, causes, and consequences of violence against women. It begins by noting that, "in all societies, to a greater or lesser degree, women and girls are subject to physical, sexual and psychological abuse that cuts across lines of income, class and culture."[44] The text proceeds to outline some of the forms of violence that women experience in the private as well as the public sphere, including rape, sexual abuse, battering, female genital mutilation, sexual harassment, trafficking

in women, forced prostitution, prenatal sex selection, female infanticide, forced pregnancy, forced abortions, and forced sterilization. All such acts of violence violate and impair or nullify women's enjoyment of their human rights.

Violence against women is closely linked to cultural norms. It is, therefore, as the *PFA* reaffirms, not a private matter but, rather, an issue requiring government action. The text sets new ground in several respects. Governments are assigned responsibility for enacting and enforcing legislation to prohibit violence against women and to punish the perpetrators of such violence. Furthermore, states not only are called upon to prevent and eliminate violence against women but also are not to invoke "any custom, tradition or religious consideration to avoid their obligation with respect to its elimination."[45] This provision closes an important loophole that has frequently been used as an excuse for not ending violence against women.

Governments are called upon to provide quality social services to assist women and girls who were threatened by violence or who were victims of violence and to counsel and rehabilitate the perpetrators of such violence. As part of the strategy for eliminating violence against women, governments are urged to root out gender-stereotyping that perpetuates lower status for women, including that portrayed in the media's images of rape and sexual slavery. Clearly, governments have the pivotal role to play, but the text also called upon employers, trade unions, NGOs, private enterprises, and educational institutions to root out all forms of violence against women. At the international level, the UN secretary-general is asked to assist the special rapporteur on violence against women and to ensure that she receives the personnel and other resources necessary to fulfil her mandate.

In some areas, Canada would have liked to go beyond the existing text. It was unsuccessful in getting other states to agree to establish a Convention on the Elimination of Violence on Women.[46] On the other hand, the section on violence against women reaffirmed the provisions of the UN *Declaration on the Elimination of Violence Against Women.* Overall, the section is strong, containing well-founded and extensive measures for combatting violence against women in both public and private spheres. As such, it addresses most of Canada's principal negotiating objectives.

National Machinery

Canada's Priorities

Canada's objective is to address the importance of a strong national machinery for the advancement of women that has adequate resources and the mandate, authority and capacity to coordinate the integration of women's concerns into policy and programmes.[47]

Provisions in the PFA

The section entitled "Institutional Mechanisms for the Advancement of Women" focuses on national machineries, though it also makes recommendations to regional and international institutions. It begins by outlining the deficiencies of mechanisms at all levels, which include unclear mandates, inadequate resources, and a lack of appropriate training, especially in the use of gender analysis. Furthermore, machineries to advance women are frequently marginalized within organizations rather than being involved in the core operations of national, regional, and international bodies. The text advocates mainstreaming a gender perspective in the development, implementation, and monitoring of all policies and programs. It calls on governments to establish and strengthen national machineries and to imbue them with clear mandates and adequate resources. Such machineries require the competence and authority both to influence the formulation and implementation of policies and programs and to evaluate their effects on women and men, respectively. The machineries are to be located at the highest possible level of government. Regional and international bodies, as well as governments, are required to collect, compile, and analyze gender-disaggregated data and information. The resulting data and analysis are to be disseminated and used in the development of new programs and policies and in revising existing ones. As discussed previously under "Economic and Social Development," provisions referring to unpaid work – most of which are included under "Institutional Mechanisms" – set important precedents and are viewed as major accomplishments by the Canadian delegation.

Media

Canada's Priorities

> Canada's objective is to reflect the important role of all forms of media, including alternative media, in promoting realistic portrayals of women and their situations; the need for research, education and training; media literacy; codes of conduct; and increased ability of women to use media, including new technologies, for enhanced networking.[48]

Provisions in the PFA

Many of the provisions in this section were drawn directly from the UNESCO Symposium held in Toronto in 1995. In its definitions of the problems and in its subsequent recommendations for action, the section addresses the concerns outlined in Canada's Objectives. It begins with the recognition that the media exercise considerable influence over public policy as well as over the attitudes and behaviours of individuals and groups. Yet, in spite of its pervasive and powerful influence, the media are not doing nearly as much as they could to advance women: "Everywhere the potential exists for the media to make a far greater contribution to the advancement of women."[49] Few women have achieved positions of seniority in the media; their influence over media policy is small. All forms of media communications – electronic, print, audio, and visual – are characterized by a lack of gender sensitivity. As a result, negative and degrading images of women, as well as gender-based stereotypes that reinforce limited roles for women, are found throughout media communications.

The recommendations urge governments to promote women's access to, and full and equal participation in, all levels and forms of the media. Such access and participation should be facilitated by supporting women's education and training and promoting research aimed at identifying problems and facilitating the mainstreaming of a gender perspective. The media are urged to present balanced and diverse images of women as creative human beings, to avoid the use of gender-based stereotypes, and to refrain from exploiting women as sexual objects and commodities. The text assigns to the media and advertising organizations the responsibility for developing self-regulating guidelines to ensure that women are portrayed in positive, nonstereotypical manners and to "address violent, degrading or pornographic materials."[50] In addition to disseminating positive, balanced, and diverse images of women, the media, NGOs, and the private sector were called upon to raise awareness of issues raised in the *PFA*, including the need for men to share equally in family responsibilities and the need to eliminate all forms of violence against women and girls. Primary responsibility for monitoring the media's performance of these tasks is allocated to NGOs, which are encouraged to establish media watch groups. NGOs and media professional associations are asked to provide women with training to enhance their understanding and knowledge of media communications and to enable them to acquire the skills necessary to use these technologies and to participate fully in media-related decision making.

Environment

Canada's Priorities

Canada's objective is to ensure that gains made for women at the United Nations Conference on Environment and Development are reflected, particularly the full involvement of women in economic and political decision-making related to the environment.[51]

Provisions in the PFA

The section reaffirmed – but did not go beyond – the language agreed to at the 1992 Rio Conference on the Environment and Development.[52] It recognizes that environmental degradation affects women to a greater extent than men and that women, especially indigenous women, have particular knowledge of the environments in which they live because they often work more closely with it than do their male counterparts. Their participation and leadership in all levels of decision making and management relating to sustainable development, the protection of the environment, and control over resources are, therefore, essential. The provisions to protect the intellectual and cultural property rights of indigenous women proved to be particularly controversial. The final text provides some protection, specifying that these rights are to be respected and that the benefits resulting from the use of such knowledge and practice are to be shared on a "fair and equitable" basis.[53] Such protection is, however, significantly weakened by the inclusion of the clause "subject to national legislation."[54] Governments, private sector institutions, and NGOs are all called upon to mainstream a gender perspective in designing, approving, and implementing policies, programs, and projects and to develop strategies for increasing the number of women actively involved at all levels of decision making. The provisions are general, "motherhood-type" pronouncements that satisfied Canada's objectives. They reinforced what already existed but did little to move the agenda ahead.

Girl Child

Canada's Priorities

Canada's objective is to promote the human rights of the girl child and the elimination of all forms of discrimination against girls; to enable girls to grow up as equal members of society, well-prepared for a productive future.[55]

Provisions in the PFA

Many of the concerns of girls, such as access to education, nutrition, and health care, were addressed in greater length in earlier sections, though they are noted here as well. The text calls for the elimination of all forms of discrimination against girls. Governments agree to root out harmful practices, such as female infanticide, early marriage, sexual abuse, sexual exploitation, female genital mutilation, and early child bearing. In addition to prescribing the eradication of these harmful practices, the text advocates the elimination of the negative stereotyping of girls and the discrimination girls face in getting access to food, nutrition, and health services. Governments, international organizations, and NGOs are urged to ensure that girls not only have access to education and training equal to that enjoyed by boys but that educational materials promote positive images of girls and women, especially in areas where they have traditionally been underrepresented. The need to end the economic exploitation of child labour and to protect girls in the workplace is also addressed.

Several issues in the section proved to be particularly controversial. References to the family triggered considerable debate. Guatemala, Benin, and other conservative states wanted the term "family" used, while Canada, the European Union, and other allies advocated the use of the term "families" in recognition that families can exist in various forms. In the end, governments agreed to accept the compromise wording contained in Chapter 2, Global Framework: "The family is the basic unit of society and as such should be strengthened. It is entitled to receive comprehensive protection and support. In different cultural, political and social systems, various forms of the family exist."[56] Thus, the compromise wording was far less inclusive than Canada's preferred term. The text did acknowledge the importance of the family and recognized that it takes various forms. In keeping with Canada's objectives, the text further specified that men as well as women must share responsibility for the upbringing of children and that motherhood is important but that this role should not be used as grounds for limiting women's ability to participate fully in society. All these provisions satisfied Canada's objectives.

The question of what balance should be struck between parental rights and responsibilities, on one hand, and the rights of the girl child, on the other, also aroused considerable debate, particularly regarding a girl's right to make decisions pertaining to her own sexuality. The Holy See, its allies, and the fundamentalist Islamic states championed parental rights, whereas Canada and other Western countries advocated increasing rights for the child as she approaches adulthood. A balance was struck giving priority to the well-being of the girl. The text recognized "the rights of the child to access information, privacy, confidentiality, respect and informed consent, as well as the responsibilities, rights and duties of parents and legal guardians to provide, in a manner consistent with the evolving capacities of the child, appropriate direction and guidance."[57] But it goes on to specify that, "in all actions concerning children, the best interests of the child shall be a primary consideration."[58] Governments, international organizations, and NGOs are to ensure that girls receive reproductive-health education, including information on family planning and sexually transmitted diseases.

As discussed in Chapter 5, Canadian negotiators were very active in the debates over inheritance. Egypt and the fundamentalist Islamic states opposed equal inheritance for girls and boys, whereas Canada and its allies argued strongly for full equality. The text calls on governments to pass and enforce "legislation that guarantees equal rights to succession and ensures equal right to inherit, regardless of the sex of the child."[59] As noted in

Chapter 5, having equal rights to inherit is not the same as having the right to inherit equally. Nevertheless, achieving this wording was seen as a major accomplishment by the Canadian delegation.

The section on the girl child was described by Mary Purcell, chair of the caucus on the girl child, as "a milestone."[60] In advocating the elimination of all forms of discrimination against girls and in promoting their human rights and their equality with boys in all realms of life, the text satisfies Canada's broad negotiating objectives as well as addressing most of its specific concerns.

Institutional and Financial Arrangements

After the strategic objectives and actions have been laid out for each of the twelve areas of concern in Chapter 4 of the *PFA*, the institutional arrangements to ensure their implementation are discussed in Chapter 5. The latter, titled "Institutional Arrangements," makes it clear that, although the primary responsibility for implementation rests with state governments, effective implementation cannot be achieved without the concerted efforts of public and private institutions at the local, national, subregional, regional, and international levels. The range of institutions included is extremely broad. It encompasses all bodies within the UN system, including the international financial institutions, regional and subregional organizations, legislative bodies, private corporations, NGOs operating at all levels from grassroots operations through to the international arena, trade unions, professional associations, academic and research institutes, religious organizations, and the media. The text specifies that improvements are necessary at all levels if implementation is to be successful. Institutions need strong, clear mandates as well as adequate resources to translate the provisions in the *PFA* into concrete actions. A gender perspective must be integrated throughout all their policies, programs, and operations. Women need to be recruited and promoted so as to achieve gender balance, especially at the highest levels of decision making. Mechanisms are needed to ensure accountability and to monitor compliance with the provisions in the *PFA*.

As discussed in Chapter 5 of this book, states held highly divergent positions on the scope of the mandates for the international bodies charged specifically with advancing women and on the level of resources to be allocated to these bodies. When the conference began, brackets remained around the provisions for the UN Commission on the Status of Women and its secretariat, the Division for the Advancement of Women, the UN Development Fund for Women, the International Research and Training Institute for the Advancement of Women, and the UN Committee on the Elimination of Discrimination Against Women. Canadian negotiators played lead roles in ensuring that the *PFA* provisions strengthened rather than weakened the UN bodies dedicated to advancing women, since these bodies would be in the forefront in advocating the implementation of the *PFA* and monitoring compliance with its provisions. The text calls for the strengthening of the CSW's mandate. Furthermore, it recommends that both financial and personnel resources be reallocated from within the regular UN budget to ensure that the CSW, the Division for the Advancement of Women, and the Committee on the Elimination of Discrimination Against Women have the means necessary to carry out their respective mandates. Both the UN Development Fund for Women and the International Research and Training Institute for the Advancement of Women were urged to review and revise their work programs to ensure the implementation of the *PFA* provisions pertaining to their respective mandates.

As the chief administrative officer of the UN, the secretary-general is allocated responsibility for mainstreaming a gender perspective throughout the UN and for overseeing the implementation of the *PFA*.[61] The secretary-general is also asked to create a high-level post within his or her office to provide advice on gender issues and to help ensure that the *PFA* provisions are implemented throughout the UN system.[62] While some states had hoped for the establishment of a new position, the text specified that the post is to be created using existing financial and personnel resources.

A further focus of debate was a proposal for designating the Fourth World Conference on Women a "Conference of Commitment," which Australia had made at the 1995 New York Preparatory Meetings. The proposal, which called on states to explain in writing their plans for implementing the *PFA*, went to Beijing in brackets. Canada opposed the idea of written commitments on the grounds that states should implement the *PFA* in its entirety rather than merely focusing on a specific set of commitments.[63] In the end, the wording in Chapter 5 of the *PFA* is considerably diluted from that of Australia's original proposal, and it merely notes that "States and the international community are encouraged to respond to this challenge [implementing the *PFA*] by making commitments for action. As part of the process, many states have made commitments for action as reflected, *inter alia*, in their national statements."[64] Australia's original proposals for documenting each government's specific commitments in an annex to the conference report was not incorporated. The text did not provide any provisions for monitoring compliance. However, the NGO community, which strongly endorsed Australia's proposal, took it upon themselves to document and publicize the commitments made in plenary speeches. The commitments were also summarized by the Secretariat of the Fourth World Conference on Women. In the end, some eighty states – less than half the countries participating at the Beijing conference – had pledged to undertake specific activities and to devote resources to ensure the implementation of the *PFA*.[65] Consistent with Canada's position on a "Conference of

Commitment," Sheila Finestone, secretary of state for the status of women, did not announce any new plans or resources to ensure the implementation of the *PFA*. When questioned about the absence of such commitments in her speech, Finestone responded, "The gender-equality program [*Setting the Stage for the Next Century: The Federal Plan for Gender Equality*] is a very significant accomplishment. I consider that quite sufficient."[66]

There are two ways of viewing Canada's position on commitments. On the one hand, it could indeed be motivated by a desire to see the whole *PFA* – rather than select provisions – implemented. On the other hand, it could be seen as a way of avoiding commitments. By its own record of progress in implementing the *PFA,* the government will indicate which view has greatest validity. For the sake of Canadian women, as well as those affected by Canada's actions and policies in other parts of the world, it is to be hoped that the first view is correct: that Canada did not make specific commitments because it intends to implement the entire text. The decision not to allocate additional resources accorded with Canada's preferences, as did the provisions to strengthen the institutional arrangements, generally, and the UN bodies dedication to the advancement of women, in particular.

The sixth and final chapter of the *PFA* addresses "financial arrangements." Negotiations on these provisions had been largely completed before the Beijing conference; relatively little text remained in brackets. Chapter 6 identifies inadequate allocations of financial and human resources as being major reasons for the slow progress made in advancing women around the world and in implementing the Nairobi *Forward-looking Strategies for the Advancement of Women*. There is considerable overlap between Chapter 5 (institutional arrangements) and Chapter 6 (financial arrangements). Both discuss the need for effective institutional arrangements to promote and monitor the implementation of the *PFA* and to oversee the mainstreaming of a gender perspective at the national, regional, and international levels, though such recommendations are dealt with in greater depth in Chapter 5. Likewise, the need to allocate adequate financial and human resources is recognized in both chapters, though the breadth and depth of the discussion is greater in Chapter 6. The latter recognizes the special requirements necessary to implement the *PFA* in Southern countries, where inadequate resources are likely to cripple efforts to achieve the objectives outlines in the *PFA*. Northern countries are requested to meet the 7 percent target for official development assistance that has been agreed to internationally, and institutions at the subregional, regional, and international levels are asked to mobilize funds to facilitate the implementation of the *PFA*.

Conclusion

How one evaluates the *PFA* depends on one's own values and priorities. As Rhonda Ferderber commented, how one assesses the outcome "all depends on one's focus: does one see the cup being half full or does one perceive it to be half empty?" For the conservative forces, much in the *PFA* is unpalatable. This view is reflected in the number of reservations registered by the Holy See and its allies and the fundamentalist Islamic countries, particularly in the areas pertaining to sexual and reproductive rights.[67] In contrast, the *Beijing Declaration* and *PFA* go a long way towards meeting many – though not all – of Canada's negotiating objectives. After comparing the language in the *Beijing Declaration* and *PFA* with Canada's stated objectives, one would have to conclude that Canada had been very successful in the negotiations. Of course, the objectives were expressed in generalities – as is the norm in instructions to Canadian delegations – which makes it hard to measure degrees of success. It is thus necessary to supplement textual analysis with the assessments of those who actually represented Canada in Beijing. While no one viewed the documents as perfect, all the government negotiators interviewed were pleased with the very considerable progress that had been made in spite of some stiff opposition and serious logistical trials. The advancement of women is always a particularly difficult endeavour: "women's rights, because they connect so basically to cultures, customs, property and the power structure itself, have to be one of the most frustrating areas for seeking world-wide commitments."[68] Yet not only was progress made but the preconference hopes and expectations of government officials were exceeded. As one Canadian negotiator comments, "I am amazed that we achieved as much as we did. We made progress on every one of our priorities. This is very unusual."[69] Canada had sought to build on the gains made at previous world conferences. The *PFA* reinforced and went beyond the language agreed to at the 1993 Vienna Conference on Human Rights, the 1994 Cairo Conference on Population and Development, and the Copenhagen Summit for Social Development.[70] Valerie Raymond describes the *PFA* as "the strongest ever international agreement on women's equality."[71]

Government officials viewed the outcome in highly positive terms, both because Canada's macro-level, and most of its micro-level, objectives were reflected in the *Beijing Declaration* and *PFA* and because its own negotiators played major leadership roles in facilitating their achievement, particularly in the areas of violence, women's human rights, reproductive rights, and unpaid work.[72]

The *PFA* contains advances for women in each of the twelve critical areas of concern. In some areas, new precedents were set, while in others, previous commitments were extended and strengthened. Yet, as the conference ended, key questions were raised in many quarters. What difference will the *Beijing Declaration* and *PFA* make to the lives of women around the globe? What will change as a result of the conference and the documents it adopted? Clearly, the answers to these questions will depend first and foremost on the political will of state governments to live up to the commitments they made in Beijing. Successful implementation will also depend on the work of private and public bodies at the international, regional, subregional, national, subnational, and local levels. On the last day of the Beijing meetings, Gertrude Mongella, secretary-general of the conference, declared: "The Fourth World Conference on Women is concluded, but the real work of transforming words into action is only now beginning. Let the spirit of organization and goal-setting which marked the preparatory phase of this Conference become the energy to propel implementation. Let the diversities of women now be channelled into making women indeed, 'the greatest multipliers of prosperity' rather than the 'greatest victims of poverty.'"[73] The *PFA* serves as a basis for dialogue within government circles, between governments and NGOs, and between governments and UN agencies. It can be cited by government officials working to advance women in their interdepartmental negotiations with other colleagues. It also provides standards by which a government's record can be measured and criticized: "It is not legally binding on nations but can be used as a good yardstick to measure, prod or rap the knuckles of government as required."[74] Within Canada, the government's commitment to the *PFA* can be cited as an important reason for not allowing roll-backs of policies and programs designed to advance women. The commitments outlined in the *PFA* can also be used to keep the government focused on critical, concrete policies because the text itself deals with tangible objectives and specific strategies for their attainment. The networks among Canadian NGOs, generally, and women's groups, in particular, expanded considerably during the Beijing process. For many, it was a valuable learning experience that has left them much better positioned to monitor the government's progress in implementing the provisions of the *PFA* and to press for greater compliance. After the Beijing conference, the CBFC produced a "Follow-up Guide" to assist groups and individuals in understanding the key provisions in each of the *PFA's* twelve critical areas of concern, to provide an assessment of Canada's performance in each area, and to provide strategies to ensure implementation of these key *PFA* provisions through working within the local community as well as through lobbying federal and provincial officials.[75] The 184-page book is clear, well organized, and user-friendly. While not an ideal document, the *PFA* does contain a lot of valuable and progressive language that can serve as a useful tool for those inside and outside government who are seeking to advance the status of women.

8
Building on the Past, Looking to the Future

Synopsis of the Case

The book began with two primary objectives. It sought to examine the interaction among Canadian government actors, both in Ottawa and on the Canadian delegations, in the development of Canada's positions and strategies for the Beijing Fourth World Conference on Women and the preparatory negotiations leading up to it. It also sought to explore the participation of Canadian NGOs in the government-sponsored mechanisms and at the international negotiations in order to assess their contributions and the extent to which they were able to exert influence in the foreign policy-making process. To set the stage for the case study, Chapter 2 provides an overview of developments and preparations leading up to the Fourth World Conference on Women, all of which influenced the tenor of Beijing negotiations and the breadth and depth of the documents adopted at the conference. It begins with overviews of the three preceding UN conferences on women and notes some of the major developments and trends that were realized during the Decade for Women. Since the path from the Third World Conference on Women to the Fourth World Conference on Women was not a straight trajectory, brief consideration is given to the conferences and summits convened by the UN in the 1990s, which significantly advanced the international language of women's rights. The remainder of the chapter focuses on the mandate of the Beijing Conference on Women and the process by which the *PFA* was drafted within the UN secretariat and negotiated in three key sets of preparatory meetings: the five regional conferences convened in 1994 by the UN's Regional Economic Commissions; the spring 1995 session of the CSW; and the informal consultations convened by the CSW in the summer of 1995. From this discussion, it is clear that the Beijing conference was very much part of an ongoing process that had begun some twenty years earlier to define women's rights and to improve the status of women around the globe. Understanding the international dimensions of the Beijing process and the historical framework in which it took place is critical to understanding the conference and the participation of Canadians – both government actors and NGO representatives. The importance of the external environment is explored in a separate section later in this chapter.

Having considered some of the major international developments and parameters in Chapter 2, the subsequent two chapters turn their attention to activities within Canada. Chapter 3 examines the interaction among federal government actors in Ottawa in the formulation of Canada's policies and strategies. The decision-making process within federal government circles functioned smoothly and, in contrast to the tenets of the governmental politics approach, its primary characteristics were cooperation and collaboration rather than conflict and competition. The governmental politics approach sees public policy resulting from a bargaining process in which diverse government actors, each with their own particular set of priorities to advance, compete to determine outcomes.[1] The approach, developed and popularized by Graham Allison, challenges the traditional concept of public policies emanating from a rational monolithic entity: the government. According to the approach, it is necessary to identify the relevant government actors and their respective goals, which are determined primarily by the mandates of their departments and agencies; to assess their relative bargaining resources and skills; and to understand the nature of the bargaining process and the influence it exerts over policy outcomes. While Allison writes about American foreign policy, he claims that his model can also be applied to the study of other national governments. In the Canadian context, Kim Richard Nossal took up the challenge, and he concludes that the bureaucratic politics model is "both useful and applicable."[2] Although Nossal finds the model to be applicable, he judges the Canadian process to be less conflict ridden and more prone to "friendly competition" than the American system and concludes that the dominant outcome of the Canadian system is compromise.[3] Governmental politics, nonetheless, continues to feature prominently in many cases involving Canadian foreign policy. During Canada's "fish war" with Spain, tensions arose between the Department of Fisheries and Oceans, on one hand, and the Department of Foreign Affairs and International Trade, on the other, over which department would assume the lead and over which approach should be used – the "quiet diplomacy" advocated by DFAIT or the more aggressive style taken by the Department of Fisheries and Oceans.[4] Interdepartmental wranglings – this time primarily involving the Department of the Environment and National Resources Canada – were also very much in evidence when positions for 1997 Kyoto negotiations for a legally binding protocol to reduce greenhouse gas emissions were being determined.[5] Governmental politics also featured prominently during the campaign to ban antipersonnel land mines as the Department of National Defence and the Department of Foreign Affairs and International Trade each wrestled to control the file and assert primary leadership.[6]

Governmental politics in the Canadian foreign policy-making process are generally viewed as being less competitive and to involve less "pulling and hauling" than is thought to be present in the American system. Yet, even taking this difference into consideration, the case of Canada and the Beijing Conference on Women involved particularly little intragovernmental competition to determine policies and strategies. The most important explanation for this degree of collegiality was that government policies had already been established to deal with all the issues in the *PFA*; there was an existing framework and set of policies to guide the development of positions and strategies for the Beijing process. Any major disagreements that had occurred had been dealt with years earlier, before cabinet had formally adopted its policies. By the time preparations for the Beijing conference were underway, there was a high degree of consensus among Canada's public servants, who were the ones who drafted Canada's positions and strategies for Beijing. Collegiality was also aided by the early and effective organization of the interdepartmental negotiations. When problems of timing occurred, they were usually externally generated, such as the late arrival of the draft *PFA* in January 1995. Finally, the calibre of the key Canadian public servants involved in this case and the continuity in their participation further facilitated smooth policy making. They had extensive experience with the issues and, in most cases, with UN negotiations. They understood the precedents that had been set at previous conferences and summits and the parameters within which they had to operate both within Canada and at the international negotiations.

The discussion in Chapter 3 of government politics focuses briefly on the provinces and territories, which frequently play important roles internationally and in the Canadian foreign policy-making process.[7] Such was not the case in this study. Working with a pre-existing framework of regular consultations, federal government officials kept their provincial and territorial counterparts informed of developments relating to the Beijing Conference on Women and solicited their response. Yet the provincial and territorial officials responsible for the status of women in their respective jurisdictions were, for the most part, minor players in the Beijing process. Their resources were minimal, and their overall priorities were domestic rather than international matters. Furthermore, the positions being formulated in Ottawa were consistent with Canada's policies and the provincial and territorial governments generally agreed with the direction and substance of federal policies on women. Yet, in spite of their relatively minimal involvement in the Beijing process, provincial and territorial officials were able to cite the UN Fourth World Conference on Women as justification for pressuring their respective governments to take further measures to advance women, just as their federal counterparts had used the conference as leverage to get cabinet approval for a new policy mandating the use of gender-based analysis in the development of Canadian policies.

The discussion in Chapter Three of governmental officials is followed by an examination in Chapter 4 of another set of Canadian actors who sought to influence Canada's positions on the *PFA*: the NGOs. Here, the discussion focuses on the principal channels within Canada for facilitating NGO input into the Canadian foreign policy-making process: the Canadian Beijing Facilitating Committee and the Canadian Preparatory Committee. These government-sponsored mechanisms served as efficient two-way conduits for communication between the government and the attentive public in Canada. Government support was critical to the participation of large numbers of geographically dispersed women's groups in the development of the composite NGO texts. These texts, in turn, assisted the Canadian NGOs in their lobbying efforts at home and at the international meetings, and facilitated their leadership in the international NGO meetings. On the other hand, the mechanisms did not result in the NGOs exerting significant influence over Canada's positions.

After exploring the policy-making process within Canada in terms of governmental politics in Chapter 3 and NGO involvement in Chapter 4, the focus switches to the international arena in Chapter 5. From this discussion, it is clear that Canadian delegations not only were active but also assumed key leadership roles at the preparatory negotiations (the 1994 Vienna Regional Meetings for Europe and North America; the 1995 New York Preparatory Meetings; and the informal consultations convened in the summer of 1995) and at the Fourth World Conference on Women. Canadian negotiators were asked to chair contact groups struck to tackle some of the toughest, most controversial issues, and they were prominent in the debates and in JUSCANZ, all of which resulted in noteworthy contributions.

In keeping with standard practice, the composition of the Canadian delegation remained the prerogative of the minister of foreign affairs. While some would have liked to have had a somewhat larger contingent of government negotiators in order to have had the added expertise and the additional human resources to handle the extremely rigorous workload of the negotiators, there is no doubt that those selected were experienced, dedicated, and recognized experts in their respective issue areas. As a result, they achieved high levels of success in achieving their negotiating objectives and made major contributions to the negotiations. The assessment of the selection of the nongovernmental observers produced more mixed results. Budgetary considerations were evident throughout. At the preparatory negotiations, Canada deserves full credit for including one, and in the case of the 1995 New York meetings, two, nongovernmental observers on its delegations when so very few other states did so. Furthermore, the individual selected to attend the preparatory meetings was appointed to the delegation on the recommendation of the CBFC, and she remained committed to facilitating the work of this constituency. On the other hand, one person could not possibly have the expertise necessary to evaluate developments in twelve issues areas nor could she cover all the negotiations; there are physical limitations to being in all places at all times. There was an expectation in Vienna and New York that the nongovernmental observer appointed on the recommendation of the CBFC would serve as a liaison between the NGO community and the Canadian delegation. Such expectations were far less apparent in the selection of nongovernmental observers for the Canadian delegation to the Fourth World Conference on Women, to which individuals rather than representatives of NGOs were appointed. The minister of foreign affairs always selects nongovernmental observers who are considered likely to further the objectives of the Canadian government. These objectives are not necessarily the same as those of the NGO community. In some cases, however, the government may consider it most expedient to include activists from the NGO community because of their expertise and, at times, in order to placate or co-opt the NGO community.

In the case of the Canadian delegation to the Beijing conference, the credentials of all the nongovernmental observers were excellent; they all had proven track records of advancing women. Together they represented a wide diversity of Canadian society, including English-speaking Canadians, French-speaking Canadians from Quebec and other parts of Canada, women of colour, Aboriginal women, and the trade union movement. Collectively they embodied a great deal of expertise relevant to the issues under negotiation. Through their discussions with a wide range of participants at the intergovernmental meetings, as well as with those attending the NGO forum, they contributed useful intelligence to the delegation. A few actively followed specific sets of negotiations and provided valuable assistance to the Canadian negotiators. Some, particularly those lacking UN experience, felt frustrated by the problems they faced in finding meaningful roles for themselves. There were, moreover, differences of opinion on the relationship that should exist between the nongovernmental observers and the Canadian NGO community. Many in the latter expected those who had been fortunate enough to have the government pay their way to the conference and to have direct access to delegation meetings to share some of the benefits derived from having access to closed negotiations and direct contact with key government negotiators. They expected systematic contact with the nongovernmental observers that was aimed at facilitating the work of the NGOs. In contrast, the Canadian government expected the nongovernmental observers to give their primary loyalty to supporting its delegation's efforts to advance official positions.[8] Some government officials went as far as to consider it a conflict of interest for nongovernmental observers to be privately briefing NGO representatives. Whether because of a concern over conflict of interest, a lack of previously established relations with the particular NGOs represented in Beijing, inexperience with UN negotiations, or disinterest, very few nongovernmental observers on the Canadian delegation maintained systematic ongoing working relationships with Canadian NGOs. This development has relevance for the "democratization" of Canadian foreign policy, discussed later in the chapter.

The focus on the international level is maintained in Chapter 6, which examines the activities and contributions of Canadian NGOs at the preparatory meetings as well as at the Fourth World Conference on Women and the NGO forum. It begins with the 1994 Vienna Regional Meetings and the 1995 New York Preparatory Meetings, which were extremely significant venues for the NGOs because of the importance of seeking input and of establishing positions and lobbying strategies early in the process. The discussion of the Fourth World Conference on Women examines the key determinants of NGO access to the negotiations and their contributions. The chapter concludes with a look at the NGO forum, where Canadian NGOs orchestrated positions for the conference and, most importantly, where they forged and further developed contacts and networks that will facilitate cooperation with NGOs from other parts of the world.

A great deal of the governmental and NGO activity throughout the Beijing process focused on influencing the scope and substance of the *PFA*. It is, therefore, fitting that Chapter 7 is devoted to assessing the extent to which Canada was successful in achieving its stated objectives pertaining to the *PFA*. From this discussion, it is clear that Canada realized its objectives in all its areas of priority. This is not to say that Canada got everything it wanted. It was, for example, unsuccessful in keeping sexual orientation in the diversity clause.

The responses of Canadian NGOs to the *PFA* were mixed.[9] Overall, feminist groups considered the *PFA* to have advanced women, though in several cases they did not consider it to have gone nearly far enough. For example, the NAC criticized the text for failing to deal with either the negative impact which globalizing is having on women or the systematic root causes of poverty. VOW considered the peace provisions pertaining to disarmament – one of its highest priorities – weak. Conservative groups opposed to the feminist agenda, such as REAL Women, opposed the overall direction of the *PFA* as well as many of its specific provisions, especially those pertaining to sexual and reproductive rights and the use of gender-based analysis, which pervades the text. Overall, however, there has been a keen recognition among Canadian NGOs, in general, and women's groups, in particular, that the *Beijing Declaration* and *PFA* not only contain language to move the agenda ahead in each of the twelve areas of critical concern but also are valuable tools in their crusades. The importance of the *PFA* as a lobbying tool has been recognized by Canadian NGOs, including the CBFC, VOW, and even the NAC, which had issued several highly critical critiques of the document right after the conference.[10] Even government officials involved with the Beijing process have recommended that NGOs use the *PFA* to hold the Canadian government responsible to the commitments it made in Beijing.[11] Canadian NGOs actively participated in the 2000 review of progress made towards the implementation of the *PFA*, and they continue to assess the government's performance vis-à-vis the strategies outlined in the *PFA*.

Having provided an overview of the case, it is now time to relate its findings to two themes in the literature on Canadian foreign policy making. The first concerns the parameters set by the external environment, whereas the second pertains to debates about the democratization of Canadian foreign policy.

External Parameters

A great deal of academic attention has been devoted to assessing Canada's place in the world and the implications of this status for Canadian foreign policy. The literature includes broad analyses of the evolving international environment and its implications for Canadian foreign policy.[12] The role and influence of the external environment have also been examined in light of specific case studies.[13] Over the past three decades, Canada's status in the international community of states and the foreign policy that it charts for itself have been subjects of lengthy debate.[14] Some argue that Canada is a principal power,[15] whereas others contend that Canada is a middle power,[16] and still others see Canada as a satellite of the United States.[17] Debating the respective merits of these broad, competing perspectives is beyond the scope of this work. It may, nonetheless, present empirical evidence of interest to those who do continue to engage in this debate. The case discusses Canada's involvement with an issue area that is definitely a low priority on its foreign policy agenda, whereas most of the assessment of Canada as a principal power, middle power, and satellite has focused on major foreign policy priorities: issues of military security and issues of trade and economics.

The literature on Canadian foreign policy and the external environment is rich and diverse. Clearly, views vary considerably over Canada's status in the international arena, over the role it can and should play in international politics, and over the degree to which its traditional focus on multilateralism and middle power diplomacy is well founded.[18] Yet, there is general agreement that the external environment constitutes a major determinant of Canada's foreign policies and that it sets the parameters within which Canadian decision makers have to operate.

In the case of Canada and the Beijing Conference on Women, the external environment and the actions of other states and UN bodies clearly set the parameters within which Canadians had to operate. The conference did not occur in a vacuum. Instead, it was convened to accelerate progress in the advancement of women, building on the work of preceding conferences and summits. Being part of an ongoing process was both an historic fact and a mindset. Government officials and NGO representatives were well aware of being part of a process. While each had objectives specific to the conference, the conference was not seen as an end in itself. In keeping with standard UN procedures for preparing for world conferences and summits, the key negotiating documents were drafted by UN public servants, in this case by those in the Secretariat of the Fourth World Conference on Women. The international community of states did have opportunities at the regional preparatory meetings as well as at the early CSW discussions of the conference to influence the breadth of issues addressed, the forms of their treatment, and the depth of their coverage. Yet, as is evident in all international venues, the negotiations in this case were not a level playing field in which all countries had equal opportunities to exert influence. There were two major negotiating blocs: the European Union and the Group of Seventy-Seven. The United States, as usual, found it easier to have its voice heard than did the lesser powers. But even a superpower cannot dictate policy. And if a superpower is unable to determine outcomes, it is clear that a much smaller power, such as Canada, will not be able to impose its will. At the preparatory meetings and at the Beijing conference, Canada was neither a superpower that could command the attention of the international community nor was it a member of either of the major negotiating blocs. Canadian negotiators had to operate within relatively narrow parameters set by the nature of the UN conference process and by the actions of the major states and blocs of states.

Canada's work as an individual country and as a member of JUSCANZ to broker compromises acceptable to the two key negotiating blocs exemplified middle-power diplomacy. Clearly, the interests of world order are best served when all countries are able to agree to norms by consensus rather than when blocs are polarized. The case does not, however, provide a good test of the extent to which Canadian foreign policy in this area is independent of (or dependent on) that of the United States, both because the positions of the two countries were fairly similar on a significant number of issues and, most importantly, because human rights, in general, and women's rights, in particular, are simply not high-enough priorities in foreign policy making to warrant Canadian concerns about deviating from US wishes. Even if Canada had taken the lead on a provision or set of provisions in face of strong US opposition, the issue would not have been important enough in the broader context of foreign policy making to have warranted any serious US retaliation. In contrast, the United States would react vehemently if Canada decided to renege on some of the NAFTA provisions.

As time went on, the parameters within which all states had to operate became increasingly narrow. The draft document that became the *PFA* was made available only shortly before the 1995 New York Preparatory Meetings. States did not, therefore, come to the meetings with a *tabula rasa;* quite to the contrary, the process required them to respond to the provisions of a draft document and to do so in short order. Early in the 1995 New York Preparatory Meetings, states registered their concerns about the text. The additions, deletions, and amendments they proposed were placed in the text in square brackets. Thereafter, the scope of the negotiations was severely limited, being confined to the removal of the square brackets. Text without square brackets was considered to reflect consensus and could not be reopened. Hence, states had to shift their priorities as the negotiations and the documents evolved. Once consensus had been reached on an issue, it no longer received attention. In contrast, issues for which there remained large sections of highly contested text either became, or continued to be, focal points commanding attention. This reality explains why health and human rights remained such key areas of concern following the 1995 New York Preparatory Meetings.

Context and timing also influenced the tenor and outcome of the international negotiations. For example, the New York Preparatory Meetings followed closely the Copenhagen Summit for Social Development. As a result, many delegates arrived in New York tired, and the Group of Seventy-Seven had not had time between Copenhagen and New York to work out consolidated positions on many of the contentious provisions in the *PFA*. Consequently, negotiating sessions had to be postponed while the Group of Seventy-Seven worked out its positions, which, in turn, slowed down progress.

The decision to hold the conference in China had many implications. Much of the early CSW meetings (i.e., pre-March 1995) were preoccupied with negotiations with China over the terms and conditions of holding the conference and, most especially, the NGO forum, on Chinese soil.[19] Considerable time and energy went into issues of visas, concerns about security, and the location of the NGO forum. Interaction between the forum and the intergovernmental conference was severely curtailed by the geographic isolation of the former from the latter. There were also problems of inadequate infrastructure. In short, the choice of location posed logistical problems for all the participants.

The external environment not only set the parameters within which Canadian decision makers had to establish Canada's positions, priorities, and strategies in this case but also offered opportunities to advance broader policy objectives. Federal public servants were able to use the Beijing conference as a lever for developing new policies and taking on new activities within Canada, as exemplified by their success in getting cabinet approval for *Setting the Stage for the Next Century: The Federal Plan for Gender Equality.*[20] In addition, the Beijing process necessitated in-depth, ongoing cooperation and collaboration among various units within the federal government concerned with advancing women. The further development and consolidation of such collaborative relations strengthened the base from which to mount future joint efforts to get the government, as a whole, to be more progressive on women's issues.

The international environment clearly set the parameters within which Canadians had to operate and greatly influenced the extent to which they were able to realize their objectives. Yet, there are important facets of the case that the international environment cannot fully explain: Canada's choice of its specific positions, priorities, and strategies, and the quality and the quantity of leadership provided by the Canadian negotiators. It is neither feasible nor credible for a delegation to push its position on every item under negotiation. Priorities need to be chosen carefully. Canada's positions and priorities were determined in Ottawa – albeit largely in response to an established text. Nonetheless, the substance of the response needed to be consistent with existing Canadian policies. Canadian negotiators cannot make proposals at international meetings that go beyond Canadian legislation. On the other hand, in areas where Canada's laws were more advanced than those of other countries, it was logical to see its negotiators taking lead roles. It was, for instance, not surprising that Canada took the lead to ensure that gender-based persecution was included in the *PFA* as grounds for refugee status, since this was an area where its legislation offered more protection to women refugees than did that of any other country.[21] Thus, Canadian decision makers had to establish Canada's policies, priorities, and strategies within the parameters set by the external environment and within the context of existing Canadian policies.

Canada's positions and strategies were worked out interdepartmentally by federal public servants and approved by the minister of foreign affairs and the secretary of state for the status of women. Government officials worked hard before the negotiations not only developing their positions in response to the provisions in the UN text but also working out strategies to maximize their influence. These preparations stood them in good stead for the negotiations, as exemplified by earlier discussions of their successes as chairs of contact groups and as effective negotiators. Canada's influence at the negotiations was not the result of its extensive power capabilities in a range of fields; instead, it stemmed from the ability of its negotiators to persuade others of the merits of their positions, to build coalitions in support of their negotiating objectives, and, at times, to bridge the gap between competing perspectives, particularly those of the European Union and the Group of Seventy-Seven. The Canadian negotiators exemplified good entrepreneurial leadership.[22] Effective entrepreneurial leadership does not depend on the structural power of a delegate's state, but it does require sound judgment, a keen sense of timing, the capacity to reformulate provisions so as to be generally acceptable, the use of conciliatory language, the ability to inspire confidence in others, and tireless efforts to persuade. The Canadian negotiators knew the issues well and demonstrated the elements of effective entrepreneurial leadership: good timing, astute diplomacy, and sheer hard work.

The domestic environment also helped set the context within which Canadian decision makers had to operate. Preparations for the Fourth World Conference on Women came at a time of major cost-cutting, accompanied by extensive reviews of programs and projects within both the federal and the provincial and territorial governments. As a result, government officials had to adjust to, as well as participate in, major restructuring within government, while at the same time carrying out the preparatory work for the Fourth World Conference on Women. A period in which programs and staff are being cut and government units are being restructured is not the most stable environment in which to develop policies. Cuts in government spending meant that those responsible for preparing for the conference were short-staffed. The ministerial decision not to allocate additional funds for conference preparations left the public servants scrambling to find ways of using existing funds to carry out the additional responsibilities, which included producing and disseminating information about the conference to a far-flung but extensive attentive public. Cuts also limited the funds available for the government-sponsored mechanisms. Furthermore, on the eve of the Copenhagen Summit for Social Development, which in turn was convened just before the 1995 New York Preparatory Meetings, the Canadian government announced massive cuts to the overall funding of NGOs. These cuts drastically hit at the core of many NGOs' operating budgets, curtailing their activities and the extent to which they could contemplate sending delegates to the New York Preparatory Meetings, let alone to China to attend the Fourth World Conference on Women. One of the most serious casualties of the cuts was the Canadian Advisory Council on the Status of Women, whose mandate included advising the Canadian government on policies and programs pertaining to women; monitoring and criticizing government performance in this area; undertaking, commissioning, and publicizing research on issues affecting women; and advising the government on emerging trends. Before being disbanded, the Canadian Advisory Council on the Status of Women had been providing the government with its analysis of the *PFA*.[23] Its demise meant that one well-positioned watchdog was no longer here to monitor the government's compliance with the commitments it made in Beijing.

The Beijing Conference on Women came at the end of a long string of UN conferences. This was both a blessing and a curse. It was advantageous in the sense that these conferences had tended to involve many of the same people and so these people were knowledgeable about the issues, understood conference procedures, and had experience working together on many of the issues in the *PFA*. In addition, mechanisms for preparing for conferences were well established and it was simply a case of plugging the specific actors and issues into an existing modus operandi. On the other hand, the fact that the conferences involved many of the same government officers also meant that these individuals were already suffering from "conference fatigue" by the time preparations for the Beijing conference began.[24] It was, therefore, more difficult to get attention for yet another conference.

The international environment also set the parameters within which Canadian NGOs had to operate. UN regulations and the decisions of its member states determined which groups could attend the intergovernmental negotiations and to which negotiations they were allowed access. The nature and format of UN negotiations also significantly influenced the format of NGO activities and type of lobbying strategies that were most likely to succeed. Like states, NGOs had to respond – sometimes at very short notice – to UN-generated documents. The nature of UN negotiations determined that the NGOs most likely to exert influence were those which understood the rules, procedures, and character of such meetings, had keen senses of timing and the ability to recognize potentially fertile opportunities for lobbying, understood UN language and the relevant precedents established in a particular issue area, and were capable of conducting line-by-line analysis and of proposing specific wording that would both reflect their concerns and be generally acceptable to the international community of states. In short, the structure, rules, procedures, and nature of the negotiations were significant determinants of which groups succeeded in having their concerns reflected in the conference documents and which groups did not.

Democratizing the Canadian Foreign Policy-Making Process?
As discussed in Chapter 1, considerable academic attention has been devoted in recent years to assessing the government's efforts to implement its promise to democratize the Canadian foreign policy-making process. The discussion below focuses on three questions:

- Which NGOs participated in the government-sponsored mechanisms?
- Did the government-supported mechanisms facilitate meaningful participation?
- Whose interests were served by the government-sponsored mechanisms?

Each of these questions is addressed individually below.

Which NGOs Participated in the Government-sponsored Mechanisms?
The selection of the CBFC's membership was remarkably democratic. Letters were sent to 2,000 women's groups across the country soliciting nominations. From these nominations, national women's groups elected six representatives of national groups, provincial and regional groups elected six representatives from their ranks, and groups representing specific constituencies (e.g., indigenous women, visible minorities, lesbians, immigrant women) elected eight representatives. The process was more democratic than that used for selecting members of the NGO coordinating committees established for the 1995 Copenhagen Summit for Social Development and the 1993 Vienna Conference on Human Rights, where lead groups in the field began the process and gravitated into the leadership positions.

The NGOs involved in the Beijing process represented large and diverse sectors of the attentive public. They included anglophone groups and francophone groups from Quebec and other parts of the country. Their numbers included women's groups, indigenous groups, peace groups, human rights groups, development groups, and environmental groups, as well as groups devoted to promoting the rights of lesbians, children, the disabled, women of colour, and seniors. In ideological terms, the vast majority of the participants were feminist in their orientation. Several prominent right-wing groups, including REAL Women, contacted government officials on numerous occasions and were on the CBFC distribution list. It is not surprising, however, that they did not exercise leadership roles in the government-sponsored mechanisms, since the CBFC membership was elected and the right-wing groups made up a very small minority of those participating. Overall, the NGOs involved in the Beijing process represented large and diverse sectors of the counterconsensus. Government efforts to facilitate this degree of participation clearly moved the process along the continuum towards democratization.[25] The NGOs had valuable insights to contribute: their voices needed to be heard and taken seriously. Yet, the question still remains: Did the Canadian foreign policy-making process allow them meaningful participation? As Sandra Whitworth states, "democracy is not just a process, it is also an outcome."[26]

**Did the Government-supported Mechanisms Facilitate
Meaningful Participation?**
Sandra Whitworth's study of the Special Joint Committee Reviewing Canadian Foreign Policy illustrates how participation cannot be equated with influence, since although diverse women's groups participated in the consultations, their concerns were not reflected to any appreciable extent in the committee's work: "While women's organizations were invited to submit briefs and appear before the Special Joint Committee, their views were largely ignored in the final report."[27] These findings further confirm the

pervasive view in the literature on Canadian foreign policy making: the dominant Canadian political culture may set broad parameters within which government officials have to operate, but the latter, nonetheless, enjoy a large degree of autonomy from civil society in the formulation and implementation of Canada's foreign policies.[28]

The question thus arises: Did the government-sponsored mechanisms facilitate NGO participation that affected policy outcomes? The answer in this case is a clear no: the members of the CBFC exerted very little influence over the direction and substance of Canada's positions. Neither the government officials nor the NGO representatives on the Canadian Preparatory Committee (CPC) thought NGOs had significantly influenced the substance of Canada's positions. There are several reasons for this lack of influence.

On the NGOs side, two factors undermined the effectiveness of their submissions to government: the timing and the format of the composite texts they submitted to government. The problem of timing was to a considerable extent externally generated, though it was clearly exacerbated by the lack of UN experience of most of key actors in the CBFC. The UN system itself militated against early preparations. Federal civil servants had been working on the issues in the *Platform for Action* for years and they were operating within guidelines set by established government policy. Their specific positions and strategies were worked out interdepartmentally before the NGOs even presented their composite texts. On the other hand, the CBFC failed to establish priorities early in the process or to develop a conceptual framework for assessing the evolving international texts. In every case, by the time NGOs had produced a composite text, the conference agenda and the government's objectives were already clearly established.

A second set of problems relate to the format of the NGO submissions to government. The problem was partly because of inadequate time, though inexperience was also a key factor. The first text the CBFC submitted to the government was described by an experienced NGO representative as a "higgledy-piggledy compilation." Yet, as time went on, the CBFC developed more effective methods of drafting composite NGO texts, and their documents became increasingly user-friendly. Although the CBFC did demonstrate a significant learning curve, it never achieved the desired goal of producing a concise, well-organized line-by-line analysis for key priorities in the *Platform for Action*. Many of NGO problems in producing effective composite texts stemmed from the inexperience of its key leaders. In contrast, the leaders of the NGO facilitating committees for the Copenhagen Summit for Social Development and the Vienna Conference on Human Rights had extensive international experience. UN negotiations are a world unto themselves. To conduct effective line-by-line analysis, one needs to know UN language, rules, procedures, and structures – the parameters within which government delegates and all participants must function. The CBFC was much more democratically constituted than were the NGO coordinating committees established for the Copenhagen Summit for Social Development and the Vienna Conference on Human Rights. However, the committees established for the latter two sets of meetings had more key members with extensive UN experience who were more effective in exerting influence in the policy-making process than was the CBFC.

Yet, even if the NGOs had had perfect timing and had presented their positions in a completely user-friendly format, there is still the question of whether government officials would have been receptive. As discussed earlier, the literature on Canadian foreign policy demonstrates that the Canadian government is fairly autonomous from civil society, in general, and the counterconsensus, in particular, in formulating foreign policy. It would be hard to argue that the government, as a whole, was particularly receptive to women's issues or to their well-being.

In sum, the government-sponsored mechanisms in our case fulfiled one, but only one, of the criteria for assessing democratization: facilitating the participation of a large and diverse range of groups and allowing the voice of the counterconsensus to be heard. Yet, if the interests of democratization were being only partially addressed, then whose interests were being served?

Whose Interests Were Served by the Government-sponsored Mechanisms?

Students of Canadian foreign policy have been sceptical of government efforts to democratize the policy-making process. There is widespread agreement that government-sponsored mechanisms to facilitate NGO participation do little to influence policy outcomes but that they are significant in serving the interests of the governing elite.[29] Kim Nossal describes stakeholder politics – the strategy of providing the stakeholders (the attentive public) with opportunities to participate – as "an excellent tool of political management for state officials. It ensures that those primarily affected by a policy area will have an opportunity to have their say, to comment on proposed policy changes, to register their objections or to offer their ideas. It thus not only protects state officials against future claims by stakeholders; it also binds the stakeholders more tightly to the policies eventually adopted."[30] Cranford Pratt has described government strategies for dealing with NGOs as "exercises in public relations, in the erosion of dissent, and in the co-option of dissenters," rather than as opportunities for meaningful dialogue in which NGOs can exert some influence.[31] Mark Neufeld argues that the very idea of democratizing the foreign policy-making process was appropriated by the government from the NGOs in the counterconsensus in order to co-opt the groups and their leaders.[32] Drawing on the work of Robert Cox, Neufeld argues that, to retain its hegemony, the ruling elite must, at times, co-opt its real critics (i.e., the leaders of key societal groups that oppose the overall direction and substance of its policies) by appropriating some of their "dangerous" ideas.[33] And, continues Neufeld, "in the Canadian case, the leaders to be co-opted were those active in the social movements which formed the core of the counter-consensus. And the 'dangerous idea' to be assimilated and domesticated was the conjoining of 'democracy and foreign policy.'"[34] Neufeld is, nevertheless, quick to point out that the NGOs' demands for democratization have been accommodated only in form, not in substance. For instance, the government was able to retain its hegemony throughout the hearings of the Special Joint Committee Reviewing Canadian Foreign Policy by carefully constructing the parameters within which they took place. It was the government that determined the timing and locations of the hearings, the list of groups invited to participate, the agenda, and the themes for discussion.[35] Sandra Whitworth agrees that the hearings exemplify techniques in political management and attempts to manufacture consent.[36] She concludes, however, that the government was not very effective in managing the views of women's groups, since the latter were largely ignored in the final report.[37] Women's groups, which make up an important component of the counterconsensus, were able to present their views, but these views were not acknowledged or represented to any appreciable extent in the outcome of the process.

When the question of whose interests were served is applied to this case, one would have to say that both NGOs and the government benefited from the arrangements. Government support of NGO participation was considerable. Within Canada, it included

- funding the CBFC to facilitate and coordinate the participation of NGOs
- providing funds to assist NGOs in preparing their positions
- establishing the CPC to facilitate consultations between the Interdepartmental Committee on the World Conference on Women and the NGO community
- disseminating information pertaining to the Fourth World Conference on Women, including comprehensive briefing packages for those attending the conference.

Government support for the NGOs attending the international negotiations included:

- funding NGO representatives to attend the 1994 Vienna Regional Meetings, 1995 New York Preparatory Meetings, and the Beijing Conference on Women

- providing substantial briefings for those attending the international meetings
- inviting nongovernmental observers on the Canadian delegations to the preparatory negotiations and the Fourth World Conference on Women.

Thus, Canadian NGOs were assisted in several important ways. First, the mechanisms ensured that important information was distributed to the attentive public on an ongoing basis. The CBFC produced an informative newsletter, *Onward to Beijing*, which, along with other relevant government and UN documents and briefing kits, was circulated to anyone who expressed an interest in being on its distribution list.

Second, the mechanisms promoted networking among a large number of diverse groups. They helped strengthen the linkages among women's groups sharing common goals and between women's groups and other members of the counterconsensus. In particular, the CPC brought together women's groups with other members of the broader counterconsensus, including labour, development groups, and human rights groups. Furthermore, government funding allowed Canadian groups to send representatives to attend the international negotiations, where they were able to forge and strengthen networks with NGOs from other countries, as well as with international NGOs.

Third, the mechanisms facilitated the formulation of joint positions and lobbying strategies. The CBFC oversaw the development of NGO composite texts, which in turn assisted them in presenting their priorities and positions to government officials at home and at the international negotiations, and facilitated assuming leadership roles in the international NGO caucuses. Without government funding, it would not have been possible for such geographically dispersed and diverse groups to have worked together to develop composite texts.

Fourth, the CPC provided a channel for presenting views directly to key government officials before each of the preparatory meetings and the Beijing conference. It guaranteed access – albeit on a somewhat limited basis – to those formulating Canada's positions.

Government support of NGO participation was not purely altruistic. It did much to enable the Canadian government to retain control of the process. Government dominance was obvious in the CPC – the principal channel for NGOs to convey their concerns and their critiques of the *PFA* to government officials. Government officials decided on the composition of the CPC, called and chaired its meetings, and set its agendas. As discussed in Chapter 4, the NGO representatives on the CPC expressed frustration at the way the meetings were structured, which left little time for substantial two-way discussions between them and the government officials about Canada's positions.

Having the ability to decide who would get what information when also constituted significant power resources for government officials. This is not to say that they generally withheld information. Quite to the contrary, they shared a great deal of information about the conference with the NGOs. Such sharing was highly beneficial to the NGOs, but it also addressed government objectives. Public interest in, and support for, the conference bolstered the importance and the legitimacy of the work being done within the Canadian government to prepare for it. Government officials were prompt in passing the draft conference document on to the NGOs. It was, after all, in the government's best interest to have the NGOs produce composite texts to serve as evidence of societal support for moving the agenda ahead. On the other hand, government officials did not hesitate to withhold information – particularly the substance of its negotiating positions at the 1995 New York Preparatory Meetings – when this tactic seemed most conducive to its interests. Government officials may have had good reasons for making these decisions but the fact remains that control over the distribution of vital information is an important trump card.

The political management referred to by Kim Nossal was also exemplified by the ways in which the government-sponsored mechanisms institutionalized participation, thereby determining which voices got central access to the policy-making process. Voices of dissension were not silenced, but they were frequently relegated to the sidelines. Likewise, the selection of nongovernmental observers to the Canadian delegation to Beijing reflected good political management. The visible presence of twelve women drawn from diverse segments of society enhanced the credibility of the Canadian delegation's claim to be speaking for Canadian women. Furthermore, the minister's decision to appoint individuals rather than representatives of specific women's groups muted internal criticism. Groups, such as the NAC, whose relations with government were more acrimonious than cooperative were not represented on the delegation.

In addition to serving as useful tools of political management, the government's provisions to facilitate NGO participation assisted the former in coping with their heavy workload. Having a CBFC to field inquiries and to distribute information reduced the amount of time government officials had to spend dealing directly with NGOs. Government officials in all the key departments received numerous queries from the attentive public, but many of these inquiries could be directed to the CBFC. Thus, governmental support for the NGOs clearly had some highly positive spin-offs for the government.

Assessing the extent to which co-option took place is more difficult. The vast majority of the groups involved agreed with the general direction of Canada's positions, so there was less need for co-option at the macro-level than would be the case when the NGOs are advocating a radically different direction to the one proposed by government. On the other hand, the NGOs did not hesitate to level criticisms in areas where they thought the Canadian government should be more proactive. For example, the VOW wanted the Canadian government to be a vigorous advocate for the inclusion of strong disarmament provisions in the *PFA*. The NAC demanded that the Canadian government pledge additional resources for women's advancement and exert pressure to have the *PFA* address the root causes of the structural inequalities inherent in capitalism. Participating in the CBFC and the CPC did not stop NGOs from criticizing Canada's stands. Madeleine Gilchrist, who had been centrally involved as a member of the CBFC and as a nongovernmental observer on Canada's delegations to the preparatory meetings, resigned from Canada's delegation to the Fourth World Conference on Women explicitly because she had found government officials to be insufficiently forthcoming in sharing information and insufficiently receptive to incorporating NGO recommendations into their official positions. She was clearly quite capable of criticizing a process in which she had been an active player. Yet as an overall trend, those leading the CBFC tended to be less critical, particularly in public, of government officials than were some of those less close to the centre. This trend may, however, have been more reflective of the nature of the relationship that already existed between CRIAW and the government than of the latter's control of the process.

From the above discussion, one can conclude that the government-sponsored mechanisms did much to facilitate the participation of NGOs, both quantitatively in terms of the broad and diverse range of the groups involved and qualitatively in terms of the amount of preparatory work they were able to achieve and the various levels on which they were able to participate. The mechanisms did not enable them to influence the substance of Canada's official positions. However, the mechanisms did assist government officials in several ways. They helped cultivate interest and support for the conference, which was a high priority for those formulating Canada's positions. They institutionalized participation, influencing which voices got central access. They did not stop the criticisms of the most vocal critics, but they did prevent them from playing the lead roles. The mechanisms could not control the NGOs, but they did assist the government in retaining control of the process.

Points to Ponder
This section begins by reiterating several premises about NGOs and the Canadian political process that are outlined in Chapter 1.

1 NGOs representatives are not chosen by the full Canadian electorate, but NGOs do nonetheless play important roles in the Canadian democratic process.[38]

2 There are structural barriers to their efficacy; the government, as a whole, is not particularly receptive to groups in the counterconsensus.

3 In light of the barriers they face and the scarce resources available to them, NGOs need to choose their targets, tactics, and timing carefully so as to maximize their efficacy.

4 The government needs to facilitate more meaningful participation of a broad range of NGOs for ethical and practical reasons.

From examining some of the recent literature on the Canadian foreign policy-making process, it is clear that NGOs have good reasons for being suspicious of government motives. Their funding has been drastically cut in recent years. Likewise, the social programs which many of them have struggled long and hard to promote have been, and continue to be, eroded. The Canadian Advisory Council on the Status of Women was disbanded only months before the Fourth World Conference on Women. NGOs have legitimate fears that closer working relations may lead to co-option. There is also the fear that being seen to work closely with government officials may lead to accusations of co-option which, in turn, could undermine the credibility of group leaders in the eyes of the group members.

On the other hand, the government is not a monolith, and there may be allies within it worth courting. Developing strategies and a broad range of tactics can be extremely useful when approaching government so that one can select the strategy or tactic most appropriate to securing one's objectives with an individual government official or a particular set of government actors. NGO resources are scarce; they must be used to greatest advantage to secure the desired results. Increased efficacy is important because the development and implementation of policies that improve the status and well-being of women – even if they are only incremental changes – nonetheless move the agenda ahead. NGOs may wish to weigh carefully the costs and benefits of working more cooperatively with government officials when developing their lobbying strategies for each particular case in which they choose to become involved. In developing such strategies, it may be useful to consider the points outlined below. They are offered specifically for consideration by women's groups, though other NGOs may also find them of use.

1. There May Be Allies within Government Worth Courting

Governments consist of individuals holding diverse viewpoints determined primarily by the mandate and ethos of the individual's department and division, as well as by the individual's own personal beliefs, experiences, and values. Women's divisions are generally more progressive on women's issues than are their colleagues in other parts of the government. As a result, they frequently face a hard sell within their own departments and in interdepartmental negotiations when they seek to ensure that Canada's policies and programs promote women's equality. Within government, they must compete to influence policy decisions with their more-numerous and generally better-funded colleagues from other departments and divisions. They need strong, credible allies from outside government (i.e., women's groups) to support their struggles to influence policy.

In the case of Canada and the Fourth World Conference, there was a high degree of consensus among the public servants formulating Canada's position. The only case of NGOs supporting one public servant over another occurred when Abby Hoffman advocated broadening and strengthening the health provisions and according them a higher priority than the public servants in SWC and DFAIT considered prudent. When these differences came to a head at the 1995 New York Preparatory Meetings, the Canadian NGOs tended to side with Hoffman. Their support was insufficient to countermand the strength of the dominant actors for the key departments. Yet, this one example must not obfuscate the fact that overall there was relatively little interdepartmental wrangling among the public servants formulating Canada's positions and so little need for them to seek external allies to bolster their bargaining positions when dealing with each other.[39] In the broader context of Canadian foreign policy making, however, there is a pervasive need for evidence of widespread and vigorous support for women's equality. Advancing women in this country – let alone women around the world – has never been a top priority for the Canadian government. It is important for those working within government to advance women to be able to point to a strong constituency of societal support to strengthen their arguments for moving the agenda ahead. In this case, it was important to have evidence of vigorous societal demands for Canada taking progressive positions at the Fourth World Conference on Women and the preparatory meetings leading up to it. The need for NGO allies was most acute at the 1995 New York Preparatory Meetings, though it was also evident at the Fourth World Conference on Women, where conservative forces were vehemently opposing much of the direction and substance of the *PFA* and were targeting Canadian negotiators for their leadership roles. Most of the key government officials in the IDC '95 and on the Canadian delegation said how much they would have appreciated greater support from Canadian women's groups and how helpful such support would have been when they encountered conservative forces at the UN meetings. The need for greater support from women's groups is not limited to the Beijing process. Quite to the contrary, officials working within government to advance women expressed a strong desire to have the support of women's groups, especially when they have to negotiate with more conservative forces within government as well as come up against the diatribes of conservative groups in society. The government is not a monolith, and there may be allies worth courting who are eager to develop mutually beneficial working relations with NGOs, generally, and with women's groups, in particular.

2. Cooperating with Government Allies in the Pursuit of Common Objectives Can Be a Useful Strategy

This point follows logically from the first consideration. Public servants in women's bureaus may not be prepared to move as far ahead on an issue as women's groups would like, but this does not necessarily preclude cooperating to advance government policy as far as possible together. The chances of moving the government as a whole ahead are generally greater if the government officials working to advance the status of women and women's groups cooperatively exert pressure for change rather than working at loggerheads and allowing the more conservative forces to exploit schisms among feminists. This is not to say that women's groups must abandon their broader agendas. That there is societal pressure to move beyond the position advocated by the women's bureaus actually lends credibility to the latter's arguments to move ahead at all.

In deciding whether or not to cooperate with potential government allies, leaders of women's groups need to weigh carefully the opportunity costs of not cooperating (and, thereby, of losing valuable opportunities to exert influence) with the concerns that cooperation may lead to co-option. The costs of co-option can include the diversion of resources from a group's primary goals, a reduction in its freedom to act, and the risk for its leaders of losing credibility with their own memberships. The choice is not necessarily an easy one; it requires a careful weighing of the costs and the benefits. Government officials form relations with NGOs primarily to maximize their own interests. Sometimes it is to fight the good fight together – in which cases women's groups may well want to collaborate with government allies – but other times, the contact may be less mutually beneficial. Government officials frequently consult both with women's groups seeking to promote gender equality and with groups opposed to this objective as a strategy for legitimizing their own position, which is portrayed as a balance between two extremes.

There are significant potential benefits to cooperating. Having allies in government facilitates getting access to information vital to effective lobbying. Not only does it facilitate getting access to important information but it also greatly enhances the chances of getting it early in the policy-making process, when there is still room to manoeuvre. Governments rarely reverse a policy decision once it has been announced publicly because of the high costs of being seen to back down. Consequently, getting access early is critical. Government allies can inform NGOs when a policy is being contemplated, allowing the latter to become involved at the start of the policy-making process. Having government allies also greatly enhances a group's chances of getting access to those formulating, approving, and implementing policies and of finding government officials more receptive to their views than they would be to the concerns of groups with whom they lack established relations.

The private sector has been particularly successful in establishing close, cooperative working relations with government departments.[40] The potential for cooperation between the government and groups in the counter-consensus has been best exemplified in recent years during the campaign to ban antipersonnel land mines. This campaign was unique and its model of government-NGO relations will not be easy to replicate for several reasons. The issue itself was clear, easily understood, and emotionally charged; it lent itself to mass mobilization. Canadians supported the ban, and there was not a strong domestic constituency advocating antipersonnel land mines. After all, who would be in favour of such diabolical weapons that leave thousands of victims, particularly women and children, killed or maimed every year? It is, moreover, much easier to maintain cohesion among a coalition of NGOs focused on one narrow, short-term objective, such as banning antipersonnel land mines, than it is to maintain solidarity among groups with broad-ranging, diverse, long-term objectives, as is evident in the women's movement.

The case of Canada and the Beijing Conference on Women is in many respects very different from the campaign to ban antipersonnel land mines. The provisions in the *PFA* were broad ranging, and the positions and priorities of the Canadian NGOs were extremely diverse. A relatively small but vocal minority was opposed to the direction and much of the substance of Canada's positions. Domestic as well as foreign policies were highly visible and under debate during the Beijing process. Thus, the case was not as conducive to government-NGO partnership as was the campaign to ban antipersonnel land mines, but there was, nonetheless, potential for a far higher degree of cooperation between the government officials and representatives of the feminist women's groups than actually occurred. If the relationship had been more cooperative, government officials would have been willing to share more information.[41] As mentioned in Chapter 5, government officials say that they became increasingly reticent to go the extra mile for groups that verbally abused them – and they were not referring only to the conservative groups. In an ideal partnership, the Canadian negotiators not only would keep NGOs apprised of developments in the negotiations but would also flag the key issues of contention and indicate which states might be prompted to take more progressive stances. The Canadian NGOs could then lobby the NGOs from the states that could potentially be brought on side in the hopes that the NGOs from these other countries would persuade their own governments to support the direction advocated by Canada and its NGOs. There were, of course, issues on which the Canadian government and the Canadian NGOs did not see eye to eye, particularly in terms of tackling the structural inequalities associated with the globalization of capitalism. There were, however, many more issues on which Canada and the vast majority of the Canadian NGOs were much stronger proponents of women's rights than were most states participating at the conference. In these cases, there was definite potential for the Canadian negotiators and most of the NGO representatives working together to move the agenda ahead at least as far as Canada's official positions.

3. Understanding the Parameters within which Government Allies Operate Helps to Facilitate Harmonious Relations

If NGOs do decide to cooperate with government officials, it is helpful to understand the parameters within which the latter operate.[42] The parameters within which government officials must operate are set by many factors, including their relative bargaining strength within government circles and their need to formulate positions consistent with existing government policy, as well as the dynamics of and power configurations at the international negotiations. Finite resources and a need to protect credibility are further factors limiting the range of options available to government officials and the number of priorities that can be pursued. Such choices are often vigorously challenged by Canadian NGOs, as exemplified during a daily briefing by the Canadian delegation in Beijing at which one of the Canadian NGO representatives expressed anger that Canada was not taking the lead on the issue of female genital mutilation – an issue that poses serious problems for some women and girls in Canada. The lack of Canadian leadership on this issue was interpreted as a lack of commitment to ensuring the elimination of the practice. The perspective of the Canadian negotiators was radically different; they were not taking the lead on this issue for three reasons.[43] First, the African countries were already providing effective leadership in this area. Second, it was more credible for the African countries to take the lead on this issue than it was for Canada to do so, since female genital mutilation affects large numbers of girls and women in Africa and relatively few in Canada. Third, no country can take the lead on all issues; each must choose its issues carefully. In this case, consensus was moving under capable African leadership in the direction Canada supported (i.e., to condemn the practice).

In addition to understanding the parameters within which allies must operate, it is helpful to have a range of tactics at one's disposal so as to be able to select the tactic most appropriate to a given time and place, a particular issue, and a particular government actor or set of actors. It may be necessary to take a very tough line when dealing with a cabinet minister who has neglected to make women's equality a high priority. On the other hand, a tough, adversarial approach generally does little to enhance constructive working relations with one's allies.

4. Policy Sessions Are Most Effective When Focused on the Development of Policies

Sharing experiences and frustrations is not only therapeutic but also valuable in identifying problems, in gaining a deeper understanding of their dimensions, and in community building. Such exercises are best conducted before the development of policies, as they can serve to derail the drafting of concrete proposals. This pattern was all too evident at the CBFC's first meeting, which was designed to facilitate the development of NGO positions but ended up serving primarily as a "bitch session." There is a time for consciousness raising; in fact, it is a vital activity, especially in the early stages of discussions, when it is important to understand the complexity of the issues and the diverse perspectives of the participants. There is also a time for developing concrete positions and strategies. Trying to combine opportunities for the extensive sharing of personal experiences with policy-making sessions often works to the detriment of the latter.

5. A Unified Stance in Public Enhances Credibility and Strengthens the Impact of Lobbying Efforts

It is healthy and necessary to discuss a wide diversity of views; in fact, it is intrinsic to feminist ideology. Such internal schisms are best debated before appearing before government officials or the media. Groups that do not appear to have a clear sense of their objectives and priorities appear less credible and are easier to dismiss. It can also make it more difficult for allies within government to argue for the group: "When cabinet ministers see NAC's loud, aggressive demonstrations and see them doing their dirty laundry on Parliament Hill, it makes it harder for Sheila Finestone [secretary of state for the status of women] to argue the need to finance them."[44] In private, there may be times for debating the content of the Canadian women's perspective and for seeking to ensure that one's own views are reflected in the perspective. There may also be times when it is necessary to accept that there will be more than one perspective – even among feminist groups. In public, it may be most advisable to focus on getting a positive outcome on a specific issue rather than arguing about perspectives. It may be easier to succeed in promoting a limited agenda on which members can agree rather than a broad range of demands on which there is internal dissension that becomes public.

6. Knowing the Intricacy of UN Negotiations
Is of Prime Importance to Participants

Seeking influence apropos UN negotiations is not the same as lobbying at home on domestic issues. To participate in international negotiations and the foreign policy-making process pertaining to them, one has to understand the UN context, rules, and procedures. Who are the key actors? How are the negotiations structured? Where are the key negotiations being conducted: in a main committee, a contact group, or the corridor? Who has access to which meetings? Why? If one is denied access to key sessions, can one cultivate contacts who do have access and who will act as two-way conduits in and out of the closed meetings? What is the precise meaning of the terminology being used? What language has already been accepted at previous summits and conferences? These are just some of the many questions to which NGOs require answers if they are to be able to function effectively within the UN.

Clearly, no one strategy or set of strategies can guarantee that a NGO or coalition of NGOs will be successful in their lobbying efforts. The extent to which government, as a whole, is likely to move to accommodate NGOs remains limited. It is, nonetheless, hoped that the points outlined above will serve as reminders of the range of factors a NGO may wish to consider when developing its lobbying strategies.

The government may wish to facilitate more meaningful participation for groups for both ethical and practical reasons. The current system is not an equal playing field in which all have equal opportunities to exert influence. Women's groups and women's divisions and departments within government share more than a concern for women's equality. They share the problem of having to compete against formidable odds to have their priorities translated into policies. Many of those currently working for women's divisions within the federal government recognize the need for outside allies in their struggle to get the government to be more receptive to the needs of women. NGOs can contribute expertise that comes from working directly in the community and from networking with other groups at home and abroad. The legitimacy of a particular government policy, position, or program is enhanced by the support of the NGO that is recognized to have expertise in the area or to speak for the affected constituency. In media interviews, parliamentary and other government hearings, public meetings, and international venues, a credible NGO can voice strong, valuable support for the positions taken by its allies in government. Such support can enhance the bargaining resources of a government ally vis-à-vis those of his or her competitors in intergovernmental bargaining, public debates, and international negotiations. As well as these practical reasons for seeking NGO allies, there is the ethical imperative to ensure that meaningful participation in the Canadian policy-making process is not reserved solely for the NGOS with the greatest resources. For all these reasons, government officials may wish to consider the points outlined below when contemplating future relations with NGOs in the counterconsensus.

1. Understanding the parameters within which NGOs operate helps facilitate harmonious relations

Women's groups are usually run by small numbers of employees and volunteers. In either case, the motivation for involvement is personal dedication to the issue. Volunteers receive no financial remuneration. Those employed by women's groups generally work for salaries and benefits that are considerably less than they would earn working in other sectors of the economy. Women's groups operate quite differently from government. The former tend to be more internally democratic and flexible, while the latter is much larger and more hierarchical. The government functions according to its own standard operating procedures through its bureaucratic channels. The very differences in their natures make it hard for NGO representatives to understand why government acts so slowly and cautiously and for government officials to understand why NGOs expect sweeping changes to come – if not overnight – then at least in relatively short order. It is particularly frustrating for individuals devoting vast amounts of time and energy to a cause they hold dear, either for no pay or for relatively low pay, to encounter intransigence on the part of government officials, or worse still, to see the gains they fought so hard to achieve being eroded. Individual public servants may not be able to redress these frustrations, but it may assist relations if the frustrations are recognized and acknowledged.

Sensitivity to NGO fears of co-option and to fears of being seen to be co-opted is also important. It would be difficult for the president of the NAC to be seen having a friendly, congenial chat with the minister of finance – after all the cuts he has made to NGO funding and to women's programs – without NAC members wondering what was going on. Image is important to NGO leaders just as it is to government officials, especially to elected politicians.

2. NGO facilitating committees that are democratically constituted, inclusive of the major NGOs in the issue area, and consisting of members with relevant expertise are likely to be most effective

The CBFC was an innovative idea that produced tangible benefits for both the federal government and the NGOs. To its credit, it was democratically constituted in the sense that 2,000 Canadian women's groups participated in open elections to select its membership. This degree of democratization was far greater than that seen in the establishment of facilitating committees for other world conferences and summits. Unfortunately, most of its core members and staff lacked UN experience and so found themselves in a new organization that was preordained to have a short life span and yet was involved in a process characterized by a long learning curve. Designing plans for future facilitating committees will require a careful balancing of several sets of criteria, which may not necessarily be compatible: (1) the selection process must be democratic, (2) the major NGOs in the field must be involved centrally, and (3) those placed in leadership roles must have expertise in UN negotiations and in lobbying the Canadian government regarding such negotiations. There are opportunity costs to ignoring any one of these sets of criteria, but what balance can be struck between the need to make the process as democratic as possible and the need for expertise to optimize the effective use of scarce resources? The procedures used in this case, of collecting nominations from large numbers of diverse groups from across the country and then having them elect a NGO facilitating committee, went a long way towards making the process democratic. The facilitating committee was not elected by the Canadian electorate but through a process that did involve a large segment of the attentive public. The need for expertise is apparent; yet, the responsibility for developing the necessary expertise should not fall solely on NGO shoulders. As discussed in point four below, government officials working to enhance the status of women may wish to give greater thought to assisting potential allies in the NGO community. The women's groups gained a great deal of experience during the Beijing process, which they continue to broaden in their post-Beijing lobbying activities: they are much better positioned today to establish and administer an effective facilitating committee than they were in 1994.

3. *Those with UN experience, in-depth knowledge of the conference*
   document, and strong ties to the NGO community are best able to
   fulfil the roles prescribed for nongovernmental observers
It is not essential that each and every nongovernmental observer have all these attributes. Trade-offs sometimes need to be made. For example, the person best positioned to represent a key sector of the NGO community may not always be the person with UN experience. It may be wise to weigh carefully the advantages and disadvantages of appointing individuals lacking one or more of the characteristics listed above. UN structures, procedures, and language are not easily mastered; those who arrive without prior knowledge of these matters will need to devote a good deal of the conference or summit to learning such specialized details. To maximize their effectiveness, nongovernmental observers also need to have a good working knowledge of the conference documents, which means that they need to have analyzed the provisions in at least one key issue area in the negotiating text before arriving at the conference or summit.

Nongovernmental observers representing diverse constituencies can play important roles in legitimizing decisions, in monitoring government policies, and in providing valuable two-way linkages with the broader NGO community. These functions can best be achieved if those selected are clearly responsible to particular NGO constituencies. One of the tasks expected of nongovernmental observers is to liaise with the NGO community. Those best able to fulfil this role are those who already have well-established, direct ties to prominent NGOs participating at the international conference or summit. Madeleine Gilchrist was nominated by the CBFC, and the nomination was accepted by the minister of foreign affairs. Although there were limits to the extent to which one individual could monitor diverse negotiations and stay in close contact with a variety of Canadian NGOs, Gilchrist did consistently serve as a two-way link between the Canadian delegation and Canadian NGOs at both the Vienna Regional Meetings and the New York Preparatory Meetings. In contrast, the decision to appoint individuals – rather than NGO representatives – to the Canadian delegation to Beijing resulted in a lack of ongoing systematic liaison between the Canadian delegation and the Canadian NGOs attending the conference. If facilitating the participation of Canadian NGOs is to remain a government objective and if the government's prescribed roles for the nongovernmental observers are to include assisting the Canadian negotiators, then it may be important to rethink the criteria used in making appointments to future Canadian delegations.

4. Assisting NGO allies to lobby effectively may be mutually beneficial
Few would disagree with the premise that if one chooses to have NGO allies, it is preferable to have allies that are more – rather than less – effective. Government officials working to enhance the status of women seem to have been more reticent to educate women groups about lobbying strategies than their colleagues in other areas of government have been to instruct their nongovernmental allies. The Department of Finance, for example, has devoted considerable time and energy to educating business allies on the ways to maximize their effectiveness on particular issues. Although SWC has a lot fewer resources, it may still wish to consider developing educational materials about participation at UN negotiations before future NGO facilitating committees are struck so that interested members of the public may be better able to assess the needs of the committee. Furthermore, most NGOs beginning preparations for a UN conference or summit could benefit from a briefing paper explaining in detail the negotiations, their structure, their agenda, their precedents, and their procedures. Such information would not only assist NGO allies to participate more effectively but could also help to curtail some of the criticism that comes when people do not fully understand the parameters of international negotiations. For instance, Jackie Claxton and Duy Ai Kien listened to many complaints

in Huairou about procedural matters that were not within their jurisdiction. Such situations are unpleasant for government officials and an ineffective use of NGO energy, which could be channelled into more productive lobbying.

In-depth briefings for the nongovernmental observers would also assist them to perform their prescribed roles more effectively. In making these suggestions, it is recognized that not all NGO representatives or nongovernmental observers will be receptive to government efforts to "educate" them. On the other hand, there were significant numbers of nongovernmental actors, both on the Canadian delegation and in the broader NGO community in Beijing, who lamented the lack of in-depth government briefings on the dynamics of the conference. These individuals would have welcomed substantial briefings, on both the process and strategies for greater efficacy, that combined practical advice and concrete examples. Training sessions held before the conference would be particularly useful. From the point of view of courting allies, those willing to receive instruction may also prove to be the most cooperative allies.

5. An adequately funded feminist think-tank would benefit all those seeking
   to advance women in Canada
Women's groups suffer from small staffs and scarce resources; hence, few produce comprehensive briefs focused on policy directives. Women's bureaus within government also face scarce resources relative to those within, as well as outside, government who are pressing opposing agendas. There is, for example, no feminist counterpart to the well-endowed Fraser Institute. There is a need for a similarly well-financed feminist think-tank that would analyze topical issues of gender and women's equality and develop concrete policy recommendations. Such an institute would enable women's bureaus and departments within the federal and provincial and territorial governments as well as NGOs to compete more effectively in Canada's policy-making process.

In conclusion, the *Beijing Declaration* and *PFA* built on progress made at previous conferences and summits. There now exists strong language to advance women and to combat the critical barriers to their empowerment. The significance of this language depends on its implementation. It is hoped that the points raised above will facilitate the work of government officials and NGO representatives to ensure that the provisions in the *PFA* are indeed translated into concrete action.

Appendices

Membership on the Canadian Beijing Facilitating Committee

Pat Beck	National Council of Women
Fernande Bergeron	Réseau national d'action éducation femmes
Linda Christansen-Ruffman	Canadian Research Institute for the Advancement of Women (CRIAW)
Shelagh Day	lesbian representative
Susan Dowse	youth representative
Marge Friedel	(co-chair) National Métis Council
Madeleine Gilchrist	Voice of Women (VOW)
Stella LeJohn	UN End of Decade Committee
Fleurette Osborne	Ontario Coalition for Visible Minority Women
Joyce Rankin	Prairies representative, Women in Trades and Technology
Estelle Reddin	Disabled Women's Network (PEI)
Micheline Simard	Conseil d'intervention pour l'accès des femmes au travail (CIAFT), Quebec representative
Lucya Spencer	National Organization of Immigrant and Visible Minority Women
Barbara Guy	YWCA, Northern Territories representative
Charlotte Thibault	(co-chair) L'Association des collaboratrices et partenaires en affaires
Vasso Vahlas	Immigrant and Visible Minority Women of BC
Felicita Villasin	National Action Committee on the Status of Women (NAC)
Janice Walker	Native Women's Association of Canada
Andrea Webb	Inuit Women's Association
Judith Wiley	YWCA of/du Canada

Source: Onward to Beijing 1, 3 (April 1995): 19.
Note: There was some turnover in the membership of the CBFC. Six of the women listed above were not on the membership list a year earlier. See *Onward to Beijing* 1, 1 (1994): 4.

Appendix 2

Membership on the Canadian Preparatory Committee

Federal Government
Rajani Alexander
Women in Development and Gender Equity
Canadian International Development Agency

Donna Balkan
External Relations
Canadian Human Rights Commission

Elizabeth Barot
Condition de la femme et Jeunesse
Commission canadienne pour l'Unesco

Louise Bergeron-de Villiers (chair)
Coordinator
Status of Women Canada

Janet Burn
Communication Services
External Relations and Communications
Status of Women Canada

Jackie Claxton
Women's Program
Social Development and Education
Department of Human Resources Development

Vivian Collins
UN World Conference on Women Secretariat
Status of Women Canada

Adèle Dion
International Women's Equality
Department of Foreign Affairs and International Trade

Rhonda Ferderber
External Relations and Communications
Status of Women Canada

Duy Ai Kien
Women's Program
Social Development and Education
Department of Human Resources Development

Sandra Lyth
Status of Women Canada

Marnee Manson
Status of Women Canada

Valerie Raymond
UN World Conference on Women Secretariat
Status of Women Canada

Women's Groups
Ruth Brown
National Council of Women of Canada

Shelagh Day
National Action Committee on the Status of Women

Fleurette Osborne
Congress of Black Women

Monique Roy
Réseau national d'action éducation femmes

Lucya Spencer
National Organization of Immigrant and Visible Minority Women

Charlotte Thibault
L'Association des collaboratrices et partenaires en affaires

Other Nongovernmental Participants

Development NGOs
Edith Mukakayumba/Maryse Tremblay
Association québécoise des organismes de coopération internationale

Enid Page
MATCH International Centre

Human Rights NGOs
Ariane Brunet
Centre international des droits de la personne et du développement démocratique

International NGOs
Francine Arsenault
Disabled Persons International/Council of Canadians with Disabilities

Labour
Carol Phillips
Canadian Labour Congress

Research
Joanna Kerr
North-South Institute

Dr. Glenda Simms
Canadian Advisory Council on the Status of Women

Rosina Wiltshire
Gender and Sustainable Development Program
International Development Research Centre

Observers
Lise Martin
Canadian Beijing Facilitating Committee

Additional Persons Receiving Information
Madeleine Gilchrist
Canadian Voice of Women for Peace

Appendix 3

Areas of Responsibility for Individual Members of Canada's Negotiating Team at the Fourth World Conference on Women

Declaration:
Louise Bergeron-de Villiers, Valerie Raymond, Ross Hynes, Sheila Regehr

Health, Girl Child:
Ruth Archibald, Diana Rivington, Valerie Raymond

Human Rights, Armed Conflict, Violence against Women:
Kerry Buck, Adèle Dion, Ross Hynes

Refugees:
Ruth Archibald, Kerry Buck, Adèle Dion

Resources:
Sheila Regehr, Diana Rivington

Poverty, Economic Issues, Education, Environment, Media, Decision Making, National Machinery:
Sheila Regehr, Diana Rivington

Institutional Arrangements:
Valerie Raymond, Kerry Buck, Sheila Regehr, Adèle Dion

Source: This list was handed out by the Canadian delegation to Canadian NGOs at the International Convention Centre (Beijing, September 3, 1995).

Appendix 4

Canadian Nongovernmental Organizations Accredited to the Fourth World Conference on Women

Aboriginal Nurses Association of Canada
Alliance Action
Alliance de la Fonction Publique du Canada
Alliance for Life
Asociacion Mundial de Radios Comunitarias, Red Internacional de Mujeres En AMARC
Association Canadienne pour les Nations Unies – Section de Québec
Baha'i Community of Canada
Campaign Life Coalition
Camrose International Institute
Canadian Association for the Advancement of Women in Sport
Canadian Beijing Facilitating Committee
Canadian Committee for UNIFEM
Canadian Council for International Development
Canadian Council for Refugees
Canadian Federation of Business and Professional Women's Clubs
Canadian Federation of University Women
Canadian Home Economics Association
Canadian Hunger Foundation
Canadian Indigenous Women's Resource Institute
Canadian Labour Congress
Canadian Nurses Association
Canadian Research Institute for the Advancement of Women
Canadian Teachers' Federation
Canadian University Service Overseas
Canadian Youth Speak International
Centre for Feminist Research, York University
Centre for International Studies/University College of Cape Breton
Centre for Refugee Studies, York University
Congress of Black Women of Canada
Conseil permanent de la jeunesse
Democratic Society of Iranian Women in Canada
Developing Countries Farm Radio Network
Disabled Women's Network
EGALE (Equality for Gays and Lesbians Everywhere)
Era Ecological Rights Association
Fédération des dames d'Acadie
Federation of Medical Women of Canada
Fédération nationale des femmes canadiennes-françaises
Femmes d'affaires sans frontières
Friends of Breastfeeding Society
Immigrant Women of Saskatchewan
Institute for the Study of Women/Mount Saint Vincent University
International Centre for Criminal Law Reform and Criminal Justice Policy
International Centre for Human Rights and Democratic Development
International Development Research Centre
International Secretariat for Water
Jewels (Justice and Equality for Women Everywhere Legally, Lawlessly and Shamelessly)
Jmj Children's Fund of Canada
Korean Canadian Women's Association
Life Ethics Education Association
Lifeline (Aid to Women)

Manitoba Action Committee on the Status of Women
Match International Centre
National Action Committee on the Status of Women
National Council of Women of Canada
National Métis Women of Canada
National Organization of Immigrant and Visible Minority Women of Canada
National Watch on Images of Women in the Media (Mediawatch)
Native Women's Association of Canada
North-South Institute
Organisation catholique canadienne pour le développement et la paix
Oxfam-Quebec
Pauktuutit (Inuit Women's Association of Canada)
Planned Parenthood Federation of Canada
Physicians for Global Survival (Canada)
Presbyterian Church in Canada
REAL Women of Canada
Réseau national d'action éducation femmes
Society for Canadian Women in Science and Technology
Sommet des femmes en Acadie
Union internationale des travailleurs et travailleuses unis de l'alimentation et du commerce
United Nations Association in Canada
West Indian-Canadian Charitable Foundation
WETV – The Global Access Television Service
Winning Women: Committee for Political Skills
Women for a Just and Healthy Planet (Toronto)
Women Inventors Project
Women's Canadian Ort
Women's Economic Network
Women's Health Interaction/Inter Pares
Women's Health in Women's Hands: A Community Health Centre for Women
Women's Studies Programme, York University
World University Service of Canada
World Women's Veterinary Association
Young Amazons

Appendix 5

Those Receiving Government Funding to Attend the 1995 New York Preparatory Meetings

Amy Angeconeb	Native Women's Association
Fernande Bergeron	Réseau national d'action éducation femmes
Colleen Burke	Voice of Women
Anna-Louise Crago	Young Amazons
Wendy Duffy	YWCA of Calgary
Margaret Dunkley	Northern Access Network
Deb Ellis	Alliance for Non-Violent Action
Amy Go	Canadian Ethnocultural Council
Liz Hardwick	Environmental Youth Alliance
Janice Henry	Métis National Council of Women
Vuyiswa Keyi	Women's Health in Women's Hands
Paulette Marchetti	Canadian Tibet Committee
Jacqueline Nadeau-Martin	Association féminine d'éducation et d'action sociale
Vasso Vahlas	Immigrant and Visible Minority Women of BC
Andrea Webb	Inuit Women's Association
Maria Yax	Nova Scotia – Beijing Women's Action Group

Source: "Funded Canadian NGO Delegates to New York," *Onward to Beijing* 1, 3 (1995): 11.

Appendix 6

Those Receiving Government Funding to Attend the NGO Forum on Women '95

Kay Anonsen	Provincial Advisory Council on the Status of Women
Michèle Asselin	L'R des centres des femmes du Québec
Fernande Bergeron	Réseau national d'action éducation femmes
Catherine Boldt	Canadian Research Institute for the Advancement of Women
Norah Calliou	Métis National Council of Women
Carla Castaneda	Trent Women's Centre
Marion Copelston	Women's Network
Françoise David	Fédération des femmes du Québec
Shelagh Day	National Association of Women and the Law
Helen Durie	Victoria Sexual Assault Centre
Cheryl Fennel	Canadian Congress of Learning Opportunities for Women
Marsha Forrest	Aboriginal Nurses' Association
Delie Gallien Chaisson	Sommet des femmes en Acadie
Amy Go	Chinese Canadian National Council
Danielle Hébert	Centrale syndicale nationale
Miche Hill	National Action Committee
Meg Hogarth	MediaWatch
Fatima Jaffer	Kinesis: Vancouver Status of Women
Lisa Jensen	Alberta Council for Global Justice
Charlotte Johnson	Federated Women's Institutes of Canada
Vuyiswa Keyi-Ayema	Women's Health in Women's Hands
Diane Lemieux	Regroupement québécois des centres d'aide et de lutte contre les agressions à caractère sexuel
Cynthia Lam	Chinese Family Services
Winnie Ng	National Action Committee
Debbie O'Connell	Groots Canada
Karen Penderson	National Farmers' Union
Joyce Rankin	Women in Trades and Technology
Sharon Selkirk	The Canadian Federation of Business & Professional Women Clubs
Sadeqa Sidiqui	South Asia Women's Community Centre
Mary Sillet	Pauktuutit
Lucya Spencer	National Organization of Immigrant and Visible Minority Women of Canada
Milana Todoroff	Canadian Women Studies and Disabled Women Network
Nicole Turmel	Public Service Alliance of Canada
Lucy Van Oldenbarneveld	Yukon Status of Women
Fellicita Villasin	Intercede
Janis Walker	Native Women's Association of Canada
Margaret Ann Wildman	National Council of Women
Dolly Williams	Congress of Black Women
Corrine Younie	Women Looking Forward

Source: "Funded Participants to Forum '95 (Fourth World Conference on Women),"
Onward to Beijing 1, 4 (1995): 18.

Notes

Preface

1 Depending on whose account one reads, the distance between Huairou and Beijing varied from 40 to 80 kilometres. The Office of the NGO Forum on Women – the UN body responsible for organizing the forum – calculated the distance between Huairou and the Beijing International Convention Centre to be 42 kilometres, and its figure is used in this book. See United Nations, NGO Forum on Women Secretariat, *NGO Forum on Women: Look at the World Through Women's Eyes, 30 August-8 September: Final Report*, 17.

Chapter 1: Introduction

1 For a concise overview of the major accomplishment of the conference, see Canada, Status of Women, *Beijing Platform for Action: Key Achievements* (Ottawa, 1995).
2 See Allison T. Graham, *The Essence of Decision: Explaining the Cuban Missile Crisis* (Boston: Little, Brown, 1971); Kim Richard Nossal, "Allison through the (Ottawa) looking glass: bureaucratic politics and foreign policy in a parliamentary system," *Canadian Public Administration* 22 (1979): 610-26; and Elizabeth Riddell-Dixon, "Deep seabed mining: a hotbed for governmental politics," *International Journal* 41, 1 (1985-86): 72-94.
3 Liberal Party of Canada, *Creating Opportunity: The Liberal Plan for Canada* (Ottawa, 1993).
4 Kim Richard Nossal, "The Democratization of Canadian Foreign Policy: The Elusive Ideal," in *Canada Among Nations 1995: Democracy and Foreign Policy*, ed. Maxwell A. Cameron and Maureen Appel Molot (Ottawa: Carleton University Press, 1995), 33-4.
5 Nossal, "The Democratization of Canadian Foreign Policy," 35.
6 The contributors to these debates include Nossal, "The Democratization of Canadian Foreign Policy," 29-43; Sandra Whitworth, "Women, and Gender, in the Foreign Policy Review Process," in *Canada Among Nations 1995: Democracy and Foreign Policy*, ed. Maxwell A. Cameron and Maureen Appel Molot, 83-98; and Mark Neufeld, "Democratization in/of Canadian Foreign Policy: Critical Reflections," *Studies in Political Economy* 58 (1999): 97-119.
7 For example, Nossal in "The Democratization of Canadian Foreign Policy" and Whitworth in "Women, and Gender, in the Foreign Policy Review Process" analyzes the Special Joint Committee Hearings. Mark Neufeld in "Democratization in/of Canadian Foreign Policy" considers the Special Joint Committee hearings but also provides a more macro-level critique of the Canadian foreign policy-making process. Cranford Pratt, in "Competing perspectives on Canadian development assistance policies," *International Journal* 51, 2 (1996): 235-58, focuses on the determinants of Canada's foreign aid.
8 Nossal, "The Democratization of Canadian Foreign Policy," 37.
9 Ibid., 39.
10 Elections Canada, preliminary results dated December 19, 2000. <www.elections.ca/ele/val/turnout_e.pdf> (January 16, 2001). My thanks to Miriam Lapp for her assistance in locating the data on the 2000 election.

11 In the 2000 election, the Progressive Conservative Party received 12 percent of the popular vote and almost 4 percent of the total seats, while the Bloc Québécois received 11 percent of the popular vote and almost 12.6 percent of the total seats. The Canadian Alliance received 25.5 percent of the popular vote and 22.3 percent of the total seats. The percentage of the popular vote that each political party received is available at Elections Canada, preliminary results dated December 19, 2000. <www.elections.ca/ele/val/totals_e.pdf> (January 16, 2001). The number of seats that each political party received is available at Globe and Mail, Election 2000 Voters' Toolkit <www.globeandmail.com/series/election/toolkit/answer-finder.html> (January 16, 2001).

12 The percentage of the popular vote that each political party received is available at Elections Canada, preliminary results dated December 19, 2000 <www.elections.ca/ele/val/totals_e.pdf> (January 16, 2001). The number of seats that each political party received is available at Globe and Mail, Election 2000 Voters' Toolkit <www.globeandmail.com/series/election/toolkit/answer-finder.html> (January 16, 2001).

13 For a more in-depth discussion of these issues, see Keith Archer, *Political Choices and Electoral Consequences* (Kingston/Montreal: McGill-Queen's University Press, 1990); Harold D. Clarke, Jane Jensen, Lawrence LeDuc, and Jon H. Pammett, *Absent Mandate: Interpreting Change in Canadian Elections,* 2nd ed. (Toronto: Gage, 1992); Jackson and Jackson, *Politics in Canada,* especially Chapter 12, 420-68; Richard Johnston, André Blais, Henry E. Brady, and Jean Crête, *Letting the People Decide* (Montreal: McGill-Queen's University Press, 1992); Miriam Lapp, "End First-Past-the Post" *Policy Options* 20, 9 (1999): 20; Henry Milner, ed., *Making Every Vote Count: Reassessing Canada's Electoral System* (Peterborough, Ontario: Broadview Press, 1999); Nancy Riche, "We Need Some Form of Proportional Representation," *Policy Options* 20, 9 (1999): 21; and Joseph Wearing, *The Ballot and Its Message: Voting in Canada* (Toronto: Copp Clark Pitman, 1991).

14 See Eugene Forsey, "Senate Reform," in *Canadian Legislatures 1987-1988,* ed. Robert J. Fleming (Ottawa: Ampersand Communications, 1988), 23-9; H. McConnell, "The Case for a Triple E Senate," *Queens Quarterly* (Autumn 1988): 683-98; Peter McCormick, "Canada Needs a Triple E Senate," in *Politics: Canada,* 7th ed., ed. Paul Fox and Graham White (Toronto: McGraw-Hill Ryerson, 1991), 522-5; Samuel C. Patterson and Anthony Mughan, eds., *Senates and the Theory of Bicameralism* (Columbus: Ohio State University, 1999), 1-31; and Randall White, *Voice of Region: The Long Journey to Senate Reform in Canada* (Toronto: Dundurn, 1990).

15 A. Paul Pross, *Group Politics and Public Policy* (Toronto: Oxford University Press, 1986), x.

16 These contributions are discussed in greater detail by Paul Pross in *Group Politics and Public Policy,* especially Chapter 4, 4-96.

17 Cranford Pratt, "Dominant class theory and Canadian foreign policy: the case of the counter-consensus," *International Journal* 39, 1 (1983-4): 100.

18 See Pratt, "Dominant class theory," especially 117-29; and Neufeld, "Democratization in/of Canadian Foreign Policy," footnote 19, 116.

19 Whitworth, "Women, and Gender, in the Foreign Policy Review Process," 84.

20 See ibid., 94.

21 Central to the debate over the relative autonomy of the government and NGOs in the foreign policy-making process are the works of Kim Richard Nossal, *The Politics of Canadian Foreign Policy,* 3rd ed. (Scarborough: Prentice Hall, 1997), especially Chapter 4, 95-137; and "Analysing the domestic sources of Canadian foreign policy," *International Journal* 39, 1 (1983-4): 1-22; and Cranford Pratt, "Competing perspectives," 235-58; and "Dominant class theory," 99-135.

22 Sandra Burt, "The Women's Movement: Working to Transform Public Life," in *Canadian Politics,* 2nd ed., ed. James P. Bickerton and Alain-G. Gagnon (Toronto: Broadview, 1994), 220.

23 Ibid., 220.

24 Sylvia Bashevkin, "Free Trade and Canadian Feminism: The Case of the National Action Committee on the Status of Women," *Canadian Public Policy* 15, 4 (1989): 364.

25 Burt, "The Women's Movement," 221.

26 Ottawa: Canada Communications Groups, 1995. These references to women included a

mention of the Fourth World Conference on Women (26), a sentence saying that Canada is "associated internationally with the promotion of the rights of women and children" (34), and two references to the need to ensure women's full and equal participation in economic development (40, 42).

27 Whitworth, "Women, and Gender, in the Foreign Policy Review Process," 84. See also Sandra Whitworth, *Feminism and International Relations: Towards a Political Economy of Interstate and Non-governmental Organizations* (London: Macmillan, 1994). In recent years, several other students of Canadian foreign policy have sought to break the silence. The macro-level problem was clearly outlined by Deborah Stienstra in "Can the Silence be Broken: Gender and Canadian Foreign Policy," *International Journal* 50, 1 (1994-5): 103-27. Others have chosen to focus on particular areas of foreign policy. For example, Kimberly Manning and Barbara Arneil examine "one essential aspect of peacebuilding that has hereto been neglected – gender." See "Engendering Peacebuilding," *Canadian Foreign Policy* 5, 1 (1997): 51-7, and "Gender and Peacebuilding: Report on a Roundtable," *Canadian Foreign Policy* 5, 1 (1997): 69-72. In "Gender, Race and the Politics of Peacekeeping," in *A Future for Peacekeeping?* ed. Edward Moxon-Browne (Macmillan: 1998), 176-91, Whitworth highlights the consequences of ignoring gendered and racial distinctions.

28 Stienstra, "Can the Silence be Broken," 105.

29 Ibid., 115.

30 Not all feminists would agree with this proposition. The main criticisms of seeking incremental change within the system come from radical feminists and Marxists, who argue that the existing structures themselves are fatally flawed and that one must work to change the existing androcentric structures rather than seeking piecemeal change from within. The counterargument, and the one supported here, is that the prospects of changing the existing structures at this point appear bleak; it is better to make less ambitious changes and to improve women's rights within the current system – flawed as it may be – than to settle for the status quo.

31 Steve Mertl, "New CLC head a smooth political operator," *Canadian Press Newswire*, May 6, 1999, 1.

Chapter 2: The Road to Beijing

1 The preamble to the *Charter of the United Nations* reaffirms "faith in fundamental human rights, in the dignity and worth of the human person, in the equal rights of men and women and of nations large and small," while Article 1.3 gives as one of the basic principles of the UN "promoting and encouraging respect for human rights and for fundamental freedoms without distinction as to race, sex, language, or religion."

2 For a more comprehensive discussion of the conferences and the Decade for Women, see Arvonne Fraser, *The U.N. Decade for Women: Documents and Dialogue* (Boulder, CO: Westview, 1987); Hilkka Pietilä and Jeanne Vickers, *Making Women Matter: The Role of the United Nations* (London: Zed Books, 1996); Deborah Stienstra, *Women's Movements and International Organizations* (New York: St. Martin's, 1994); Irene Tinker and Jane Jaquette, "UN Decade for Women: Its Impact and Legacy," *World Development* 15, 3 (1987): 419-27; and R.J. Harrison, "Women's Rights: 1975-1985," in *Global Issues in the United Nations Framework,* ed. Paul Taylor and A.J.R. Groom (London: Macmillan, 1989), 226-44.

3 The UN CSW is an intergovernmental body, established in 1946. Its forty-five member states now meet annually to develop policies and recommendations for the advancement of women. It also serves as the preparatory body for UN conferences focusing on gender issues. NGOs with consultative status with the United Nations Economic and Social Council are allowed to send observers to the commission's meeting.

4 Deborah Stienstra, *Women's Movements and International Organizations,* 125. In spite of opposition from some Western states, the Mexico conference also adopted a "Declaration on the Equality of Women and their Contribution to Development and Peace" which, in contrast to the *Plan of Action,* "was quite explicit about the relationship between the lack of equality for women and their political and economic context." Ibid.

5 Elisabeth Friedman, "Women's Human Rights: The Emergence of a Movement," in *Women's Rights, Human Rights: International Feminist Perspectives,* ed. Julie Peters and

Andrea Wolper (New York: Routledge, 1995), 23. By the end of the decade, the convention had been ratified by 65 governments. By 1995, the number of ratifications had risen to 143.

6 Deborah Stienstra, "From Mexico to Beijing: International Commitments on Women," *Canadian Woman Studies* 16, 3 (1996): 14.

7 The tendency of state participants to raise geopolitical issues was by no means unique to the UN conferences on women. As Arvonne Fraser points out, "virtually all nations use these [UN] conferences to present and make points about old and new – and sometimes what may seem to be extraneous – political conflicts or tensions between nations." *The U.N. Decade for Women*, 10.

8 Tinker and Jaquette, "UN Decade for Women," 421.

9 United Nations, Fourth World Conference on Women, *International Community to Seek Full and Equal Partnership Between Women and Men to Meet Challenges of Twenty-First Century*, press release, WOM/82, (New York, 1995), 2.

10 United Nations, Department of Public Information, Boutros Boutros-Ghali, "Overview," in *The United Nations and the Advancement of Women: 1945-1996*, UN Blue Book Series, vol. 6, rev. ed. (New York, 1996), 5-6.

11 Ibid., 3.

12 Stienstra, *Women's Movements and International Organizations*, 152.

13 Amrita Basu, "Reflections on Forum '85," *Signs* 11, 3 (1986): 604-5.

14 "Mexico Conference Launches Plan of Action for Women," *UN Chronicle* 12, 7 (1975): 44-5.

15 "Mexico to Copenhagen to Nairobi: 'An irresistible momentum,'" *UN Chronicle* 22, 7 (1985): ii.

16 Judy Klemesrud, "International Women's Year World Conference Opening in Mexico," *New York Times*, June 19, 1975, 41.

17 "Mexico to Copenhagen to Nairobi," ii.

18 Fraser, *The U.N. Decade for Women*, 80-1.

19 Ibid., 81.

20 Ibid., 3.

21 Stienstra, *Women's Movements and International Organizations*, 130-1.

22 Rounaq Jahan, "The International Women's Year Conference and Tribune," *International Development Review*, 3 (1975): 38.

23 United Nations, Department of Public Information, *From Beijing, a Platform for Action and a clear mandate for women's progress*, DPI/1749 (New York, 1995), 5.

24 Ibid., 5.

25 Charlotte Bunch, Mallika Dutt, and Susana Fried, "Beijing '95: A Global Referendum on the Human Rights of Women," *Canadian Woman Studies* 16, 3 (1996): 8.

26 United Nations, Fourth World Conference on Women, "Platform for Action," *Report of the Fourth World Conference on Women (Beijing 4-15 September 1995)*, A/Conf.177/20 (New York, October 1995), Annex II, paragraph 124(a), 54.

27 Thanks are due to Margaret Leahy for her insights into this conceptual evolution.

28 Examples of such international NGOs are discussed in Chapter 6.

29 According to Elisabeth Friedman, "at least 300,000 people from 123 countries signed the petition to demand that the World Conference on Human Rights address women's human rights." "Women's Human Rights," footnote 1, 32.

30 Bunch, Dutt, and Fried, "Beijing '95."

31 The Nairobi conference itself called for the convening of another world conference on women before the year 2000.

32 For an assessment of the progress being made towards the integration of gender analysis within the Office of the UN High Commissioner for Human Rights and the Centre for Human Rights, see Elizabeth Riddell-Dixon, "Mainstreaming Women's Rights: Problems and Prospects within the Centre for Human Rights," *Global Governance* 5, 2 (1999): 149-71.

33 Cited in United Nations, Department of Public Information, *From Beijing, a Platform for Action and a clear mandate for women's progress*, 1.

34 Hégel Goiter, "Women," *The Courier* 154 (1995): 48.

35 Hilary Charlesworth, "Women as Sherpas: Are Global Summits Useful for Women?" *Feminist Studies* 22, 3 (1996): 543. The Informal Contact Group on Gender met on May 16 and 31, 1995, and produced a statement read by the president of the Conference in Beijing. See United Nations, Fourth World Conference on Women, *Report of the Informal Contact Group on Gender*, A/Conf.177/L.2 (New York, 1995).

36 Bunch, Dutt, and Fried, "Beijing '95," 7.

37 United Nations, Department of Public Information, Fourth World Conference on Women, *Conference to Set Women's Agenda into Next Century*, DPI/1424, rev. 1 (New York, 1994), 1.

38 *ECOSOC resolution recommending that a world conference on women be held in 1995 and requesting the CSW to act as preparatory body*, E/Res/1990/12 (New York, 1990).

39 *General Assembly resolution endorsing the ECOSOC recommendation that a world conference on women be held in 1995*, A/Res/45/129, (New York, 1990).

40 The mandate for the Fourth Conference on Women is outlined in United Nations, Department of Public Information, *Fourth World Conference on Women: Action for Equality, Development and Peace, Beijing, China, 4-15 September 1995*, 94-24102/DPI/1468 (New York, 1994).

41 Interview with Rhonda Ferderber, director, External Relations and Communications Directorate, Status of Women Canada, Ottawa, December 9, 1997.

42 Ibid.

43 Interview with Kristen Timothy, deputy director/coordinator, United Nations Fourth World Conference on Women Secretariat, Division for the Advancement of Women, New York, June 22, 1995.

44 Madeleine Gilchrist, *Report on the United Nations Commission on the Status of Women Inter-sessional Working Group, 10-14 January 1994* (Toronto: n.p., 1994), 1.

45 United Nations, Commission on the Status of Women, 38th Session, *Draft Platform for Action: Annex to Resolution 38/10 of the Commission on the Status of Women*, E/CN.6/1994/10 (New York, 1994).

46 Interview with Timothy.

47 United Nations, Economic and Social Council, *Preparations for the Fourth World Conference on Women: Action for Equality, Development and Peace: Reports from Regional Conferences and Other International Conferences*, E/CN.6/1995/5 (New York, 1995).

48 United Nations, Economic and Social Council, *ECOSOC Resolution adopting the recommendations and conclusions arising from the first review and appraisal of the implementation of the Nairobi Forward-looking Strategies for the Advancement of Women to the year 2000 and urging Governments to implement the recommendations*, E/RES/1990/15 (New York, 1990). A second review was done in 1994, but the results were published too late to have served in the preparation of the draft *PFA*. See "Overview of the report of the Secretary-General on the second review and appraisal of the implementation of the Nairobi Forward-looking Strategies for the Advancement of Women (extract)," E/CN.6/1995/3, January 10, 1995, and E/CN.6/1995/3 Add.1, New York, February 24, 1995.

49 For the executive summary of the survey, see ST/ESA/241, April 1, New York, 1995.

50 United Nations, General Assembly, *Report of the Secretary-General to the General Assembly on the Status of the Convention on the Elimination of All Forms of Discrimination against Women (extract)*, A/49/308 (New York, 1994).

51 Department of Economics and Social Affairs, ST/ESA/STAT/SER.K/8, 1991. An updated version, *The World's Women 1995: Trends and Statistics*, ST/ESA/STAT/SER.K/12 (New York, 1995), came out too late in 1995 to be used in drafting the *PFA*, though it was available prior to the conference.

52 Interview with Timothy.

53 United Nations, Commission on the Status of Women, 39th Session, *Preparations for the Fourth World Conference on Women: Action for Equality, Development and Peace: Draft Platform for Action*, E/CN.6/1995/2, Annex (New York, 1995).

54 Prior to the March 1995 preparatory meetings, 75 percent of the *PFA* had never been negotiated. Interview with Timothy.

55 The Holy See is the Roman Catholic Church's supreme organ of government whose membership consists of the Pope, the College of Cardinals, and the Church's central

government bodies. It is considered by the UN to be a nonmember state with permanent observer status. Nevertheless, at most recent UN conferences, including the Beijing Conference on Women, it has been a full participant with a vote. The contrast between the Holy See's status as a full participant and the observer status of the UN Committee on the Elimination of Discrimination Against Women did not go unnoticed. The Holy See did not oppose all provisions in the *PFA*. For example, it supported education for the girl child. On the other hand, it opposed many of the provisions related to sexual and reproductive rights.

56 Marie-Andrée Roy, professor of Religious Studies at the University of Quebec in Montreal, defines fundamentalism as "a religious movement which tries not only to resist modernity, secularity, separation of Church and the state, but also wants to impose its values and belief system on the whole population. Religious Fundamentalism rejects all other interpretations of tradition – in fact it positions itself as the only thinking authorized interpreter." See "Fundamentalism at the NGO Forum," *Onward From Beijing: The FINAL Newsletter of the Canadian Beijing Facilitating Committee* (December 1995), 16.

57 United Nations, Fourth World Conference on Women, *Proposals for Consideration in the Preparation of a Draft Declaration and Draft Platform for Action,* A/Conf.177/L.1 (New York, 1995).

58 Interview with Valerie Raymond, executive director, UN World Conference on Women Secretariat, Status of Women Canada, Ottawa, July 18, 1995.

59 Lynn Wagner and Langston James Goree VI, "Fourth World Conference on Women Informal Consultations," brief 1, *Linkages: A Multimedia Resource for Environment and Development Policy Makers* (Winnipeg, International Institute for Sustainable Development, December 9, 1998). <www.iisd.ca./linkages/4wcw/brief1.html>

60 Ibid., 1

61 International Institute for Sustainable Development, "A Brief History of the Conference," *Earth Negotiations Bulletin* 14, 21 (1995): 2.

62 United Nations, Fourth World Conference on Women, *Report on the Informal Consultations Convened by the Chairperson of the Commission on the Status of Women,* A/Conf.177/L.3 (New York, 1995).

63 United Nations, Department of Public Information, *The United Nations and the Advancement of Women, 1945-1996,* UN Blue Books Series, vol. 6, rev. ed. (New York: 1996), 65.

64 This point was made by Kristen Timothy at a briefing for the NGOs held at the NGO forum in Huairou on September 2, 1995.

Chapter 3: Governmental Politics

1 Graham Allison's "bureaucratic politics" model challenged the then prevalent concept of public policies emanating from a rational, monolithic entity: the government. According to the bureaucratic politics model, public policies result from a bargaining process in which diverse government actors compete to determine outcomes. See Graham T. Allison, *The Essence of Decision: Explaining the Cuban Missile Crisis* (Boston: Little Brown, 1971), Chapter 5, 144-84. The model is discussed in somewhat greater depth in Chapter 8.

2 The major participants included Status of Women, Foreign Affairs and International Trade, the Canadian International Development Agency, Heritage, Justice, Health, Human Resources Development, Environment, Indian Affairs and Northern Development, National Defence, Citizenship and Immigration, and the Privy Council Office.

3 Interview with Adèle Dion, departmental coordinator, International Women's Equality, Human Rights, Women's Equality and Social Affairs Division, Department of Foreign Affairs and International Trade, Ottawa, July 17, 1995.

4 Ibid. Marnie Girvan concurred on the centrality of these objectives. Interview with Girvan, director, Women in Development and Gender Equity Division, Canadian International Development Agency, Ottawa, July 17, 1995.

5 Interview with Rhonda Ferderber, director, External Relations and Communications Directorate, Status of Women Canada, Ottawa, November 21, 1995.

6 For a discussion of the provinces and Canadian foreign policy, see Kim Richard Nossal,

The Politics of Canadian Foreign Policy, 3rd ed. (Scarborough: Prentice Hall, 1997), especially 292-314.

7 Ibid., 189.
8 "Ouellet was to spend so much time attending to provincial concerns – such as dispensing patronage and taking an active role in referendum politics – that in the Pearson Building, some officials took to calling him Mr. Five Per Cent, for the amount of time he was devoting to foreign affairs. While the characterization was no doubt less than fair, it did underscore the degree to which Ouellet, not unlike the prime minister himself, was not as energized by the portfolio as many of his predecessors had been." Ibid., 189.
9 Interview with Dion, December 11, 1997. This information was confirmed by Valerie Raymond in her letter of September 30, 1999.
10 Interviews with Abby Hoffman, executive director, Women's Health Bureau, Health Canada, Ottawa, July 10, 1996; and Dion, July 17, 1995.
11 Canada, Status of Women, *Status of Women Canada* (Ottawa, 1989), 1.
12 Canada, Status of Women, *Directory of Federal Government Programs and Services for Women* (Ottawa, 1989), 11.
13 Canada, Secretary of State, *The Women's Program and the Role of Women's Voluntary Organizations in Promoting Change* (Ottawa, 1985), 1.
14 Interview with Dion, December 11, 1997.
15 Interview with Sheila Regehr, senior policy analyst, Policy and Analysis Directorate, Status of Women Canada, Ottawa, November 23, 1995.
16 Canada, Secretary of State, *The Women's Program,* 5.
17 Interview with Duy Ai Kien, policy officer, Women's Program, Status of Women Canada, Ottawa, November 27, 1995.
18 Canada, Department of Finance, *1996/1997 Canada Estimates,* part 3 (Ottawa, 1996): 5.
19 Interview with Dion, November 21, 1995.
20 Confidential interviews with federal government officials.
21 Interview with Ruth Archibald, director, Refugee, Population and Migration Division, Department of Foreign Affairs and International Trade, Ottawa, July 11, 1996.
22 Interview with Dion, November 21, 1995.
23 Interview with Archibald.
24 The consultations with the Department of Justice were in addition to her regular contacts with the Legal Operations Division in her own department. Interview with Dion, December 11, 1997.
25 Interviews with Dion, November 21, 1995; and Archibald.
26 Canadian International Development Agency (CIDA), *Engendering Development: Women in Development and Gender Equity* (Hull, 1995), 3.
27 Ibid., 4.
28 Ibid., 4.
29 Interview with Girvan, July 17, 1995.
30 Ibid.
31 Ibid.
32 Ibid.
33 CIDA was first to fund the International Women's Tribune Centre, which was established in 1975 after the First World Conference on Women. This NGO continues to provide information, education, training resources, and technical assistance to women and women's groups in Africa, Asia, the Pacific, Latin America, the Caribbean, and the Middle East.
34 Interview with Girvan, July 17, 1995.
35 Ibid.
36 Ibid.
37 Canadian International Development Agency (CIDA), *CIDA Funding Criteria and Mechanisms* (Ottawa, 1993), 1-2. My thanks to Marnie Girvan for sharing this document with me.
38 Interview with Girvan, July 17, 1995.
39 Ibid.
40 CIDA personnel selected those who would receive funding to attend the international

negotiations. Interview with Girvan. The administration of this CIDA funding was delegated to Match International, an Ottawa-based NGO dedicated to improving the standards of livings of women around the world and to enhancing their participation in all
levels of decision making.
41 Interview with Girvan, July 17, 1995.
42 Interview with Ferderber, December 9, 1995.
43 Ibid.
44 Interview with Hoffman.
45 Ibid.
46 Interview with Ferderber, December 9, 1997.
47 Interview with Hoffman.
48 Ibid.
49 Interview with Ferderber, November 21, 1995.
50 Canada was the only country to grade its own performance in achieving the goals laid
    out in the *Forward-looking Strategies* on an ongoing basis. Before the 1995 World Confer-
    ence on Women, five editions of the *Fact Sheets* were produced.
51 Interview with Ferderber, November 21, 1995.
52 Ibid.
53 Ibid.
54 Interview with Dion, July 17, 1995.
55 Interview with Dion, December 11, 1997.
56 Interview with Ferderber, November 21, 1995.
57 Ibid.
58 Interview with Dion, December 11, 1997.
59 Interview with Ferderber, November 21, 1995.
60 Membership in the working groups consisted of representatives from those departments
    most concerned with the issue area. For example, the health working group included rep-
    resentatives from Health, CIDA, SWC, and DFAIT. Interview with Archibald.
61 Interview with Girvan, July 17, 1995.
62 The new policy was outlined in Canada, Status of Women, *Setting the Stage for the Next
    Century: the Federal Plan for Gender Equality* (Ottawa, 1995).
63 Interview with Valerie Raymond, executive director, UN World Conference on Women
    Secretariat, Status of Women Canada, Ottawa, July 18, 1995.
64 Interview with Diana Rivington, senior policy advisor, Women in Development and
    Gender Equity Division, Policy Branch, Canadian International Development Agency,
    Ottawa, November 23, 1995.
65 Interviews with Raymond, July 18, 1995; and Rivington.
66 Interview with Raymond, July 18, 1995.
67 United Nations, Secretariat of the Fourth World Conference on Women and the Division
    for the Advancement of Women, "International UNESCO Symposium on Women and
    the Media: Access to Expression and Decision-making," *Women on the Move* 8 (1995): 10.
68 Canada, Status of Women, "From New York ... to Beijing: NGO Funding for Beijing,"
    Beijing Update (Spring 1995), 2.
69 United Nations, Department of Public Information, *Draft Platform for Action*, A/Conf.177/
    L.1, (New York, 1995).
70 Interview with Raymond, July 18, 1995.
71 Interview with Dion, December 11, 1997.
72 Interview with Hoffman.
73 Ibid.
74 Interview with Dion, December 11, 1997.
75 Interview with Hoffman.
76 Interview with Dion, December 11, 1997.
77 Ibid.
78 Interview with Raymond, November 22, 1995.
79 For a clear, concise discussion of the provinces and foreign policy, see Nossal, *The Politics
    of Canadian Foreign Policy*, 292-331.

80 Canada, Task Force on Program Review, *Citizenship, Labour and Immigration: A Plethora of "People" Programs* (Ottawa: Supply and Services Canada, 1985), 112.
81 Interview with Ferderber, November 21, 1995.
82 Ibid.
83 Ibid.
84 Ibid.
85 Interview with Archibald.
86 Interview with Dion, July 17, 1995.
87 Interview with Archibald.
88 Interview with Ferderber, November 21, 1995.
89 This experience parallels the findings of several prominent authors who have studied decision-making patterns in groups where the membership is predominately female. See, for example, A. Touraine, "Social Movements: Participation and Protest," *Scandinavian Political Studies* 10, 3 (1987): especially 221; and M. Fuentes and A.G. Frank, "Ten Theses on Social Movements," *World Development* 17, 2 (1989): especially 181. See also Kathy E. Ferguson, *The Feminist Case Against Bureaucracy* (Philadelphia: Temple University Press, 1984); Nancy Adamson, Linda Briskin, and Margaret McPhail, *Feminist Organizing for Change: The Contemporary Women's Movement in Canada* (Toronto: Oxford University Press, 1988); and Virginia Sapiro, *The Political Integration of Women: Roles, Socialization and Politics* (Chicago: University of Illinois Press, 1983).
90 For an examination of the interbureaucratic struggles involved in the formulation of Canada's policies for the UN Third Conference on the Law of the Sea, see Elizabeth Riddell-Dixon, *Canada and the International Seabed: Domestic Determinants and External Constraints* (Montreal: McGill-Queens University Press, 1989), especially Chapter 5, 57-95.

Chapter 4: Nongovernmental Organizations within Canada
1 There were a few government officials who credited specific categories of NGOs with having some influence, largely at the level of agenda and parameter-setting. Adèle Dion, for example, explained that the Human Rights, Women's Equality and Social Affairs Division in the DFAIT enjoyed good relations with human rights groups and that the former were receptive to the latter's concern for the rights of women in armed conflict and adopted this issue area as a priority. Interview with Adèle Dion, departmental coordinator for International Women's Equality, Human Rights, Women's Equality and Social Affairs Division, Department of Foreign Affairs and International Trade, Ottawa, December 11, 1997.
2 This point was made by Jackie Claxton and Duy Ai Kien, who were the ones directly responsible for the relations with, and the participation of, NGOs. Interview with Jackie Claxton, director, Women's Program, Status of Women Canada, and Duy Ai Kien, policy officer, Women's Program, Status of Women Canada, Ottawa, February 25, 1998.
3 Interview with Nancy Riche, executive vice-president, Canadian Labour Congress, Ottawa, July 11, 1996.
4 Interview with Joan Grant-Cummings, president, National Action Committee on the Status of Women, Toronto, July 16, 1996.
5 For example, NAC representatives attended the 1985 Nairobi Conference on Women, the 1993 Vienna Conference on Human Rights, the 1994 Cairo Conference on Population and Development, and the 1995 Copenhagen Summit for Social Development, as well as the preparatory meetings leading up to the Fourth World Conference on Women and the 1995 Beijing Conference itself.
6 Duy Ai Kien, speech to the "Second Canadian Conference on International Health: Health Reform Around the Globe: Towards Equality and Sustainability?" (Ottawa, November 12, 1995). See also *Canadian Woman Studies* 15, 2/3 (1995). Some 1,500 copies of this volume were distributed at the Fourth World Conference on Women.
7 Interview with Rhonda Ferderber, director, External Relations and Communications Directorate, Status of Women Canada, Ottawa, November 21, 1995.
8 Interviews with Claxton, November 24, 1995; and Ferderber, November 21, 1995.
9 Interview with Ferderber, November 21, 1995.
10 Interviews with Madeleine Gilchrist, member of Canadian Voice of Women for Peace and

the Canadian Beijing Facilitating Committee and nongovernmental observer on the Canadian delegations to the 1994 Vienna Regional Meetings, the 1994 CSW Intersessional Working Group, and the 1995 New York Preparatory Meetings, Toronto, July 15, 1996; and Pat Beck, National Council of Women, member of the Canadian Beijing Facilitating Committee, and nongovernmental observer on the Canadian Delegation to the Fourth World Conference on Women, Beijing, September 1995.

11 Interview with Beck.
12 Interview with Ferderber, November 21, 1995.
13 Interview with Claxton, February 25, 1998.
14 Interview with Beck.
15 The national women's groups represented at the meetings included the Congress of Black Women of Canada, NAC, National Council of Women of Canada, National Métis Women of Canada, Réseau national d'action éducation femmes, Women's Legal Education and Action Fund, VOW, YWCA, and Zonta.
16 Interview with Gilchrist, July 15, 1995. At that point, VOW was accredited to the UN Disarmament Committee in Geneva and New York. In 1995, it received accreditation from the UN Economic and Social Council.
17 This study was subsequently published as *Strategies for the Year 2000: A Woman's Handbook* (Halifax, NS: Fernwood, 1995).
18 The members of the steering committee were Pat Beck, National Council of Women of Canada; Marge Friedel, National Métis Women of Canada; Keith Fulton, Lesbian Forum; Madeleine Gilchrist, Voice of Women: Monique Hébert, Réseau national d'action éducation femmes; Nayyar Javed, NAC; Stella LeJohn, MATCH International (chairperson); Fleurette Osborne, Congress of Black Women of Canada; Gillian Phillips, Women's Environment, Education and Development Foundation; Louise Shaughnessy, National Association of Women and the Law; Muriel Smith, United Nations Association of Canada; Laura Stelmen, National Anti-Poverty Organization; and Mary Stuart, YWCA.
19 Interview with Gilchrist, July 15, 1996.
20 According to Gilchrist, five women expressed an interest in being briefed after the Vienna meetings. Interview July 15, 1996.
21 Interview with Grant-Cummings.
22 Confidential interview with a member of the CBFC.
23 Interview with Joanna Kerr, senior researcher, North-South Institute, Ottawa, July 10, 1996.
24 Interview with Claxton, February 25, 1998.
25 Ibid.
26 Joanna Kerr, "Canadian NGOs Preparing for Beijing 1995" (n.p.: North-South Institute, 1993).
27 Interview with Kerr.
28 Ibid.
29 Ibid.
30 Ibid.
31 Ibid.
32 Interviews with several participants at the July 1993 meeting.
33 Interview with Kerr.
34 Interviews with participants at the July 1993 meeting.
35 The idea of funding NGO participation was, however, not unique to the Beijing conference. For example, funds were also provided by the Canadian government to facilitate NGO preparations for the Copenhagen Summit for Social Development and the Rio Conference on the Environment and Development.
36 Interviews with Raymond, November 22, 1995; and Gilchrist, July 15, 1996.
37 *Onward to Beijing: For Equality, Development and Peace* (newsletter of the Canadian Beijing Facilitating Committee) 1, 2 (1994), 23.
38 The decision to canvass only women's groups was contentious. Several environmental and development groups resented being excluded and argued that they had important contributions to make to a conference with the themes of development, equality, and peace. The women's groups responded that those other groups had already had conferences

devoted to their primary interests in which they had been full participants and that it was now the turn of women's groups. Interview with Kerr.

39 REAL Women had a representative on the initial ballot, but she was not elected to the CBFC. The organization remained on the CBFC database and was sent all the latter's mailings.

40 Interview with Claxton, November 24, 1995.

41 Ibid., February 25, 1998.

42 Interviews with Gilchrist, April 12, 1995; and Grant-Cummings.

43 Interview with Lise Martin, Canadian Beijing Facilitating Committee, Ottawa, July 18, 1995.

44 Interviews with Claxton, February 25, 1998; and Martin.

45 Interview with Gilchrist, July 15, 1996.

46 Interview with Martin.

47 Ibid.

48 Interview with Claxton, February 25, 1998.

49 Interview with Martin.

50 The CBFC board met for the first time in April 1994, again in January 1995, and a final time in October 1995. Interview with Martin.

51 Ibid.

52 Interviews with government and NGO participants.

53 Interview with Shelagh Day, women's rights activist and representative for the National Association of Women and the Law and EGALE (Equality for Gays and Lesbians Everywhere) at the Fourth World Conference on Women, Toronto, April 13, 1995.

54 Pauline Comeau, "Canadian NGO process to Beijing falls off the rails," *Human Rights Tribune* 2, 3(September/October 1994): 22.

55 Ibid.

56 Ibid.

57 Interview with Day.

58 Interviews with Day and Grant-Cummings.

59 Interview with Beck.

60 Interviews with government and NGO representatives.

61 Interview with Gilchrist, April 12, 1995.

62 *Onward to Beijing*, 1, 2 (1994), 18.

63 Interview with Martin.

64 Ibid.

65 Interview with Gilchrist, July 15, 1996.

66 Ibid.

67 Ibid.; and interview with Martin.

68 Interview with Gilchrist, July 15, 1996.

69 Ibid.

70 Canadian Beijing Facilitating Committee (CBFC), *Proposed line by line changes to the* Platform for Action *made by the 10 lead groups working on the CBFC's COORDINATED RESPONSE* (Ottawa: CBFC, 1995).

71 Interview with Gilchrist, July 15, 1996.

72 Interview with Martin. By submitting their document on March 9, the CBFC was actually four days ahead of the deadline specified as necessary for reviewing comments. In a bulletin issued February 23, 1995, SWC announced that it had just received the working draft of the *PFA* and requested that comments on the draft be submitted either through the CBFC or directly to SWC by March 13, 1995, "to ensure sufficient time to review." Canada, Status of Women, *United Nations Fourth World Conference on Women: Beijing, China, September 4-15, 1995: Platform for Action* (Ottawa, 1995).

73 Interview with Gilchrist, July 15, 1996.

74 Ibid.

75 The CPC facilitated government-NGO consultations not only in the development of positions regarding the *PFA* but also in the preparation of other related documents, including Canada, Status of Women, "Women's Equality in Canada: Progress in Implementing the

Nairobi Forward-looking Strategies for the Advancement of Women, January 1992 to April 1995," *Fact Sheet* 5 (Ottawa, 1995).

76 The membership of the CPC appears in Appendix 2.

77 Interview with Claxton, November 24, 1995.

78 For example, the North-South Institute and MATCH International had close relations with CIDA. Interviews with Girvan, July 17, 1995; Rivington; and Kerr. The Canadian Labour Congress had well-established contact with Human Resources Development. Interview with Riche.

79 The decision as to which women's groups would be nominated to sit on the CPC was made by the CBFC board at its first meeting in April 1994. Interview with Martin.

80 Interview with Kerr.

81 Ibid.

82 Interview with Day.

83 Interview with Martin.

84 Interview with Claxton, November 24, 1995.

85 Madeleine Gilchrist comments, "I cried when I, as a member of the Canadian delegation, saw the official government position. The government had paid no attention to the NGO line-by-line analysis." Interview with Gilchrist, July 15, 1996.

86 Ruth Archibald, director, Refugee, Population and Migration Division, Department of Foreign Affairs and International Trade, Ottawa, July 11, 1996.

87 The issue of state autonomy and the nature of the relationship between the government and civil society is explored in greater depth in the concluding chapter.

88 Interview with Claxton, November 24, 1995.

89 Interview with Kien, November 27, 1995.

90 Interview with Claxton, November 24, 1995.

91 Interview with Grant-Cummings.

92 Ibid.

93 Ibid.

94 Ibid.

95 Ibid.

96 Ibid.

97 Ibid.

98 The president of the NAC negatively contrasted the relationship between her organization and the secretary of state for SWC during the Beijing process with the NAC's relationship with the minister of justice: "A healthy respect developed between the NAC and the Ministry of Justice through the use of a consulting mechanism. When legislation was being considered by the Department of Justice, the NAC gave input in the form of what it considered unacceptable and what was considered acceptable in principle but in need of some revisions. Prior to their meetings, the NAC and the Department of Justice discussed the agenda and who should be invited to participate. The process did not mean that the minister of justice gave the NAC everything it demanded, but it did foster a healthy working relationship. In meetings with SWC, by contrast, it was the former which set the agenda and decided on the participants." Interview with Grant-Cummings.

99 Interview with C. Gwendolyn Landolt, national vice-president, REAL Women of Canada, Beijing, September 1995.

100 Interview with Landolt.

101 REAL Women, "Fourth World Conference on Women in Beijing September 4-15, 1995 [and] Non-Governmental Organization Forum (NGO) August 30-September 8, 1995" (paper presented at the NGO forum in Huairou, September 1995), 1.

102 REAL Women, "Unrepresentative Canadian Delegation Funds Feminist NGOs to Support its Extremist Policies" (paper distributed at the International Convention Centre, September 1995), 1.

103 Confidential interview with a Canadian negotiator.

104 Interview with Dion, July 17, 1995.

105 Interview with Day.

106 Interview with Gilchrist, July 15, 1996.

107 Interview with Grant-Cummings.
108 National Action Committee on the Status of Women (NAC), *Women in Canada After Beijing: Left Out, Left Over, Left Behind* (Toronto: NAC, 1997).

Chapter 5: Canadian Delegation

1   Letter from Valerie Raymond, former executive director, UN World Conference on Women Secretariat, Status of Women Canada, Ottawa, September 30, 1999, 3.
2   United Nations, Second World Conference on Human Rights, *Vienna Declaration and Programme of Action*, A/Conf.157/23 (1993).
3   Madeleine Gilchrist, "Report on the Vienna Intergovernmental Meetings," *Onward to Beijing: For Equality, Development and Peace* 1, 2 (1994): 13.
4   Ibid., 13.
5   Ibid., 13.
6   Ibid., 13.
7   Interviews with Madeleine Gilchrist, member of Canadian Voice of Women for Peace and the Canadian Beijing Facilitating Committee and nongovernmental observer on the Canadian delegations to the 1994 Vienna Regional Meetings, the 1994 CSW Intersessional Working Group, and the 1995 New York Preparatory Meetings, Toronto, July 15, 1996; and Pat Beck, National Council of Women, member of the Canadian Beijing Facilitating Committee, and nongovernmental observer on the Canadian Delegation to the Fourth World Conference on Women, Beijing, September 1995.
8   Interview with Gilchrist, July 15, 1996.
9   Ibid.
10 Ibid.
11 Interview with Joanna Kerr, senior researcher, North-South Institute, Ottawa, July 10, 1996.
12 Ibid.
13 The Copenhagen Summit for Social Development was held March 6-12, 1995.
14 Confidential interview with a staff member in the Secretariat of the Fourth World Conference on Women, 1995.
15 REAL Women, "Canadian Women Object," press release, New York, March 30, 1995, 1.
16 Interview with Rhonda Ferderber, director, External Relations and Communications Directorate, Status of Women Canada, Ottawa, December 9, 1997.
17 Ibid.
18 Confidential interview with a Canadian negotiator 1995.
19 Canada, Status of Women, "From New York ... To Beijing: NGO Funding for Beijing," *Beijing Update* (Spring 1995), 1.
20 Interview with Abby Hoffman, executive director, Women's Health Bureau, Health Canada, Ottawa, July 10, 1996.
21 Interviews with Hoffman; Shelagh Day, women's rights activist and representative for the National Association of Women and the Law and EGALE (Equality for Gays and Lesbians Everywhere) at the Fourth World Conference on Women, Toronto, April 13, 1995; and Madeleine Gilchrist, July 15, 1996.
22 Interview with Diana Rivington, senior policy advisor, Women in Development and Gender Equity Division, Policy Branch, Canadian International Development Agency, Ottawa, November 23, 1995.
23 Canada, Status of Women, "From New York ... To Beijing," 1.
24 Fewer than twenty countries included NGO representatives on their official delegations. Interview with Lise Martin, coordinator, Canadian Beijing Facilitating Committee, Ottawa, July 18, 1995.
25 Gulzar Samji, "Reflections of an NGO Representative on the Canadian Government Delegation," *Onward to Beijing* 1, 4 (1995): 10.
26 Interview with Gilchrist, July 15, 1996.
27 Ibid.
28 Interviews with Hoffman and Day.
29 Interview with Martin.
30 Interview with Gilchrist, July 15, 1996. These sentiments were echoed by Shelagh Day.

31 Interview with Martin.
32 Relations between the Canadian NGOs and government officials at the international negotiations are discussed further in Chapter 6.
33 United Nations, Economic and Social Council, *Informal Consultations on the Draft Platform for Action of the Fourth World Conference on Women*, 1995/225 (New York, June 1, 1995).
34 Letter from Raymond, September 30, 1999.
35 United Nations, Fourth World Conference on Women, *Report of the Informal Consultations Convened by the Chairperson of the Commission on the Status of Women*, A/Conf.177/L.3 (New York, 1995).
36 Kristen Timothy, deputy director/coordinator, United Nations Fourth World Conference on Women Secretariat, address at the NGO forum '95, Huairou, September 2, 1995.
37 UN conferences and summits generally negotiate a text that identifies the key issues, outlines objectives, and recommends strategies and actions for achieving these objectives – in this case the *PFA*. They also negotiate a declaration – in this case the *Beijing Declaration* – that is designed to establish a framework by setting out core principles and broad approaches to overcoming identified problems.
38 The amount of the per diem is set by the Treasury Board of Canada for all government travel.
39 Interview with Adèle Dion, departmental coordinator, International Women's Equality, Human Rights, Women's Equality and Social Affairs Division, Department of Foreign Affairs and International Trade, Ottawa, July 17, 1995.
40 Ibid.
41 Interviews with Dion, December 11, 1997; and Ferderber, December 9, 1997.
42 Interview with Ruth Archibald, director, Refugee, Population and Migration Division, Department of Foreign Affairs and International Trade, Ottawa, July 11, 1996.
43 Interview with Dion, November 21, 1995.
44 Interview with Penny Ballantyne, assistant deputy minister, Health and Social Services, Government of the Northwest Territories, Beijing, September 1995.
45 Interview with Ferderber, November 21, 1995.
46 Interview with Gilchrist, July 15, 1996.
47 Interview with Martin.
48 In contrast, five members of the NGO facilitating committee for the UN Conference on the Environment and Development were appointed to the official delegation.
49 Interview with Gilchrist, July 15, 1996.
50 The selection of candidates to fill the twelve nongovernmental observer positions was made so as to reflect regional diversity, and to include English- and French-speaking women, those working in the key issue areas, and those representing particular constituencies (e.g., youth, indigenous women, and women of colour).
51 Interview with Dion, December 11, 1997.
52 Ibid.
53 The major exception was Nancy Riche. Two years before the Beijing conference, André Ouelette, minister of foreign affairs, had offered the CLC places on the Canadian delegations to the Copenhagen Summit for Social Development and the Beijing Conference on Women. The CLC saw these offers as important endorsements by the Canadian government of its work and contributions. Interview with Riche, executive vice-president, Canadian Labour Congress, and nongovernmental observer on the Canadian Delegation to the Fourth World Conference on Women, Ottawa, July 11, 1996.
54 Interviews with Lorraine Michael, coordinator, Women and Economic Justice, Ecumenical Coalition for Economic Justice, and nongovernmental observer on the Canadian Delegation to the Fourth World Conference on Women, Beijing, August 21, 1996; and Riche.
55 Interview with Michael, August 21, 1996.
56 Ibid.
57 Canada, Status of Women, "Two Young Women Selected to Attend Conference," *Beijing Update* (Summer 1995): 1-2.
58 Interview with Dion, December 11, 1997.

59 Sally Armstrong, "Mean-spirited attack was uncalled for," *Toronto Star,* September 12, 1995, A16.
60 Canada, Status of Women, "Two Young Women Selected to Attend Conference," 2.
61 Interview with Gilchrist, July 15, 1996. Her sentiments were widely shared. For example, Joanna Kerr supported the idea of sending youth to the conference but she did not agree with the decision to allocate two of the nongovernmental positions on the delegation to them. The wisdom of having "raffled off" two places on the delegation to youth was severely criticized by then president of the NAC, Sunera Thobani, as cited by Paul Watson in "Ottawa stacking forum, feminist charge," *Toronto Star,* September 6, 1995, A3.
62 Interview with Dion, December 11, 1997.
63 Interview with Michael, August 6, 1996.
64 The details of the organization of the work at the Fourth World Conference on Women are outlined in United Nations, Fourth World Conference on Women, *Organization of Work, Including the Establishment of the Main Committee,* A/Conf.177/3 (New York, 1995).
65 Working Group One dealt with Chapter 1: Mission Statement; Chapter 2: Global Framework; Chapter 3: Critical Areas of Concern; Chapter 5: Institutional Arrangements; and Chapter 6: Financial Arrangements. It also handled the following critical areas of concern in the *PFA*: health, the media, and the girl child. Working Group Two addressed the remaining issues in the *PFA*, including human rights, diversity, armed conflict and peace, power and decision-making, education, violence, the environment, national machinery, and poverty.
66 Interview with Ferderber, December 9, 1997.
67 Interview with Marnie Girvan, director, Women in Development and Gender Equity Division, Canadian International Development Agency, Ottawa, July 17, 1995.
68 Interview with Girvan, July 17, 1995.
69 Interview with Riche, July 11, 1996.
70 Interview with Girvan, July 18, 1995.
71 Interview with Ferderber, December 9, 1997.
72 Ibid.
73 Ibid.
74 Ibid. Cathy McRae was the chief of Environmental Analysis in the External Relations and Communication Directorate at SWC.
75 Interview with Ferderber, December 9, 1997.
76 Ibid.
77 Interview with Ruth Archibald, director, Refugee, Population and Migration Division, Department of Foreign Affairs and International Trade, Ottawa, July 11, 1996.
78 Interview with Rivington.
79 Interview with Sheila Regehr, senior policy analyst, Policy and Analysis Directorate, Status of Women Canada, Ottawa, November 23, 1995. Half-way through the conference, the Canadian delegation distributed a list to all who attended the briefings for Canadian NGOs indicating which government negotiator was responsible for which issues. See Appendix 3.
80 Interview with Dion, July 17, 1995.
81 Interview with Dion, December 11, 1997.
82 Letter from Raymond, September 30, 1999, 3.
83 Interview with Rivington.
84 Interview with Archibald. July 11, 1996.
85 Dianne Rinehart, "Canada's team wins praise at women's conference," Canada Press, September 7, 1995.
86 It was decided to refer back to the section where agreement had been reached and not to repeat language in this section. Interview with Archibald.
87 Interview with Dion, December 11, 1997.
88 Interview with Girvan, July 17, 1995.
89 Interview with Dion, December 11, 1997.
90 Interview with Archibald, July 11, 1996.
91 Interview with Michael, August 21, 1996.

92 Rape had been defined as a war crime in the UN *Declaration on the Elimination of Violence Against Women.* The *PFA,* however, goes beyond that definition by making the link to genocide.
93 Interview with Archibald, July 11, 1996.
94 Interview with Ferderber, December 9, 1997.
95 Duy Ai Kien, speech to the "Second Canadian Conference on International Health: Health Reform Around the Globe: Towards Equality and Sustainability?" (Ottawa, November 12, 1995).
96 As further evidence of a commitment to NGO participation, Raymond had established a process within DFAIT for consulting with NGOs in the human rights field, prior to being seconded to SWC.
97 Interviews with government officials on the Canadian delegation.
98 Canada, Status of Women, *Briefing Book for the Canadian Delegation* (Ottawa, 1995), 3.
99 Lorraine Michael, *UN World Conference on Women, Beijing, September 4-15, 1995: Report by Lorraine Michael* (Toronto: n.p., 1995), 2.
100 Interview with Dion, December 11, 1997.
101 Michael, "UN World Conference on Women," 1.
102 Nancy Riche was a nongovernmental observer on the Canadian delegation to the Copenhagen Summit for Social Development, while Lorraine Michael was a nongovernmental observer on the Canadian delegation to the Third Preparatory Meetings for the Copenhagen Summit.
103 Interview with Michael, August 21, 1996.
104 Interview with Dion, December 11, 1997.
105 Interviews with nongovernmental observers, Beijing, September 1995.
106 Such requests were made by at least two nongovernmental observers – Lorraine Michael and Nancy Riche – and one parliamentarian – Audrey McLaughlin.
107 Interview with Gilchrist, July 15, 1996.
108 Interview with Regehr. This view was corroborated by Ruth Archibald, who described their contributions as "very helpful and useful."
109 Interview with Regehr.
110 Interview with Michael, August 21, 1996. These sentiments were echoed by Nancy Riche.
111 Interview with Dion, December 11, 1997.
112 Ibid.
113 Confidential interview with a nongovernmental observer, Beijing, September 1995.
114 As noted earlier, the major exception here was Nancy Riche, who knew two years in advance that she was to attend as the representative of the CLC. In contrast, Glenda Simms was given only three weeks' notice. Interview with Simms, past president, Canadian Advisory Council on the Status of Women, and nongovernmental observer on the Canadian Delegation to the Fourth World Conference on Women, Beijing, September 1995.
115 Interviews with nongovernmental observers on the Canadian delegation, Beijing, September 1995.
116 Interview with government officials, Beijing, September 1995.
117 Interview with Dion, December 11, 1997.
118 Interview with Archibald, July 11, 1996.
119 Ibid.
120 Interviews with Riche, July 11, 1996; and Michael, August 21, 1996.

Chapter 6: Canadian NGOs at the International Negotiations

 1 Duy Ai Kien, speech to the "Second Canadian Conference on International Health: Health Reform Around the Globe: Towards Equality and Sustainability?" (Ottawa, November 12, 1995).
 2 Ibid. A list of those accredited appears in Appendix 4.
 3 Under Article 71 of the United Nations Charter, the Economic and Social Council is authorized to "make suitable arrangements for consultation with nongovernmental organizations which are concerned with matters within its competence." Consultative status

not only allows a NGO to interact with the council and its specialized agencies but also facilitates contact with the UN secretariat.

4 United Nations, Office of the NGO Forum on Women '95, "UN Briefs NGOs on Accreditation Process," *Daily NGO Bulletin* (March 28, 1995), 1.

5 International Peace Bureau, *The Other Side of Beijing: Problems* (New York: International Peace Bureau, 1995). This update was distributed by Debra Guzman on July 28, 1995, at <Debra@oln.comlink.apc.org>.

6 United Nations, Economic and Social Council, *Economic and Social Council Approves Eight Additional Non-Governmental Organizations for Participation in World Conference on Women*, ECOSOC/5617 (New York, 1995).

7 Eleven groups included on the list compiled by the secretariat were denied accreditation. See ibid., 1.

8 Ibid.

9 On August 21, 1995, "organizers admitted 2,800 confirmation letters had still not left China." Rod Mickleburgh, "Women's Forum delegates lack visas: Despite positive spin from organizers, many problems remain as Beijing's NGO conference approaches," *Globe and Mail*, August 23, 1995, A8.

10 Judy Rebick, "Beijing Dairy: The women's conference the media missed," *Canadian Forum* 74, 845 (1995): 27.

11 Sunera Thobani, "Beijing and Beyond," *Action Now* (Quarterly publication of the NAC) 5, 8 (1995): 2.

12 Carole Samdup, "Tibetan Women Triumph in Beijing," *Onward From Beijing* (December 1995), 9.

13 Interview with Jackie Claxton, director, Women's Program, Status of Women Canada, Ottawa, February 25, 1998; and Duy Ai Kien, policy officer, Women's Program, Status of Women Canada, Ottawa, February 25, 1998.

14 As cited in "Report of the 39th Session of the Commission on the Status of Women (Fourth World Conference on Women Prepcom) 15 March-7 April," *Earth Negotiations Bulletin* 14, 9 (1995): 9.

15 Interview with Lorraine Michael, coordinator, Women and Economic Justice, Ecumenical Coalition for Economic Justice, and nongovernmental observer on the Canadian Delegation to the Fourth World Conference on Women, Beijing, August 21, 1996.

16 By the end of April 1995, 36,000 had registered for the NGO Forum on Women.

17 Reuters News Agency, "China rejects plea to move forum," *Globe and Mail*, May 25, 1995, A17.

18 Rod Mickleburgh, "China angers UN organizers: Plan to move NGO forum outside Beijing 'unbelievable'," *Globe and Mail*, April 6, 1995, A16.

19 Irene Santiago as cited in Rod Mickleburgh, "Moving women's forum out of Beijing sparks outcry," *Globe and Mail*, April 22, 1995, A9.

20 Reuters News Agency, "China rejects plea to move forum," *Globe and Mail*, May 25, 1995, A17.

21 Pauline Comeau, "Access becomes the key issue for the UN World Conference on Women," *Human Rights Tribune* 3, 2 (June/July 1995): 9.

22 United Nations, NGO Forum on Women Secretariat, *NGO Forum on Women: Look at the World Through Women's Eyes, 30 August-8 September: Final Report* (New York, 1995), 18.

23 *Onward to Beijing* 1, 1 (1994): 2.

24 Quoted in Rod Mickleburgh, "China angers UN organizers."

25 Catherine Boldt, "Frustrations and Challenges," *Onward from Beijing* (December 1995), 11.

26 Canada's negotiating objectives are discussed in Chapter 7.

27 "Health Canada's Women's Health Bureau," in Canada, Health, *Women's Health: Fourth World Conference on Women* (Ottawa, 1995), Attachment 3, 1.

28 Interview with Claxton, November 24, 1995. See Appendix 5 for a list of those funded to attend the 1995 New York Preparatory Meetings and Appendix 6 for a list of those funded to attend the NGO Forum on Women '95.

29 Support for NGOs to attend the women's conference and NGO Forum in China came from government departments such as SWC, CIDA, DFAIT, Human Resources Development,

Health, Agriculture, Justice, Indian and Northern Affairs, Heritage, and the Canadian Mortgage and Housing Corporation.

30 Interview with Claxton and Kien, February 25, 1998.
31 Interview with Madeleine Gilchrist, member of Canadian Voice of Women for Peace and the Canadian Beijing Facilitating Committee and nongovernmental observer on the Canadian delegations to the 1994 Vienna Regional Meetings, the 1994 CSW Inter-sessional Working Group, and the 1995 New York Preparatory Meetings, Toronto, April 12, 1995.
32 Interview with Joan Grant-Cummings, president, National Action Committee on the Status of Women, Toronto, July 16, 1996.
33 Interview with Claxton and Kien.
34 Memorandum from Duy Ai Kien, September 6, 2000.
35 Interview with Claxton and Kien.
36 Letter from Lise Martin and Jackie Claxton to all those on the CBFC distribution list (Ottawa, March 13, 1995), 1-2. Emphasis in the original.
37 Canada, Status of Women, "From New York ... To Beijing: NGO Funding for Beijing," *Beijing Update* (Spring 1995), 1.
38 Interview with Claxton and Kien.
39 See Appendix 6.
40 Interview with Claxton and Kien.
41 Interview with Gilchrist, July 15, 1996.
42 Interview with Joanna Kerr, senior researcher, North-South Institute, Ottawa, July 10, 1996.
43 Interview with Claxton, November 24, 1995.
44 Canadian Beijing Facilitating Committee, "NGO Regional Meeting in Vienna: Forum 94," *Onward to Beijing: For Equality, Development and Peace* 1, 2 (1994): 12.
45 Madeleine Gilchrist, "Report on the Vienna Intergovernmental Meetings," *Onward to Beijing: For Equality, Development and Peace* 1, 2 (1994): 13.
46 Interview with Gilchrist, April 12, 1995.
47 Ibid.
48 Interview with Kerr.
49 E/ECE/RW/HCM/L.3/Rev.1.
50 Interview with Gilchrist, April 12, 1995.
51 Interview with Gilchrist, July 15, 1995.
52 International Peace Bureau, *Final Preparatory Meeting for Beijing: Fraught with Problems* (New York: International Peace Bureau, 1995), 1. This update was distributed by Debra Guzman on July 28, 1995, at <Debra@oln.comlink.apc.org>.
53 Interview with Lise Martin, coordinator, Canadian Beijing Facilitating Committee, Ottawa, July 18, 1995.
54 Women's Linkage caucus, August 30, 1995.
55 Valerie Raymond, "Talking Points for Valerie Raymond, Executive Director, UN World Conference on Women Secretariat, to the Professional Association of Foreign Service Officers" (Ottawa: Department of Foreign Affairs and International Trade, 1995), 5.
56 Interview with Gilchrist, July 15, 1996.
57 Interview with Ruth Archibald, director, Refugee, Population and Migration Division, Department of Foreign Affairs and International Trade, Ottawa, July 11, 1996.
58 Interview with Archibald.
59 Ibid.
60 Ibid.
61 Interview with Katherine McDonald, president of the Advisory Council for the Status of Women in Nova Scotia and member of the Board of Directors, International Planned Parenthood Federation, Beijing, September 9, 1995.
62 See Deborah Stienstra, "Can the Silence be Broken? Gender and Canadian Foreign Policy," *International Journal* 50, 1 (1994-5): 116; and Kathleen E. Mahoney, "Human Rights and Canada's foreign policy," *International Journal* 47, 3 (1992): 594.
63 Interview with Kerry Buck, deputy director, Human Rights, Humanitarian Affairs and International Women's Equality Division, July 5, 2000.

64 It must be noted that in both these cases, the good working relations extended well beyond the Beijing process.

65 Interview with Riche.

66 Ibid.

67 Sunera Thobani, "Beijing and Beyond," *Action Now* 5, 8 (1995): 2-3.

68 Interview with Grant-Cummings.

69 Ibid.

70 Ibid.

71 Interview with C. Gwendolyn Landolt, national vice-president, REAL Women of Canada, Beijing, September 1995.

72 The emphasis appears in the original document. REAL Women of Canada, "Fourth World Conference on Women in Beijing, September 4-15, 1995 [and] Non-Government Organization Forum August 30-September 8, 1995" (paper presented at the NGO forum in Huairou, September 1995), 1. Similar phraseology was used in other documents circulated by the group at the conference and the NGO forum, as illustrated by the titles chosen: "Beijing Platform of [sic] Action – A Racist Document" and "REAL Women of Canada Rejects Western Cultural Imperialism in the Beijing Platform for Action."

73 Interview with McDonald.

74 Ibid.

75 There were 3,250 media representatives accredited to the Fourth World Conference on Women. United Nations, Department of Public Information, *From Beijing, a Platform for Action and a clear mandate for women's progress*, DPI/1749 (New York, 1995), 5. Over 3,000 international journalists attended the NGO forum. United Nations, NGO Forum on Women Secretariat, *NGO Forum on Women, Final Report*, 18.

76 Judy Rebick, "Beijing Diary," 30.

77 Interview with Riche.

78 Interview with McDonald.

79 Interview with Kerr.

80 Madeleine Gilchrist, "Beijing '95 and the Canadian Press," *Onward From Beijing* (December 1995), 18.

81 Ibid., 18.

82 United Nations, NGO Forum on Women Secretariat, *NGO Forum on Women, Final Report*, 4. Of the 30,000 participants, only 1,400 were men. Ibid., 63.

83 Ibid., 4. The number of workshops and panels in Huairou was "a quantum leap from the 200 in 1975 in Mexico and 1,500 in Nairobi," United Nations, NGO Forum on Women Secretariat, "Thousands Come to Huairou for Largest Gathering on Women," *NGO Forum on Women '95 Bulletin* (December 1995), 1.

84 United Nations, NGO Forum on Women Secretariat, *NGO Forum on Women, Final Report*, 23.

85 Ibid., 24.

86 Interview with Janis Alton, United Nations representative, Voice of Women, Toronto, April 12, 1995.

87 Interview with Claxton, February 25, 1998.

88 Judy Rebick, "Beijing Diary," 30.

89 Interview with Alton.

90 Shelagh Day as cited in *Onward From Beijing* (December 1995), 9.

Chapter 7: Canada and the *Beijing Declaration* and *Platform for Action*

1 United Nations, Development Program, *Fourth World Conference on Women, Beijing, 4-15 September: Declaration and Platform for Action Break New Ground in International Efforts for Advancement of Women to Year 2000*, press release, WOM/871 (New York, 1995), 2.

2 United Nations, Fourth World Conference on Women, *Platform for Action* (hereafter *PFA*), Chapter 1, 10, par. 1. The *PFA* constitutes most of the United Nations, Fourth World Conference on Women, *Report of the Fourth World Conference on Women (Beijing, 4-15 September 1995)* A/Conf.177/20 (New York, October 1995).

3 *PFA*, Chapter 1, 10, par. 2.

4 *PFA,* Chapter 3, 19, par. 44.
5 Chapter 4 consists of 100 of the 126 pages in the *PFA.*
6 United Nations, Department of Public Information, *From Beijing, a Platform for Action and a clear mandate for women's progress,* DPI/1749 (New York, 1995), 1.
7 Canada, Status of Women, "Overview of Canadian Objectives and Priorities for the Platform for Action," in Canada, Status of Women, *Briefing Book for the Canadian Delegation* (Ottawa, 1995), 2. The same text also appeared in "Canadian priorities and Objectives for the PFA," which was part of the NGO kits produced by SWC for the Beijing conference.
8 In particular, the *Briefing Book for the Canadian Delegation* refers to the 1990 New York Summit for Children, the 1992 Rio Conference on the Environment and Development, the 1993 Vienna Conference on Human Rights, the 1994 Cairo Conference on Population and Development, and the 1995 Copenhagen Summit for Social Development. According to the *Briefing Book,* "Of particular importance are agreements reached on rights for girl children, on the promotion and protection of women's rights as human rights, including reproductive health and rights, on the empowerment of women and on the critical place of gender equality in reducing poverty and achieving sustainable economic and social development." (Canada, Status of Women, "Overview of Canadian Objectives," 1.)
9 As cited in Canada, Department of Foreign Affairs and International Trade, "Ouellet Announces Delegation to the Fourth World Conference on Women," *This Week in Trade and Foreign Policy* (August 24-30, 1995), 4.
10 Interview with Valerie Raymond, executive director, UN World Conference on Women Secretariat, Status of Women Canada, Ottawa, November 22, 1995.
11 Canada, Status of Women, "Overview of Canadian Objectives," 2-4.
12 My thanks to Kerry Buck, deputy director, Human Rights, Humanitarian Affairs and International Women's Equality Division, for her valuable insights into this issue, the debate it sparked, and its final resolution at the Fourth World Conference on Women.
13 See *PFA,* Chapter 2, 11, par. 9.
14 Seth Faison, "Fragile Pact Gives Women 'Glimmer' of New Hope," *International Herald Tribune,* September 16, 1995.
15 Canada, Status of Women, "Canada's Priorities for the 12 Critical Areas of Concern in the Platform for Action," in Canada, Status of Women, *Briefing Book for the Canadian Delegation,* 1-3. These priorities accurately reflect the instructions to the Canadian negotiators. Interview with Adèle Dion, departmental coordinator, International Women's Equality, Human Rights, Women's Equality and Social Affairs Division, Department of Foreign Affairs and International Trade, Ottawa, December 11, 1997.
16 Interview with Dion, December 11, 1997.
17 Canada, Status of Women, "Overview of Canadian Objectives," 2.
18 *PFA,* Chapter 4, 21, par. 46.
19 For a detailed account of the debate and of the chair's decision, see Shelagh Day, "Women's Sexual Autonomy: Universality, Sexual Rights, and Sexual Orientation at the Beijing Conference," *Canadian Woman Studies,* 16, 3 (1996): 46-54.
20 Shelagh Day, "Women's Sexual Autonomy," 50.
21 International Institute for Sustainable Development, "The Main Committee," *Earth Negotiations Bulletin* 14, 21 (1995): 8.
22 Mary Sillett, "Ensuring Indigenous Women's Voices are Heard: The Beijing Declaration on Indigenous Women," *Canadian Woman Studies* 16, 3 (1996): 62-3.
23 Canada, Status of Women, "Overview of Canadian Objectives," 3.
24 *PFA,* Chapter 4(A), 23, par. 56.
25 The issue has been included in this section because this is where Canada categorized its objectives regarding unpaid work. It is important to note, however, that most of the paragraphs dealing with unpaid work appear in the *PFA* under Institutional Mechanisms for the Advancement of Women.
26 Non Governmental Organisation (NGO) BEIJING DECLARATION, September 15, 1995. <www.igc.org/beijing/ngo/ngodec.html>.
27 Canada, Status of Women, "Overview of Canadian Objectives," 3.

28 Ibid., 3.
29 Ibid., 4.
30 In 1993, Canada had become the first country in the world to include the well-grounded fear of sexual violence and other gender-based persecutions as legitimate grounds for claiming refugee status in Canada.
31 *PFA*, Chapter 4(E), 64, par. 145(d).
32 Interview with Dion, December 11, 1997.
33 Ibid.
34 Interviews with Madeleine Gilchrist, member of Canadian Voice of Women for Peace and the Canadian Beijing Facilitating Committee and nongovernmental observer on the Canadian delegations to the 1994 Vienna Regional Meetings, the 1994 CSW Inter-sessional Working Group, and the 1995 New York Preparatory Meetings, Toronto, July 15, 1996; and Pat Beck, National Council of Women, member of the Canadian Beijing Facilitating Committee, and nongovernmental observer on the Canadian Delegation to the Fourth World Conference on Women, Beijing, September 1995.
35 Canada, Status of Women, "Canada's Priorities," 1.
36 United Nations, Division for the Advancement of Women/Department of Public Information, *Beijing Declaration and Platform for Action (Summary)* (New York: 1996). The document can be found at <www.undp.org/fwcw/plat.htm>.
37 Canada, Status of Women, "Canada's Priorities," 1.
38 Canada, Status of Women, *Beijing Platform for Action: Key Achievements* (Ottawa, 1995), 2.
39 Canada, Status of Women, "Canada's Priorities," 1.
40 *PFA*, Chapter 4(C), 39, par. 95.
41 Canada, Status of Women, "Beijing Platform for Action," 2.
42 *PFA*, Chapter 4(C), 39, par. 96.
43 Canada, Status of Women, "Canada's Priorities," 1.
44 *PFA*, Chapter 4(B), 51, par. 113.
45 Ibid., Chapter 4(D), 54, par. 124a.
46 Interview with Rhonda Ferderber, director, External Relations and Communications Directorate, Status of Women Canada, Ottawa, December 9, 1997.
47 Canada, Status of Women, "Canada's Priorities," 2.
48 Ibid., 2.
49 *PFA*, Chapter 4(J), 102, par. 234.
50 Ibid., 105, par. 244.
51 Canada, Status of Women, "Canada's Priorities," 3.
52 Interview with Diana Rivington, senior policy advisor, Women in Development and Gender Equity Division, Policy Branch, Canadian International Development Agency, Ottawa, November 23, 1995.
53 *PFA*, Chapter 4(K), 108, par. 253(c).
54 Ibid., 108, par. 253(c).
55 Canada, Status of Women, "Canada's Priorities," 3.
56 *PFA*, Chapter 2, 15, par. 29.
57 *PFA*, Chapter 4(L), 114, par. 267.
58 Ibid., 114, par. 267.
59 Ibid., 115, par. 274(d).
60 Mary Purcell, International Federation of University Women and chair of the caucus on the girl child, as cited in United Nations, Fourth World Conference on Women, *Girls of Today are the Women of Tomorrow,* press release, September 13, 1995, 1.
61 On November 10, 1995, UN Secretary-General Boutros Boutros-Ghali committed himself to ensuring that a gender perspective was mainstreamed throughout the workings of the UN. United Nations, General Assembly, 50th Session, "Implementation of the Outcome of the Fourth World Conference on Women: Action for Equality, Development and Peace: Report of the Secretary-General," A/50/744 (November 10, 1995).
62 On December 28, 1995, UN Secretary-General Boutros Boutros-Ghali announced that his senior adviser, Assistant Secretary-General Rosario Green, would serve as his adviser on gender issues.

63 Rod Mickleburgh, "Canada backs platform boosting women," *Globe and Mail,* September 7, 1995, A12.
64 *PFA,* Chapter 5, 123. par. 293.
65 United Nations, Commission on the Status of Women, 40th Session, *Statement by Ms. Rosario Green, Special Adviser to the Secretary-General for Gender Issues* (New York, 1996), 2.
66 As cited by Mickleburgh, "Canada backs platform boosting women," A12.
67 Many in this group also object to a reduction in parental control over children. Equal inheritance for girls was unacceptable to most of the fundamentalist Islamic states.
68 Editorial, "Some leadership from Canada," *Edmonton Journal,* September 10, 1995, A10.
69 Interview with Dion, December 11, 1997.
70 Interview with Rivington.
71 Valerie Raymond, "Talking Points for Valerie Raymond, Executive Director, UN World Conference on Women Secretariat, to the Professional Association of Foreign Service Officers" (Ottawa: Department of Foreign Affairs and International Trade, 1995), 1.
72 Interview with Ferderber, December 9, 1997.
73 As cited in United Nations, Development Program, *Fourth World Conference on Women, Beijing, 4-15 September: Declaration and Platform for Action Break New Ground,"* 2.
74 Jane Foy, "UN conference on women confirms value of unpaid work," *London Free Press,* September 25, 1995, 16.
75 Canadian Beijing Facilitating Committee (CBFC), *Take Action for Equality, Development and Peace: A Canadian Follow-up Guide to Beijing '95* (Ottawa: CBFC, 1996).

Chapter 8: Building on the Past, Looking to the Future
1 Graham T. Allison, *The Essence of Decision: Explaining the Cuban Missile Crisis* (Boston: Little, Brown, 1971), Chapter 5, 144-84. Allison uses the term "bureaucratic politics" in his writings about the American policy-making process. In the Canadian context, the term would imply a focus on the public service and the exclusion of their political masters. In order to include both levels of government actors, the term "governmental politics" is being used here.
2 See Kim Richard Nossal, "Allison through the (Ottawa) looking glass: bureaucratic politics and foreign policy in a parliamentary system," *Canadian Public Administration* 22 (1979), 610.
3 Nossal, "Allison through the (Ottawa) looking glass," 626. For other examinations of the model in the Canadian context, see Nossal, "Bureaucratic politics and the Westminster model," in Robert O. Matthews, Arthur G. Rubinoff, and Janice Gross Stein, eds., *International Conflict and Conflict Management: Readings in World Politics* (Scarborough: Prentice Hall, 1984), 230-7; Michael M. Atkinson and Kim Richard Nossal, "Bureaucratic politics and the New Fighter Aircraft decisions," *Canadian Public Administration* 24 (1981): 531-62; and Elizabeth Riddell-Dixon, "Deep seabed mining: a hotbed for governmental politics," *International Journal* 41, 1 (1985-6): 72-94; and "Winners and Losers: formulating Canada's policies on international technology transfers," *International Journal* 47, 1 (1991-2): 159-83.
4 See Cooper, *Canadian Foreign Policy: Old Habits and New Directions* (Scarborough: Prentice Hall, 1997), 157. See also 158-72.
5 See Douglas Macdonald and Heather A. Smith, "Promises made, promises broken: Questioning Canada's commitments to climate change," *International Journal* 55, 1 (1999-2000): 107-24.
6 Brian W. Tomlin, "On a Fast Track to the Ban: The Canadian Policy Process," *Canadian Foreign Policy* 5, 3 (1998): 3-23.
7 See Kim Richard Nossal, *The Politics of Canadian Foreign Policy,* 3rd ed. (Scarborough: Prentice Hall, 1997), Chapters 11 and 12, 212-331.
8 Interview with Adèle Dion, departmental coordinator, International Women's Equality, Human Rights, Women's Equality and Social Affairs Division, Department of Foreign Affairs and International Trade, Ottawa, December 11, 1997.
9 For a sampling of their views, see *Onward From Beijing* (December 1995).
10 See CBFC, *Onward from Beijing* (December 1995), and Canadian Beijing Facilitating

Committee (CBFC), *Take Action for Equality, Development and Peace: A Canadian Follow-up Guide to Beijing '95* (Ottawa: CBFC, 1996); Canadian Voice of Women for Peace, *Priorities for Actions in the Area of Peace*, distributed January 3, 1996, by Bruna Nota at bruna@web.apc.org; and National Action Committee on the Status of Women (NAC), *Women in Canada After Beijing: Left Out, Left Over, Left Behind* (Toronto: NAC, 1997).

11 See Louise Bergeron-de Villiers, "Everyone Has a Role in Realizing the Promise," *Canadian Woman Studies* 16, 3 (1996): 18-20.

12 See, for examples, Denis Stairs, "Canada and the security problem: Implications as the millennium turns," *International Journal* 54, 3 (1999): 386-403; Andrew F. Cooper, *Canadian Foreign Policy: Old Habits and New Directions* (Scarborough, Prentice Hall, 1997), especially Chapter 1, 1-25; Nossal, *The Politics of Canadian Foreign Policy*, especially 19-94; Tom Keating, *Canada and World Order: The Multilateralist Tradition in Canadian Foreign Policy* (Toronto: McClelland and Stewart, 1993); and David Black and Claire Turenne Sjolander, "Multilateralism Re-constituted and the Discourse of Canadian Foreign Policy," *Studies in Political Economy* 49 (1996): 7-36.

13 See, for instance, Macdonald and Smith, "Promises made, promises broken," 107-24; and Elizabeth Riddell-Dixon, *Canada and the International Seabed: Domestic Determinants and External Constraints* (Montreal: McGill-Queens University Press, 1989), especially 159-64.

14 Excellent overviews of this literature are provided by Cooper, *Canadian Foreign Policy*, especially 6-25; and David R. Black and Heather A. Smith, "Notable exceptions? New and arresting directions in Canadian foreign policy literature," *Canadian Journal of Political Science* 26, 4 (1993): 745-74.

15 David Dewitt and John Kirton, *"Canada as a Principal Power"* (Toronto: John Wiley, 1983). Almost a decade earlier, James Eayrs had sought to elevate perceptions of Canada's standing in the world by arguing that it had many resources that conferred power; hence, that it should be termed a "foremost power." See "Defining a new place for Canada in the hierarchy of world power," *International Perspectives* (May/June 1975), 15-24. See also John J. Kirton, "Canada as a principal financial power: G-7 and IMF diplomacy in the crisis of 1997-9," *International Journal* 54, 4 (1999): 603-24.

16 Some of the key recent contributions to this literature include Cooper, *Canadian Foreign Policy*, especially 6-25; and Andrew Cooper, Richard A. Higgott, and Kim Richard Nossal, *Relocating Middle Powers: Australia and Canada in a Changing World Order* (Vancouver: University of British Columbia Press, 1993). For critical reviews of the concept, see Mark Neufeld, "Hegemony and Foreign Policy: The Case of Canada as a Middle Power," *Studies in Political Economy* 48 (1995): 7-29; and Black and Turenne Sjolander, "Multilateralism Reconstituted."

17 For examples see Marci McDonald, *Yankee Doodle Dandy: Brian Mulroney and the American Agenda* (Toronto: Stoddart, 1995); Wallace Clement, "Continental political economy: an assessment of relations between Canada and the United States," *Canadian Review of American Studies* 10, 1 (1979): 77-87; and Stephen Clarkson, ed., *An Independent Foreign Policy for Canada?* (Toronto: McClelland and Stewart, 1968).

18 Based on the premise that Canada cannot play an effective role in the full range of international decision making but that it must instead select those areas where it can make the greatest contributions and best satisfy its own interests, significant efforts have been made within the last decade to carve out appropriate "niches" for Canadian foreign policy. See Duane Bratt, "Niche-Making and Canadian Peace-making," *Canadian Foreign Policy* 6, 3 (1999): 73-84; Andrew F. Cooper, "In Search of Niches: Saying 'Yes' and Saying 'No' in Canada's International Relations," *Canadian Foreign Policy* 3, 3 (1995): 1-13; and Evan Potter, "Niche Diplomacy and Canadian Foreign Policy," *International Journal* 52, 1 (1996-7): 25-38. For a critique of niche diplomacy, see Heather A. Smith, "Caution Warranted: Niche Diplomacy Assessed," *Canadian Foreign Policy* 6, 3 (1999): 57-72.

19 Interview with Rhonda Ferderber, director, External Relations and Communications Directorate, Status of Women Canada, Ottawa, November 21, 1995.

20 Canada, Status of Women, *Setting the Stage for the Next Century: The Federal Plan for Gender Equality* (Ottawa, 1995).

21 The provisions in the *PFA* are not as advanced as is Canadian practice. Confidential interview with a Canadian negotiator.

22 Oran Young defines the entrepreneurial leader as one who "uses negotiating skill to influence the manner in which issues are presented in the context of institutional bargaining and to fashion mutually acceptable deals bringing willing parties together on the terms of constitutional contracts yielding benefits for all." See Oran Young, "Political Leadership and Regime Formation: On the Development of Institutions in International Society," *International Organization* 45 (1991): 281-308. Canada's negotiators frequently demonstrate effective entrepreneurial leadership, and their skill in this regard needs to be recognized more fully. For a discussion of effective entrepreneurial leadership by Canadian public servants in quite a different venue, see Elizabeth Riddell-Dixon, "Individual Leadership and Structural Power," *Canadian Journal of Political Science* 30, 2 (1997): 257-83.

23 Interview with Glenda Simms, past president, Canadian Advisory Council on the Status of Women, and nongovernmental observer on the Canadian Delegation to the Fourth World Conference on Women, Beijing, September 1995.

24 Interview with Ferderber, November 21, 1995.

25 This finding coincides with Sandra Whitworth's conclusion regarding the hearings of the Special Joint Committee Reviewing Canadian Foreign Policy: "the direct involvement of Canadian citizens in the consultation process is at least a partial step toward greater democratization." Sandra Whitworth, "Women, and Gender, in the Foreign Policy Review Process," in *Canada Among Nations 1995: Democracy and Foreign Policy*, ed. Maxwell A. Cameron and Maureen Appel Molot (Ottawa: Carleton University Press, 1995), 94.

26 Ibid., 94.

27 Ibid., 84.

28 See Nossal, *The Politics of Canadian Foreign Policy*, especially Chapter 4, 95-137; and "Analysing the domestic sources of Canadian foreign policy," *International Journal* 39, 1 (1983-4): 1-22; and Cranford Pratt, "Competing perspectives on Canadian development assistance policies," *International Journal* 51, 2 (1996); "Dominant class theory and Canadian foreign policy: the case of the counter-consensus," *International Journal* 39, 1 (1983-4): 99-135; and *Internationalism Under Strain: the North-South Policies of Canada, the Netherlands, Norway and Sweden* (Toronto: University of Toronto Press, 1989), especially 51-2.

29 See Whitworth, "Women, and Gender," 83-98; Mark Neufeld, "Democratization in/of Canadian Foreign Policy: Critical Reflections," *Studies in Political Economy* 58 (1999): 97-119; and Cranford Pratt, "Dominant class theory," 99-135.

30 Nossal, "The Democratization of Canadian Foreign Policy: The Elusive Ideal," in *Canada Among Nations 1995: Democracy and Foreign Policy*, ed. Maxwell A. Cameron and Maureen Appel Molot (Ottawa: Carleton University Press, 1995), 38.

31 Pratt, "Dominant class theory," 120.

32 Neufeld, "Democratization in/of Canadian Foreign Policy," 104-7

33 Ibid., 104.

34 Ibid., 104-5.

35 Ibid., 106.

36 Whitworth, "Women, and Gender," 93.

37 Ibid., 94.

38 As Paul Pross points out, NGOs monitor the government in the development and implementation of policy, provide important venues for citizens to articulate shared interests and positions to government, contribute unique expertise and experience to the policy-making process, and act as sources of vitality and creativity. See Paul Pross, *Group Politics and Public Policy* (Toronto: Oxford University Press, 1986), especially Chapter 4, 84-107.

39 For an example of a case where there was a good deal of competition between sets of government actors, each seeking to influence policy outcomes, and factions using the strategy of courting nongovernmental actors to bolster their respective bargaining positions in the interdepartmental negotiations, see Elizabeth Riddell-Dixon, *Canada and the International Seabed*.

40 Cranford Pratt points out that in the Canadian political system, "not only is the government particularly responsive to the requirements of capitalism but separate business interests in pursuit of specific and immediate interests interact with government with an ease, intimacy, and influence not achieved by other interest groups." See "Competing perspectives," 245.
41 Interviews with government officials on the Canadian delegation to the Fourth World Conference on Women.
42 Of course, the converse is also true: the relationship between government officials and NGOs is more likely to flourish if the former recognizes the demands and constraints faced by NGO leaders. This level of recognition is included in the points that government officials may wish to ponder.
43 Interview with Sheila Regehr, senior policy analyst, Policy and Analysis Directorate, Status of Women Canada, Ottawa, November 23, 1995.
44 Confidential interview with a public servant in SWC, Ottawa, 1995.

Interviewees

Government

Ruth Archibald, Director, Refugee, Population and Migration Division, Department of Foreign Affairs and International Trade, Ottawa, July 11, 1996.

Cherril Baker, Violence Prevention Unit, Ontario Women's Directorate, Toronto, November 19, 1997.

Penny Ballantyne, Assistant Deputy Minister, Health and Social Services, Government of the Northwest Territories, Beijing, September 1995.

Kerry Buck, Second Secretary, Canadian Mission to New York, New York, June 21, 1995 and Deputy Director, Human Rights, Humanitarian Affairs and International Women's Equality Division, July 5, 2000.

Janet Burn, Chief, Communications Services, External Relations and Communications Directorate, Status of Women Canada.

Jackie Claxton, Director, Women's Program, Status of Women Canada, Ottawa, November 24, 1995 and February 25, 1998.

Adèle Dion, Departmental Coordinator, International Women's Equality, Human Rights, Women's Equality and Social Affairs Division, Department of Foreign Affairs and International Trade, Ottawa, July 17, 1995, November 21, 1995 and December 11, 1997.

Rhonda Ferderber, Director, External Relations and Communications Directorate, Status of Women Canada, Ottawa, November 21, 1995 and December 9, 1997.

Marnie Girvan, Director, Women in Development and Gender Equity Division, Canadian International Development Agency, Ottawa, July 17-18, 1995.

Sue Heron-Herbert, Director Community Justice, Justice, Government of the Northwest Territories, Beijing, September 1995.

Abby Hoffman, Executive Director, Women's Health Bureau, Health Canada, Ottawa, July 10, 1996.

Ross Hynes, Minister-Counsellor, Permanent Mission of Canada to the United Nations, New York, 2000.

Duy Ai Kien, Policy Officer, Women's Program, Status of Women Canada, Ottawa, November 27, 1995 and February 25, 1998.

Valerie Raymond, Executive Director, UN World Conference on Women Secretariat, Status of Women Canada, Ottawa, July 18, 1995 and November 22, 1995.

Sheila Regehr, Senior Policy Analyst, Policy and Analysis Directorate, Status of Women Canada, Ottawa, November 23, 1995.

Diana Rivington, Senior Policy Advisor, Women in Development and Gender Equity Division, Policy Branch, Canadian International Development Agency, Ottawa, November 23, 1995.

UN Officials

Patsy Robertson, Senior Advisor on Media and Public Relations, Fourth World Conference on Women, United Nations, New York, 1995.

Kristen Timothy, Deputy Director/Coordinator, United Nations Fourth World Conference on Women Secretariat, Division for the Advancement of Women, New York, June 22, 1995.

Canadian NGOs

Janis Alton, United Nations Representative, Voice of Women, Toronto, April 12, 1995.

Pat Beck, National Council of Women, Member of the Canadian Beijing Facilitating Committee and Nongovernmental Observer on the Canadian Delegation to the Fourth World Conference on Women, Beijing, September 1995.

Allison Brewer, Director, The Morgentaler Abortion Services Clinic and Representative for EGALE (Equality for Gays and Lesbians Everywhere) at the Fourth World Conference on Women, Beijing, September 1995.

Shelagh Day, Women's Rights Activist and Representative for the National Association of Women and the Law and EGALE (Equality for Gays and Lesbians Everywhere) at the Fourth World Conference on Women, Toronto, April 13, 1995.

Cecilia Forsyth, National President, REAL Women of Canada, Beijing, September 1995.

Joan Grant-Cummings, President, National Action Committee on the Status of Women, Toronto, July 16, 1996.

Madeleine Gilchrist, Member of Canadian Voice of Women for Peace and the Canadian Beijing Facilitating Committee and Nongovernmental Observer on the Canadian delegations to the 1994 Vienna Regional Meetings, the 1994 CSW Inter-sessional Working Group and the 1995 New York Preparatory Meetings, Toronto, April 12, 1995 and July 15, 1996.

Joanna Kerr, Senior Researcher, North-South Institute, Ottawa, July 10, 1996.

C. Gwendolyn Landolt, National Vice-President, REAL Women of Canada, Beijing, September 1995.

Emmie Leung, Chief Executive Officer, International Paper Industries Limited and Nongovernmental Observer on the Canadian Delegation to the Fourth World Conference on Women, Beijing, September 1995.

Katherine McDonald, President of the Advisory Council for the Status of Women in Nova Scotia and Member of the Board of Directors, International Planned Parenthood Federation, Beijing, September 9, 1995.

Lise Martin, Coordinator, Canadian Beijing Facilitating Committee, Ottawa, July 18, 1995.

Lorraine Michael, Coordinator, Women and Economic Justice, Ecumenical Coalition for Economic Justice, and Nongovernmental Observer on the Canadian Delegation to the Fourth World Conference on Women, Beijing, September 12, 1995 and Toronto, August 21, 1996.

Maureen O'Neil, President, North-South Institute, and Deputy Head of the Canadian Delegation to the Third World Conference on Women, Ottawa, August 18, 1994.

Nancy Riche, Executive Vice President, Canadian Labour Congress and Nongovernmental Observer on the Canadian Delegation to the Fourth World Conference on Women, Ottawa, July 11, 1996.

Glenda Simms, Past President, Canadian Advisory Council on the Status of Women and Nongovernmental Observer on the Canadian Delegation to the Fourth World Conference on Women, Beijing, September 1995.

Madeleine Dion Stout, Director, Centre for Aboriginal Education, Research and Culture and Nongovernmental Observer on the Canadian Delegation to the Fourth World Conference on Women, Beijing, September 1995.

Charlotte Thibault, Directrice générale, Association des collaboratrices et partenaires en affaires, New York, March 30, 1995.

Penny Van Esterik, World Alliance for Breastfeeding Action, Toronto, April 11, 1995.

International NGOs

Joanne M. Hanrahan, SSND, PhD Director of Women's Institute, College of Notre Dame of Maryland, New York, March 1995.

Rosalind W. Harris, Past President, Conference of Non-Governmental Organizations in Consultative Status with the UN Economic and Social Council. June 19, 1995.

Annelise Riles, Observer on Fijian Delegation, New York, March 30, 1995.

Lily C. Tang, Soong Ching Ling Foundation, Huairou, September 1995.

Steven Tang, Soong Ching Ling Foundation, Huairou, September 1995.

Selected Bibliography

Canadian Government Documents

Canadian International Development Agency (CIDA). *Engendering Development: Women in Development and Gender Equity*. Hull, 1995.

–. *CIDA Funding Criteria and Mechanisms*. Ottawa, 1993.

Department of Foreign Affairs and International Trade. "Canada Welcomes Gains for Women at the United Nations World Conference on Women in Beijing." *This Week in Trade and Foreign Policy* (September 14-20, 1995): 3.

–. "Ouellet Announces Delegation to the Fourth World Conference on Women." *This Week in Trade and Foreign Policy* (August 24-30, 1995): 4.

Health. *Women's Health: Fourth World Conference on Women*. (Information kit.) Ottawa, 1995.

Secretary of State. *The Women's Program and the Role of Women's Voluntary Organizations in Promoting Change*. Ottawa, 1985.

Status of Women. *Beijing Platform for Action: Key Achievements*. Ottawa, 1995.

–. *Beijing Update: Canadian Update on the Fourth United Nations World Conference on Women, Beijing, China, September 1995* 1 (1994) to 4 (1995).

–. *Briefing Book for the Canadian Delegation*. Ottawa, 1995.

–. *Canada's National Report to the United Nations for the Fourth World Conference on Women, September 1995, Beijing, China*. Ottawa, 1994.

–. *Highlights of Canada's International Activities to Promote the Advancement of Women*. Ottawa, 1993.

–. *Key Accomplishments at the 4th U.N. World Conference on Women*. Beijing, 1995.

–. "Nairobi Forward-looking Strategies for the Advancement of Women: Issues and the Canadian Situation." *Fact Sheets*. Ottawa, 1992.

–. *The Royal Commission on the Status of Women: An overview 25 years later*. Ottawa, 1995.

–. *Setting the Stage for the Next Century: The Federal Plan for Gender Equality*. Ottawa, 1995.

–. *Statement by the Secretary of State (Status of Women and Multiculturalism) of Canada, the Honourable Sheila Finestone at the Fourth United Nations World Conference on Women*. Beijing, 1995.

–. *UN Convention on the Elimination of All Forms of Discrimination against Women – Fourth Report of Canada*. Ottawa, 1995.

–. *United Nations Fourth World Conference on Women: Beijing, China, September 4-15, 1995: Platform for Action*. Ottawa, 1995.

–. *United Nations World Conference on Women, Beijing September 1995*. (Information kit) Ottawa, 1995.

–. *Women in Canada – A Statistical Report*. 3rd ed. Ottawa, 1995.

–. "Women's Equality in Canada: Progress in Implementing the Nairobi Forward-looking Strategies for the Advancement of Women, January 1992 to April 1995." *Fact Sheet* 5. Ottawa, 1995.

United Nations Documents
1994 Update of the World Survey on the Role of Women in Development. ST/ESA/241. 1995.
Report of the Secretary-General to the General Assembly on the Status of the Convention on the Elimination of All Forms of Discrimination against Women (extract). A/49/308. 1994.
The World's Women: Trends and Statistics. ST/ESA/STAT/SER.K/8. 1991.
The World's Women 1995: Trends and Statistics. ST/ESA/STAT/SER.K/12.
"After Beijing: Emphasis on poverty eradication." *UN Chronicle* 2 (1996): 74-6.
Commission on the Status of Women. 38th Session. *Draft Platform for Action: Annex to Resolution 38/10 of the Commission on the Status of Women.* E/CN.6/1994/10. New York, 1994.
–. 39th Session. *Commission on the Status of Women, Concluding Thirty-Ninth Session, Approves Draft Platform for Action for Beijing Conference.* Press release. WOM/834. New York, 1995.
–. 39th Session. *NGO Amendments to the Draft UN Platform for Action.* E/CN.6/1995/2. New York, 1995.
–. 39th Session. *Preparations for the Fourth World Conference on Women: Action for Equality, Development and Peace: Reports from Regional Conferences and Other International Conferences.* E/CN.6/1995/5. New York, 1995.
–. 39th Session. *Preparations for the Fourth World Conference on Women: Action for Equality, Development and Peace: Draft Platform for Action.* E/CN.6/1995/2. New York, 1995.
–. 39th Session. *Second Report on Nairobi Forward-looking Strategies.* E/CN.6/1995/3. New York, 1995 and *Women and Poverty* E/CN.6/1995/3/Add.1. New York, 1995.
–. 40th Session. *Statement by Ms. Rosario Green, Special Adviser to the Secretary-General for Gender Issues.* New York, 1996.
-. *Fourth World Conference on Women: Action for Equality, Development and Peace, Beijing, China, 4-15 September 1995.* 94-24102/DPI/1468. New York, 1994.
–. Fourth World Conference on Women. *Conference to Set Women's Agenda into Next Century.* DPI/1424. Rev. 1. New York, 1994.
–. *From Beijing, a Platform for Action and a clear mandate for women's progress.* DPI/1749. New York, 1995.
–. *The United Nations and the Advancement of Women, 1945-1996.* UN Blue Books Series. Vol. 6. Rev. ed. New York, 1996.
Development Program. *Fourth World Conference on Women, Beijing, 4-15 September: Declaration and Platform for Action Break New Ground in International Efforts for Advancement of Women to Year 2000,* press release. WOM/871. New York, 1995.
Division for the Advancement of Women/Department of Public Information. *Beijing Declaration and Platform for Action (Summary).* New York, 1996.
Economic and Social Council. *Economic and Social Council Approves Eight Additional Non-Governmental Organizations for Participation in World Conference on Women.* ECOSOC/5617. New York, 1995.
–. *ECOSOC Resolution adopting the recommendations and conclusions arising from the first review and appraisal of the implementation of the Nairobi Forward-looking Strategies for the Advancement of Women to the year 2000 and urging Governments to implement the recommendations.* E/RES/1990/15. New York, 1990.
–. *Informal Consultations on the Draft Platform for Action of the Fourth World Conference on Women.* 1995/225. New York, 1995.
-. *Preparations for the Fourth World Conference on Women: Action for Equality, Development and Peace: Reports from Regional Conferences and Other International Conferences.* E/CN.16/1995/5. New York, 1995.
Educational, Scientific and Cultural Organization. *Toronto Platform for Action.* (Adopted by the participants in the International Symposium: Women and the Media, Access to Expression and Decision-making, held in Toronto from February 28 to March 3, 1995.) Toronto, 1995.
"Effective implementation of 'Beijing Declaration and Platform for Action' called for." *UN Chronicle* 33, 1 (1996): 83-4.
Fourth World Conference on Women. *Draft Platform for Action.* A/Conf.177/L.1. New York, 1995.

–. *Fourth World Conference on Women: Action for Equality, Development and Peace, to Convene in Beijing, 4 to 15 September: International Community to Seek Full and Equal Partnership Between Women and Men to Meet Challenges of Twenty-First Century.* Background Release. WOM/842. New York, 1995.

–. *General Exchange of Views on the Second Review and Appraisal for the Implementation of the Nairobi Forward-Looking Strategies for the Advancement of Women to the Year 2000: The extent to which gender concerns have been included in the activities of the United Nations human rights mechanisms.* A/Conf.177/9. New York, 1995.

–. *General Exchange of Views on the Second Review and Appraisal for the Implementation of the Nairobi Forward-Looking Strategies for the Advancement of Women to the Year 2000: 1994 World Survey on the Role of Women in Development.* A/Conf.177/5. New York, 1995.

–. *General Exchange of Views on the Second Review and Appraisal for the Implementation of the Nairobi Forward-Looking Strategies for the Advancement of Women to the Year 2000: Update of the World's Women: Trends and Statistics.* A/Conf.177/6. New York, 1995.

–. *Girls of Today are the Women of Tomorrow.* Press release. New York, 1995).

–. *International Community to Seek Full and Equal Partnership Between Women and Men to Meet Challenges of Twenty-First Century.* Press release. WOM/82. New York, 1995.

–. *Organization of Work, Including the Establishment of the Main Committee.* A/Conf.177/3. New York, 1995.

–. *Proposals for Consideration in the Preparation of a Draft Declaration and Draft Platform for Action.* A/Conf.177/L.1. New York, 1995.

–. *Report of the Fourth World Conference on Women (Beijing, 4-15 September 1995).* A/Conf.177/20. New York, October 1995.

–. *Report on the Informal Consultations Convened by the Chairperson of the Commission on the Status of Women.* A/Conf.177/L.3. New York, 1995.

–. *Report of the Informal Contact Group on Gender.* A/Conf.177/L.2. New York, 1995.

General Assembly. *Report of the Secretary-General to the General Assembly on the Status of the Convention on the Elimination of All Forms of Discrimination against Women (extract).* A/49/308. New York, 1994.

International Research and Training Institute for the Advancement of Women. "Women and the United Nations: Measuring Women's Unpaid Work." *WIN News* 21, 1 (1995): 7-8.

NGO Forum on Women Secretariat. *NGO Forum on Women: Look at the World Through Women's Eyes, 30 August-8 September: Final Report.* New York, 1995.

–. *NGO Forum on Women: Look at the World Through Women's Eyes, 30 August-8 September: Program Book.* New York, 1995.

–. *NGO Forum on Women: Look at the World Through Women's Eyes, 30 August-8 September: Schedule of Activities.* New York, 1995.

–. "Thousands Come to Huairou for Largest Gathering on Women." *NGO Forum on Women '95 Bulletin.* December 1995: 1.

Second World Conference on Human Rights. *Vienna Declaration and Programme of Action.* A/Conf.157/23. 1993.

Secretariat of the Fourth World Conference on Women and the Division for the Advancement of Women. *Women on the Move* 1 (1994) – 8 (1995).

Third World Conference on Women. *Report of the World Conference to Review and Appraise the Achievements of the United Nations Decade for Women: Equality, Development and Peace, Nairobi, 15-26 July 1985.* A/Conf.116/29. 1985.

Books, Articles, and Speeches

Adamson, Nancy, Linda Briskin, and Margaret McPhail. *Feminist Organizing for Change: The Contemporary Women's Movement in Canada.* Toronto: Oxford University Press, 1988.

Allison, Graham T. *The Essence of Decision: Explaining the Cuban Missile Crisis.* Boston: Little, Brown, 1971.

Atkinson, Michael M., and Kim Richard Nossal. "Bureaucratic politics and the New Fighter Aircraft decisions." *Canadian Public Administration* 24 (1981): 531-62.

Basu, Amrita. "Reflections on Forum '85." *Signs* 11, 3 (1986): 604-5.

Brewer, Allison. "Canadian Government Sort of Comes Out in Support of Lesbians." *Herizons* 10 (Winter 1996): 6-7.

Burt, Sandra. "The Women's Movement: Working to Transform Public Life." In *Canadian Politics*, 2nd ed., edited by James P. Bickerton and Alain-G. Gagnon. Toronto: Broadview, 1994: 207-33.

Cameron, Maxwell A. "Democratization of Foreign Policy: the Ottawa Process as a Model." *Canadian Foreign Policy* 5, 3 (1998): 147-65.

Canadian Beijing Facilitating Committee (CBFC). *An Agenda for Action: Priorities for Canadian NGOs in Beijing*. Ottawa: Canadian Beijing Facilitating Committee, 1995.

–. *Canadian Beijing Facilitating Committee: National Consultations, Winnipeg, August 19-21, 1994*. Ottawa: Canadian Beijing Facilitating Committee, 1994.

–. *Onward from Beijing: The FINAL Newsletter of the Canadian Beijing Facilitating Committee (CBFC)*. December 1995.

–. *Onward to Beijing: For Equality, Development and Peace* 1, 1 (May 1994) to 1, 5 (August 1995).

–. *Proposed line by line changes to the* Platform for Action *made by the 10 lead groups working on the CBFC's COORDINATED RESPONSE*. Ottawa: Canadian Beijing Facilitating Committee, 1995.

–. *Take Action for Equality, Development and Peace: A Canadian Follow-up Guide to Beijing '95*. Ottawa: Canadian Beijing Facilitating Committee, 1996.

Canadian Woman Studies 16, 3 (1996).

Charlesworth, Hilary. "Women as Sherpas: Are Global Summits Useful for Women?" *Feminist Studies* 22, 3 (1996): 537-47.

Clark, Ann Marie, Elisabeth Friedman, and Kathryn Hochstetler. "A Comparison of NGO-State Lines of Conflict at Global UN Conferences on the Environment, Women, and Human Rights." Paper presented to the 39th Conference of the International Studies Association, Minneapolis, MN, March 1998.

Comeau, Pauline. "Access becomes the key issue for the UN World Conference on Women." *Human Rights Tribune* 3, 2 (June/July 1995): 7-11.

–. "Canadian NGO process to Beijing falls off the rails." *Human Rights Tribune* 2, 3 (September/October 1994): 21-3.

Cook, Rebecca J., ed. *Human Rights of Women: National and International Perspectives*. Philadelphia: University of Pennsylvania Press, 1994.

Cooper, Andrew F. *Canadian Foreign Policy: Old Habits and New Directions*. Scarborough: Prentice Hall, 1997.

Dorsey, Ellen. "The Global Women's Movement: Articulating a New Vision of Global Governance." In *The Politics of Global Governance: International Organizations in an Interdependent World*, edited by Paul F. Diehl. Boulder, CO: Lynne Rienner, 1997: 335-59.

Ecumenical Coalition for Economic Justice. "Numbers that Lie." *Economic Justice Report* 6, 4 (1995): 1-8.

Ferguson, Kathy E. *The Feminist Case Against Bureaucracy*. Philadelphia: Temple University Press, 1984.

Fraser, Arvonne. *The U.N. Decade for Women: Documents and Dialogue*. Boulder, CO: Westview, 1987.

Friedman, Elisabeth. "Women's Human Rights: The Emergence of a Movement." In *Women's Rights, Human Rights: International Feminist Perspectives*, edited by Julie Peters and Andrea Wolper. New York: Routledge, 1995: 18-35.

Fuentes, M., and A.G. Frank. "Ten Theses on Social Movements." *World Development* 17, 2 (1989): 179-91.

Gilchrist, Madeleine. *Report on the United Nations Commission on the Status of Women Intersessional Working Group, 10-14 January 1994*. Toronto: n.p., 1994.

Goiter, Hégel. "The 'hundred flowers' of women's diplomacy in Beijing." *The Courier* 154 (1995): 49-53.

–. "Women." *The Courier* 154 (1995): 48.

Harrison, R.J. "Women's Rights: 1975-1985." In *Global Issues in the United Nations Framework*, edited by Paul Taylor and A.J.R. Groom. London: Macmillan, 1989: 226-44.

International Development Research Centre. *Transcript: Public Forum on the Fourth UN World Conference on Women with Gertrude Mongella, Secretary-General.* Ottawa: International Development Research Centre, 1993.

International Institute for Sustainable Development. *Earth Negotiations Bulletin* 14, 21 (1995).

International Peace Bureau. *Final Preparatory Meeting for Beijing: Fraught with Problems.* New York: International Peace Bureau, 1995.

–. *The Other Side of Beijing: Problems.* New York: International Peace Bureau, 1995.

International Women Count Network. *Governments agree to measure and value unwaged work.* Press release. London, England: 1996.

Kerr, Joanna. *Ours by Right: Women's Rights as Human Rights.* London: Zed Books, 1993.

Kien, Duy Ai. Speech to the "Second Canadian Conference on International Health: Health Reform Around the Globe: Towards Equality and Sustainability?" Ottawa, November 12, 1995.

Liberal Party of Canada. *Creating Opportunity: The Liberal Plan for Canada.* Ottawa, 1993.

Meyer, Mary K., and Elisabeth Prugl. *Gender Politics in Global Governance.* Lanham, MD: Rowman and Littlefield, 1999.

Michael, Lorraine. *UN World Conference on Women, Beijing, September 4-15, 1995: Report by Lorraine Michael.* Toronto: n.p., 1995.

National Action Committee on the Status of Women. "Beijing and Beyond." *Action Now* 5, 8 (1995): 3-4.

–. *Women in Canada After Beijing: Left Out, Left Over, Left Behind.* Toronto: National Action Committee on the Status of Women, 1997.

Neufeld, Mark. "Democratization in/of Canadian Foreign Policy: Critical Reflections." *Studies in Political Economy* 58 (1999): 97-119.

–. "Hegemony and Foreign Policy: The Case of Canada as a Middle Power." *Studies in Political Economy* 48 (1995): 7-29.

Nossal, Kim Richard. "Allison through the (Ottawa) looking glass: bureaucratic politics and foreign policy in a parliamentary system." *Canadian Public Administration* 22 (1979): 610-26.

–. "Analysing the domestic sources of Canadian foreign policy." *International Journal* 39, 1 (1983-4): 1-22.

–. "Bureaucratic politics and the Westminster model." In *International Conflict and Conflict Management: Readings in World Politics,* edited by Robert O. Matthews, Arthur G. Rubinoff, and Janice Gross Stein. Scarborough: Prentice Hall, 1984: 230-7.

–. "The Democratization of Canadian Foreign Policy: The Elusive Ideal." In *Canada Among Nations 1995: Democracy and Foreign Policy,* edited by Maxwell A. Cameron and Maureen Appel Molot. Ottawa: Carleton University Press, 1995: 29-43.

–. *The Politics of Canadian Foreign Policy.* 3rd ed. Scarborough: Prentice Hall, 1997.

O'Neil, Maureen. "Women's Rights: Canada's Role and the UN Challenge." *Policy Options* 11, 8 (1990): 9-11.

Pietilä, Hilkka, and Jeanne Vickers. *Making Women Matter: The Role of the United Nations.* London: Zed Books, 1996.

Pratt, Cranford. "Competing perspectives on Canadian development assistance policies." *International Journal* 51, 2 (1996): 235-58.

–. "Dominant class theory and Canadian foreign policy: the case of the counter-consensus." *International Journal* 39, 1 (1983-4): 99-135.

–. *Internationalism Under Strain: The North-South Policies of Canada, the Netherlands, Norway and Sweden.* Toronto: University of Toronto Press, 1989.

Pross, A. Paul. *Group Politics and Public Policy.* Toronto: Oxford University Press, 1986.

Raymond, Valerie. "Talking Points for Valerie Raymond, Executive Director, UN World Conference on Women Secretariat, to the Professional Association of Foreign Service Officers." Ottawa: Department of Foreign Affairs and International Trade, 1995.

REAL Women of Canada. "Fourth World Conference on Women in Beijing September 4-15, 1995 [and] Non-Governmental Organization Forum (NGO) August 30-September 8, 1995." Paper presented at the NGO Forum in Huairou, September 1995.

Rebick, Judy. "Beijing Diary: The women's conference the media missed." *Canadian Forum* 74, 845 (1995): 27-30, 35-6.

Riddell-Dixon, Elizabeth. *Canada and the International Seabed: Domestic Determinants and External Constraints.* Montreal: McGill-Queen's University Press, 1989.

–. "Deep seabed mining: a hotbed for governmental politics." *International Journal* 41, 1 (1985-6): 72-94.

–. "Mainstreaming Women's Rights: Problems and Prospects within the Centre for Human Rights." *Global Governance* 5, 2 (1999): 149-71.

–. "Winners and Losers: formulating Canada's policies on international technology transfers." *International Journal* 47, 1 (1991-2): 159-83.

Sapiro, Virginia. *The Political Integration of Women: Roles, Socialization and Politics.* Chicago: University of Illinois Press, 1983.

Stairs, Denis. "Canada and the security problem: Implications as the millennium turns." *International Journal* 54, 3 (1999), 386-403.

Stienstra, Deborah. "Can the Silence be Broken? Gender and Canadian Foreign Policy." *International Journal* 50, 1 (1994-5): 103-27.

–. *Women's Movements and International Organizations.* New York: St. Martin's, 1994.

Stienstra, Deborah, and Barbara Roberts. *Strategies for the Year 2000: A Woman's Handbook.* Halifax, NS: Fernwood, 1995.

Thobani, Sunera. "Beijing and Beyond." *Action Now* 5, 8 (1995): 2-3.

Tinker, Irene, and Jane Jaquette. "UN Decade for Women: Its Impact and Legacy." *World Development* 15, 3 (1987): 419-27.

Touraine, A. "Social Movements: Participation and Protest." *Scandinavian Political Studies* 10, 3 (1987): 207-22.

Wagner, Lynn, and Langston James Goree VI. "Fourth World Conference on Women Informal Consultations." *Linkages: A Multimedia Resource for Environment and Development Policy Makers.* Briefing notes 1-5. Winnipeg, International Institute for Sustainable Development, December 9, 1998. <www.iisd.ca./linkages/4wcw/brief1.html>.

Whitworth, Sandra. *Feminism and International Relations: Towards a Political Economy of Interstate and Non-governmental Organizations.* London: Macmillan, 1994.

–. "Women, and Gender, in the Foreign Policy Review Process." In *Canada Among Nations 1995: Democracy and Foreign Policy*, edited by Maxwell A. Cameron and Maureen Appel Molot. Ottawa: Carleton University Press, 1995: 83-98.

Winslow, Anne, ed. *Women, Politics, and the United Nations.* Westport, CT: Greenwood, 1995.

Women's Linkage Caucus. *Recommendations on Bracketed Text in the WCW Draft Platform for Action (A/Conf.177/L.1 and A/Conf.177/L.3).* New York: Women's Linkage Caucus, 1995.

–. *Take the Brackets Off Women's Lives! Women's Linkage Caucus Advocacy Chart.* New York: Women's Linkage Caucus, 1995.

Index